"There have been very few books written lately in which all the elements of civilized life—political, religious and economic —are combined to give a rounded and complete picture of the world we live in and of its history and to point with conviction and clarity to a road which may take us out of our present stagnation. *Faith and Freedom* is one such book, and is for that reason a very rare and precious document. To say that it is a book of great erudition, originality and scope would be to say very little and to miss its essential merit. What is important is that the author combines learning with a deep religious sense and faith."   *Time and Tide*

"An amazing book. For breadth of scholarship and an ordered complexity of detail it is difficult to think of any work which is its equal."   *Catholic Times*

"It faces the problems of the present with a realistic eye. You may not agree with it in all details—who could expect that? —but you can be proud to present it as a Catholic view of the world today."   *Catholic World*

"Stimulating, perceptive book."   *The Progressive*

"Deeply thoughtful, brilliantly written . . . amounts to a history of Western civilization from its earliest beginnings. Yet it is so short and concise that it can be read almost at a sitting."   *St. Louis Post-Dispatch*

"It is masterly. A more profound statement of the Christian Democratic position, as grounded in theology, anthropology, economics, and plain human experience, would be hard to imagine."   *The Sign*

"Her prose—always persuasive and luminous—attains a new level of eloquence, a grace and nobility not unworthy of 'the height of this great argument.'"   *Saturday Review*

"*Faith and Freedom* is a book of real greatness." *Pulpit Digest*

Barbara Ward

FAITH
and
FREEDOM

IMAGE BOOKS

A Division of Doubleday & Company, Inc.
Garden City, New York

IMAGE BOOKS EDITION 1958
by special arrangement with
W. W. Norton & Company, Inc.

Image Books edition published September 1958
1st printing .... *August 1958*

COVER BY SYDNEY BUTCHKES
TYPOGRAPHY BY JOSEPH P. ASCHERL

Printed in the United States of America

Contents

AUTHOR'S NOTE

This book, which is one writer's attempt to wrestle with the angel of history, could not have been written without continuous reliance upon the wisdom and learning of others. In particular, the writings of Christopher Dawson, Jacques Maritain, Reinhold Niebuhr, Arnold Toynbee, and R. H. Tawney have exercised so great an influence that the author wishes, at the very outset, and with warmth and gratitude, to acknowledge the debt.

ONE

FOUNDATIONS

Age of Uncertainty

SURELY no previous age has known the sense of foreboding that hangs over the modern world. True, there were catastrophes and calamities in other days. Cities were sacked and great empires dissolved in ruin. Yet for the mass of the people, war and peace, prosperity and disaster, came even-handedly from the gods, and the future, which had never promised much, could not much disappoint either. This low pitch of expectation excluded the feverish extremes of either hope or fear.

But modern man, until the day before yesterday, breathed in with his earliest breath the conviction that the future would be better than the past. However divided men might be in their philosophy or politics or economic interest, one belief they shared, the belief in progress, in continuous enlightenment, in the dispelling of darkness and the growth of reason and truth. Almost to our own day, the monuments of buried civilizations, which nineteenth-century archeologists were laying bare in the desert, seemed only to underline the stability of a society which had produced no ruins and whose material equipment was growing with each decade. Victorian travelers, surveying the foundations of dead cities or gazing at the pillars of broken temples, were not much moved by the spectacle of human transience. They rather saw confirmed the peculiar solidity of their own achievement.

Yet within little more than a single generation, the great complacency has been shattered. After two world wars, the ruins have appeared in modern society. Men have walked through their own cities and seen in one night damage which the Goths or the Vandals could hardly have inflicted in fifty years. Ahead of them lies the risk of other and worse destructions, of atomic destruction which may blast the fertility of the soil and twist the biological forms of human life. And, short of complete physical catastrophe, another horror has been conjured up in the shape of social orders so inhuman that they seem better fitted to termites than to men and women. The anti-Utopias, the "Brave New Worlds," the "Nineteen Eighty-fours" project into the future a vision of society more dark than the deepest pessimism of the ancient world ever conjured up.

This collapse of confidence has occurred in a few decades. To some it gives listlessness and despair, to some nostalgia and a hankering for what is past, to others fear and the ugly anger that springs from fear. To all, it gives anxiety, a sense of searching, and an awareness that even the most settled aspects of our world are precarious. Compared with the certainties of the past, the new mood is unhappy and uneasy. Yet in the great crisis of our times it may well be a safer mood than the old complacency. It was, after all, during the period of fullest confidence that the powder chain was laid and lighted which led to the explosions of the twentieth century. Men do not learn when they believe they already know. That arrogance brings blindness and that "pride goeth before a fall" are the universal teachings not only of the world's great sages and philosophers but also of all the myth and folklore and legend in which lies deposited the secular wisdom of the human race. In our new sense of uncertainty, we are more likely than our predecessors to seek to know the truth about ourselves and our society and to search for it at the only source from which some enlightenment can flow.

This source is history. Indifference to the past, patronage not unmixed with contempt for the failure of other men in other ages—these are moods which belong to the vanished era of overconfidence. We who have walked among the blackened ruins of London or seen the rubble piled to the height of the rooftops in Essen or Dusseldorf must consider with new eyes the ruins of the past—the broken arches of the Caesars, the abandoned temples of Angkor or Yucatan, the sea city of Knossos sacked and abandoned in a night, the drift and litter of dead civilizations from one end to the other of the habitable globe. They tell us what we fear—that our own society may, like them, be under sentence of extinction. But their story may tell us, too, why the sentence was passed and whether we have any hope of avoiding or postponing the catastrophe.

At this point, however, we already confront a decisive question: whether men can in fact apply their wisdom and experience to the working out of history. They can do so only if there is, in human affairs, a margin for choice. But is there such an area of free decision? The fixities of environment, of climate, and of geography on the one hand, and the fixities of human passion and fear on the other, drive history forward on predetermined tracks; and the notion that a man can, by taking thought, alter that headlong passage by as much as a hairbreadth may be no more than a delusion. We cannot learn from history unless we are free to learn. We cannot profit by the lesson unless we are free to act. Here, at the outset of any discussion of the contemporary crisis, men need to know whether or not freedom is an illusion. Is the life of civilizations and the life of men predetermined by unshakable physical causation, each event following inexorably from the previous event? Or is there some place left in the immensities of the physical universe for the creative intervention of man?

II

This book is an attempt to find some answer to the question. Its themes are the interaction between what is conditioned and what is free in human affairs and the pattern which this interaction has created in the brief span of human history. For brief it is compared with the eons of geological time. Man himself is a newcomer on the earth—a mere hundred thousand years old in billennia of planetary existence. As for his attempts at civilization, they are perhaps six or seven thousand years old. Civilization, which seemed to our grandfathers so stable and secure, is in fact—on any balanced calculation—experimental, new, and highly precarious.

By far the longest stretch of human history has been passed within the framework of primitive tribal society; and there, it seems obvious, the compulsions of physical existence must have been overwhelmingly strong. It is difficult for us to make any mental picture of the men who lived in the vast forests and swamps of the early world, surrounded by unknown and unpredictable hazards and depending for very existence upon the food that could be snatched from dangerous thickets and river banks. In the millennia of that way of life, two great vitalities of human existence dominated all others; and these, it can be argued, have survived through all later experiments of civilization as the fundamental raw material from which society is formed.

One of these great vitalities is the protective association of the tribe. In a world in which everything was strange, the instinct to cling together against the unknown fixed in man deeply rooted loyalties to his own community and as deep a tendency to hate and reject the stranger beyond the gate. This tribal pattern has taken different forms in different societies. In some, the sense of kinship rested upon devotion to a dynasty, to a temple, to a god, in others upon the memory of tribal relationships, in our own upon the coincidence of frontiers and language. But whatever the principle of cohesion, its essence has been inward-looking loyalty and outward-looking suspicion and hate.

The other great vitality was the sheer urge for survival. The hunting grounds and the fishing rivers of the tribe were the guarantee of life. If others encroached upon them, existence itself was at stake. As society became more complex and the division of labor produced different classes with different functions, the struggle to secure the means of survival could occur inside the community as well as in its relations with the outside world.

As we come to the level of recorded history, we find that the great crises seem invariably to be concerned with one or other of these fundamental human vitalities—the urge to collective solidarity against the stranger and the determination to keep for one's community or for oneself the means of life. In the worst crises, moreover, both vitalities may run amok. While state fights state for survival and destroys the substance of living, the pressure of need and despair causes internal revolt. Civil war adds its horrors to the international struggle. The clearest instance of this double catastrophe is to be found in our own Western antecedents. Augustus imposed his Roman empire upon a Hellenic world devastated by the hideous wars of Greece and Italy in the four centuries before Christ. These wars had taken every conceivable form of violence. War between the Greek city states began the cycle. Then followed a period of wars of conquest. While Alexander conquered the East, Rome spread its power over the Italian peninsula and, with the Scipios, on into Spain and Africa. In the next phase, civil war between the rival leaders of Rome carried the fighting from one end of the Mediterranean to the other. As an undercurrent, there were fierce sporadic outbreaks of class war —the struggle between patricians and plebeians in Rome, the despairing outburst of the slaves led by Spartacus, and such horrible internecine fights as those which broke out between the factions at Corcyra in the course of the Peloponnesian wars.

So all-pervasive and inescapable do these forces of national rivalry and brute survival seem, that it is difficult to interpret history in any other terms. Chance sets a certain tribe in hunting fields which no longer support its growing numbers. Or drought or cold force it to seek new ground. A clash with other tribes must follow. The stronger wins and takes possession of the land. The more developed and populated an area, the more violent the rivalry and the more disastrous the struggle. Tribes flourish and fail. Kingdoms rise and perish. Empires prosper and are crushed. At whatever level of development, this is the cycle of man's history: a melancholy repetition of conquest and defeat, a wheel of existence grinding out an endless repetition of human presumption and human collapse. If in our own day, in spite of the advances of science and the elaboration of industrial society, we tremble before the possibility of atomic destruction, we are only conforming to the oldest fatality of history, according to which what goes up must also come down and the greater the rise the steeper the fall.

Compared with these fundamental forces of rivalry and struggle, the arts, philosophies and religions of society are no more than a superstructure—entertainments, distractions, rationalizations with which men hide from themselves the harsh outlines of earthly life. Above all, freedom in any real sense is only a delusion for no human decision has strength enough to stand against the avalanche of material happenings which pours through the lives of men and societies. A man may have the illusion of directing the movement of events—as a small boy in a runaway car may believe he is in control. But climate and soil, the location of resources, markets, trade routes, the distribution of property, the rivalries of states—all these make up such an inexorable mass of interlocking facts that history moves by their weight alone and man's little will and puny decisions rest on their surface with as small an impact as that of a summer gnat on the waters of a stream.

III

Yet such a view of history seems to allot to man a passivity which accords very uneasily with what we know of his achievements in recorded time. How does it cover, for example, those instances in which different men and different communities have reacted in opposite ways to the same crisis in their external environment? It is, for instance, known that at the dawn of history, the rich grasslands on the southern shores of the Mediterranean were turned to desert by a desiccation of the general climate. Some of the peoples of the steppe retreated to the South, following the withdrawal of fertility. Their remote descendants may be found today still in their primitive condition, among the Shilluks and the Dinkas in the swamps of the upper Nile. But another group of men did not follow the conditioned line of drift and retreat. They mastered the drought by inventing the elaborate irrigation system of the Nile and on its foundations they laid the basis of the first civilization known to history. At about the same time, a similar crisis of drought seems to have called forth the same act of creation from the dwellers by the Euphrates and the Tigris, who built the system of irrigation upon which Sumerian civilization could begin to grow.

It is thus at least arguable that there are two sides or aspects to man and his history. There is a conditioned aspect, a drift, a submission to the pressure of material events which can be so extreme as to deprive the man or the community of any attribute of freedom. The lives of some men and some communities would seem to be spent wholly under the compulsions of environment. The immense extension in time of primitive tribal society—probably through some eighty or ninety millennia—shows how normal it is for human beings to establish a fixed relationship with their surroundings and to continue in it without creative change. Yet on the other hand, with both individual men and with races and societies, there comes a time when the material conditions of life seem to be no longer the strict determinant of existence but rather the raw materials which man, as artist and creator, molds into new forms of life and new heights of creative achievement. The men who retreated before the drought were the passive sufferers of material change. The men who stayed and mastered irrigation were the active agents of rational and ordered change. Man, in short, is not only the tool of circumstance. He also has the power to master material things.

If history has this dual character, its unfolding is likely to disclose a curious weaving together of the conditioned and the free. Where men react blindly and passively to the great vitalities of material existence—to the pressure of the tribe, to the needs and hungers of survival—history will wear an aspect of uniformity. There is a dreary sameness about wars of conquest or about the ferocities which accompany civil strife. Some states of pressure and counterpressure appear to produce almost identical reactions even though millennia may lie between the events. The struggles between the Greek city states in the terrible war between Athens and Sparta—the alliances, the betrayals, the reversals of loyalty, the final denouement of exhaustion and of conquest at the hands of an outside power—offer an unhappy parallel with the Renaissance wars in Italy or with the struggle for hegemony in Europe in the last eighty years. When states are driven by fear and ambition, their reactions seem to have the lack of spontaneity, the predictability, the conditioned air of puppets dangling on a manipulator's string. The pattern is the same. The puppets repeat the same gestures. Fear and greed dance the same dance throughout the centuries, and the recurrences upon which so many theories of history are built spring simply from the repetition of the same material causation.

When, however, in history, men transcend their material drives by reason, by enlightenment and by their search for the ideal, the blind necessities are held at bay. The puppets no longer jerk and dance. For a time, a breath of freedom blows through society. The fatalities are reversed. There is a quickening, a springtime of growth and hope. Before the Greek experiment was extinguished in bloodshed, three or four hundred years of creative response had produced the marvel of Athens—"the education of Hellas." Solon devised and Cleisthenes elaborated a political constitution which gave aristocrats and ordinary citizens a balanced part in political life. Solon, too, was responsible for an economic revolution which substituted, for subsistence farming on overcrowded land, the commercial cultivation of the grape and the vine and the sending out of colonists to uncultivated land overseas. When the outward pressure of colonization encountered the hostility of the mighty Persian empire, it was Athens that gave the lead to a victorious alliance of Greek states that might have been the nucleus of a free federation. Up to that point, the pulse of creativity beat strongly in Greek society. The arts, learning, civic life, all gave evidence of the same mastery and sense of freedom. Yet after the triumph of victory over the Persians, pride of state and greed for gain—the old vitalities of tribe and property—undermined the Greek achievement. Athens lost its moral leadership and seemed to impose an increasingly imperialist control. Sparta led the revolt against Athenian predominance and wealth. In the long years of the Peloponnesian wars, the sense of freedom and creation ebbs. Hatred and anger and rivalry set the puppets dancing again. After being the education not simply of Hellas but of the world, Athens becomes no more than yet another state crippled by violence and war.

In this cycle of one of the greatest and most productive communities the world has ever known we can discern the double web of necessity and freedom—the freedom which comes from reason, generosity, and imaginative experiment, the necessity which is embodied in blind nationalism, blind greed, and the blind pursuit of self-interest. And we can see, too, some hint of the answer to the puzzle of why so many great civilizations have already crumbled away. No social order can stand more than a given degree of rivalry, national assertiveness, and class conflict. Once these blind forces take control of the social organism, its powers of growth and adaptation are shaken out of it and it passes into the puppet dance of continuous violence and ultimate collapse. The maritime empire of Knossos fell at the hands of its Achaean colonies. Sumeria collapsed after the aggressions of King Sargon. Assyria shattered Hittite and Syrian society before falling victim to the uncontrolled violence it had unleashed. The death throes of the Hellenic world, as we have seen, were in the four hundred years of perpetual war before the birth of Christ. Such is the "melancholy wheel" of rising and falling civilizations, such the meaningless maze of violence into which so much of human history has seemed to degenerate. Such, too, seems to be the unhappy rhythm of our own day.

IV

The theme which these chapters will attempt to pursue is the interrelation between this freedom and this necessity. In primitive and archaic society, so runs the argument, the human race, in spite of great material achievements, still lived on the whole under the sign of necessity. Material environment and a more or less blind reaction to it mark the earliest ages of man. There follows a period of worldwide awakening when, with the coming of the world religions, man begins to reflect upon his nature and destiny and to contemplate the range of reason and freedom. Then in our own society—with its unique antecedents in Greece and Jewry—we can trace the argument between freedom and necessity down to our own day.

There is, however, one caution to be made. When we, to-day, try to assess the balance between forces—the conditioning forces of environment and of man's blind reaction to them on the one hand and his free acts of insight, reason, creation and control on the other—we are insensibly biased toward a belief in determinism. The belief that material events alone are real and condition everything else—in other words, determinism—is the stuff of so much modern popular thinking that it must be counted the most widespread belief of our day. For at least a third of the human race—in Russia and China—it is not only widespread but obligatory. Far beyond the totalitarian frontier, however, popular determinism has its hold. In their personal lives, for instance, men believe that environment and heredity make them precisely what they are—the former in the shape of class or race and the latter in the shape of genes, chromosomes, drives, and instincts. In social life the struggle for survival, class interest, and racial antagonism are held to be the very web of history.

It is, of course, easy to understand the hold that material explanation has gained on the modern mind. This century is the first to follow the elaboration of the idea of evolution. If our universe began in stellar gas among the whirling nebulae and life emerged over infinite ages from the amoeba evolving in shallow water through legged fish to land animals and on to mammals and at last to primitive man, each advance conditioned by its superior adaptation to environment, then it is easy to conclude that the process continues to this day and that all the phenomena connected with human existence represent only more and more refined manifestations of matter and more and more elaborate adaptation to natural surroundings. Thought, the mind itself, is simply the last projection of the physical brain, comparable, say, to the waves transmitted by radioactive materials. Values are determined for the human herd by trial and error in the long struggle for survival. The good is what has been proved socially useful, justice represents the rules which have helped dominant species to survive. From the first planetary explosion a thousand million or more years ago down to the cold wars and atom bombs of our contemporary world there is no reason to invoke other explanations than that of a closed material system producing of its own momentum and according to rigidly predetermined laws all the incredible variety, the inexhaustible riches, the bewildering plethora of animate and inanimate life around us.

This vision of a vast materially conditioned universe has been rendered more vivid to our imagination in the last hundred years both by the pressure of our material environment and by the unquestioned successes of science in elaborating the laws governing material things. In this century, men's lives have been turned upside down by material changes, by the internal-combustion engine and the electric generator, by atomic energy and the jet. The industrial process makes so violent and sweeping a change in the human environment that it is easy to be obsessed by the material agents of the upheaval and forget the minds at work behind it. It has been, too, an epoch when the nearest human equivalent to "forces"—mass workers at work in mass factories and mass votes organized in mass political parties—have marched in strength into the arena of human history. There is a sense in which such party leaders as Hitler or Stalin seem to be more the products of the anonymous swarm—of hive and hill—than despots of strongly marked personal individuality.

This has also been a time when the absorbed study of the external universe in its material character—in other words, of those parts of it that can be weighed and measured—has scored stupendous triumphs for science and revealed a vast universe everywhere obeying material laws. This picture of material uniformity would not have surprised the Greeks, who expected the cosmos to be orderly and to demonstrate law; but it has certainly intoxicated some modern minds into believing that since the methods of weighing and measuring give such startling results they must be the only reliable methods of establishing what is reality.

It is a natural and legitimate procedure in science to attempt to bring together manifold phenomena within a single order of explanation. The more the field of observation can be unified, the greater the certainty with which the scientific laws controlling material things—in other words, predictions of their likely future behavior—can be established. But equally science depends upon complete scrupulousness in the formulating of its laws. Science will not confidently unify phenomena which cannot legitimately be brought under one head. It may have good guesses—indeed, science has progressed again and again by intuitions subsequently verified—but they are not elevated to laws until they have been rigorously checked. The controls of science are minute, intricate, and absolute. The checks and counterchecks cover every available fact and try to allow for every possible variation. Even the most watertight of laws is in essence still a hypothesis, waiting to be modified in the light of further discoveries.

Modern popular thinking about the universe and man's place in it has been to a great extent formulated by men who have imitated the methods of science but not its caution. With great slapdash sweeps of paint on the canvas, they have sketched in a picture of history as a materially conditioned process and man as strictly a product of what can supposedly be weighed and measured in life—class interest, property rights, material needs. Then they have proclaimed that since this is a "unified" explanation of the universe, with all save material factors left out, it is therefore scientific. This hectic method—of which Marxists, for all their claim to scientific accuracy, are the chief exponents—is the antithesis of science. There are no controls. There are no laboratory experiments. Nine-tenths of the material cannot be weighed or measured. And for some of the theories, for instance those on prehistory, there are not even facts to work on. Even if the results can be claimed to be good guesses, there is no justification for the extravagant certainty and dogmatism with which the hypotheses are declared to be the only truth—and men and women "purged" for doubting it. In a very real sense the whole method is a vast and tragic sleight of hand. Yet it has upon it the stamp of the scientific and hence can count upon an easier and more unthinking acceptance than other more elaborate and complex explanations of reality.

The Marxists may be the most rigorous exponents of determinism, but they have not been alone. The notion that society is bound by iron economic laws was the popular justification of the early excesses of capitalism. Such honest and public-spirited men as John Bright or Richard Cobden defended the labor of little children in factories on the grounds that to tamper with the workings of industrialism would destroy the automatic processes upon which prosperity was based. Even in our own day, men can be heard to argue that free enterprise —a certain method of organizing economic life—is the cause and source of political freedom. In other words, they imply that economic factors condition the social, political, and even spiritual nature of our society. This argument, for all its supposed defense of free enterprise, is undilutedly Marxist.

But it would be a mistake to attribute today's widespread popularity of determinism only to specifically modern conditions. There is a sense in which determinism fits in with deep and permanent instincts in human nature. All life is hedged around with fatalities. We are born we know not why and we die without our own choosing. Much of our life is determined for us by the family into which we are born and the age in which we have to live. Again and again, the existence we might have planned is twisted out of recognition by external catastrophes—by war or economic ruin or the onslaught of disease. And if these eruptions of necessity into daily life were not enough, no one with any imagination can have failed at some time to be impressed to the point of being dwarfed and cast down by the immensity of planetary space, by the infinity of time during which life has moved on this globe, and by the contrast between these vastnesses and man's pitifully brief and uncertain existence. And since this sense of being overshadowed by vast anonymous forces is so constant an element in human experience, it is not surprising that determinism, far from being a modern mode of thought, is probably one of the most ancient and one of the most natural to mankind. Certainly, it is the mode we discover when we look back to the first recognizable types of human society and examine what we can of the earliest activities of man.

The Dawn of Wisdom

WE KNOW something of primitive society from its partial survival into our own day. In North America, in Siberia, in Central Africa, and in Australia tribal life has persisted into the modern world and brought us a glimpse of what is, by any reckoning, the longest experiment in human living. It is an elaborate society with strong social disciplines, fixed routines, and developed ceremonies. But it is also a society strongly conditioned by physical necessity—by the unity and safety of the tribe and by the overriding need to secure the means of survival. These groups of hunters and food gatherers are men whose life is woven into a certain fixed pattern by the search for food.

Their religion seems to be what rationalists declare all religion to be—a projection of their physical needs and a species of magic by which they hope to satisfy them. By imitating the behavior of animals, by drawing them on the walls of their caves, they hope to obtain power over them and to insure good hunting and plentiful supplies. These animals upon whom life itself depends become the tutelary deities of the tribe, the totem—bear and buffalo in North America and Siberia, kangaroo and witchetty grub in Australia.

Such magical religions seem to be in essence reflections of the primitive economy, attempts to master the physical world and compel it to deliver the supplies of life. They can even be compared to modern science in its basic aim of controlling the material environment, however fantastic may be the primitive methods of incantation, fetish, and spell.

This fundamental concern with the community's powers of

survival reappears at the next stage of human advance, the great cycle of archaic civilizations which during the sixth and fifth millennia before Christ appear in Egypt and Sumeria, in the valley of the Indus and along the Yellow River in China. The starting point of these experiments in social organization was probably, as we have already seen, a crisis or challenge presented by the physical environment, in the face of which some men succumbed and others lived to find the answer. Yet it seems likely that one fundamental feature of the transformation—the change from hunting and food gathering to settled agriculture—had been prepared during the long centuries of primitive religion. If, for instance, one studies the Pueblo Indians, a very advanced form of tribal society probably comparable to that of the Neolithic peoples of Europe, one finds them already embarked on the first operations of agriculture. Their whole social order, their religion, their ceremonies, turn upon the cultivation of maize and upon its cycle of planting and watering and harvesting. It is not too fanciful to believe that the attempts of primitive magical religion to control animals and vegetation by imitating them and reproducing their images in pictures and carvings led first to a close study and observation of the natural life of beasts and plants, then to an imitation of nature's processes, and finally therefore to a mastery of the technique of sowing and cultivating and bringing to harvest. Similarly, the animal totems demanded, for their ceremonies, the preservation and taming of a ritual animal; and here may be the germ of the later domestication of animals for human use.

If this is indeed the clue to the transformation of life from the pursuit of game and the gathering of fruit on ever changing hunting grounds to the establishment of settled living in farms and fields and cities, it is not surprising to find that the ritual center of all the great archaic civilizations is the great cycle of agriculture. As the years revolve with their orderly recurrent round of warmth and cold, rains and sunshine, sowing and harvest, life and death, so man's daily existence is a recurring cycle of work and prayer in conformity with the vast forces of nature on which he depends. In most archaic cultures, the processes of nature are symbolized in the Great Mother, the goddess of fertility—Ishtar or Cybele or Astarte or Isis—whose son or lover dies and is resurrected with the rhythm of winter and spring, of barren fields and returning vegetation.

In these early civilizations, the idea of the recurrence of nature tended to become more and more elaborate and the ritual cycle based upon it came to cover more and more of human existence. It led, therefore, to a marked increase in astronomical and chronological knowledge. The orderly movement of the sun, moon, and stars became part of the ritual cycle. The Chaldeans in Babylonian society made startling discoveries in astronomy and derived from them a total fatalism according to which all events in the life of the community and of individual men were conditioned absolutely by the movements of the stars. The great Mayan calendar in Central America provided not only an astronomical calendar but a daily program of human conduct and worship. At the other end of the world, in ancient China, the calendar had a similar ritual significance. The emperor was guardian of the "way of heaven" and his performance of the ritual cycle was the point at which cosmic and social forces met and conformed. Indeed, his great palace—the Ming T'ang—was arranged in a series of rooms representing the different seasons and through them in the course of the year the emperor passed, changing his clothes, his food, and even his music to conform to the great ritual pattern of heaven and earth.

During this phase of archaic civilization, man's mastery of material things increased to a degree probably equaled only by the scientific achievements of the last two centuries. To the men of those ages we owe discoveries without which none of our modern progress would have been conceivable. They invented the alphabet and written language. They laid the foundations of mathematics. They discovered the calendar, the making of metals, the basis of engineering, boatbuilding, seafaring, and the elaboration of many forms of agriculture. Their gigantic monuments—Egypt's pyramids, the irrigation systems of Babylonia, the vast temples of Mayan society—are reminders of an architectural and physical achievement unsurpassed in our own day. Who shall say whether the gap between the hunting nomads' skin tent and the temples of Thebes is not as great as the distance which divides us today from the engineers and astronomers of ancient Egypt?

Yet this material progress did not alter the continuing dependence of the social order on the great vitalities of tribe and economic need. The tribal community was now more elaborate. It might be differentiated by devotion to a particular god. Communities were formed by amalgamating the gods of conquered tribes into the pantheon of a new and enlarged community. But to the new order was transferred the exclusive loyalty of the old and all archaic records bear witness to the clash between rival states and tribes, the perpetual warfare and conquest, the military triumphs and defeats. At the same time, the social order as a whole, including its religious aspect, remained indissolubly united to the processes of agriculture— in other words, to the basic means of survival. Between these necessities—the discipline of the state and the discipline of the economic process—the life of man was a conditioned cycle which expressed "the will of the gods"—the fatalism of unchangeable destiny.

It is not surprising that in such an order of society, the natural outlook of mankind was to see life in terms of the great orderly repetitions of nature. All living things went through the cycle of birth and death. Nature and man shared the same transience and each human generation seemed no more than the passage of the plant from seed and flower to fruit and fall. The stars in their motions followed the same orderly sequence. All things, it appeared, were subject to the law of renewal and departure, birth and death, disappearance and return. The remnants of archaic thinking which survive in the outlook of later ages are all completely deterministic. Life, history, the whole of time is tied to a revolving wheel, a "melancholy wheel" of recurrent birth and death from which man may not deviate by as much as a hairbreadth. The spectacle of this complete bondage gives, as one might imagine, a profound melancholy to the whole of this philosophy, a melancholy which echoes in the words of the greatest disciple of Greek Stoic philosophy, the Roman Emperor Marcus Aurelius, who declared: "Up and down, to and fro, round and round: this is the monotonous and meaningless rhythm of the universe. A man of ordinary mental powers who has reached the age of forty has experienced everything that has been and is and is to come."

II

It seems, no doubt, a far cry from the earth gods and fertility rites of ancient Sumeria and the melancholy determinism of archaic philosophy to our modern rationalism with its picture of a closed material universe or to modern Marxism with its single economically conditioned historical process. Yet it may be that our supposedly modern ideas have more in common with these submerged civilizations than with the two or three thousand years of human history which lie in between. It may be, when we examine modern determinism more closely, that it will appear something of a throwback to ancient ways of thought, a relapse into earlier intuitions and a relinquishing of a significant part of mankind's intellectual and moral heritage.

The first great resemblance between the two modes of thought is that reality, for each, is a single closed process. For modern rationalism there is material Nature self-subsisting and self-renewing: every thought, idea, custom, aspiration, or belief can be reduced to a material explanation. From stellar gas to the mind of Einstein, the whole process is the conditioned reflex of original matter or energy or power. In archaic civilization, too, the whole of reality was conceived of as a single, undifferentiated process. This was the case not because religion was held to be the projection of material activities but because material activities and religious worship were one. Men did not distinguish between plowing and praying, between agriculture and the fertility cults. They were simply different phases in the same ritual existence which conditioned every aspect of life from cradle to grave.

Modern man is the creature of Nature or Natural Selection or Evolution or Economic Necessity or the Historical Process. These are the names we give now to the whole of reality in which we are completely plunged and which determines all our acts and thoughts. In ancient civilization, men were similarly plunged in the material process of life and death. Agriculture was not a secular occupation distinct from the showing forth of the gods of fertility and vegetation. They were each different manifestations of a single reality. The Great Mother brought forth the fruits of the earth. Isis and Osiris, Cybele and Attis were the deities presiding over the rhythm of birth and death, renewal and decay, rise and fall in human history. Today, Evolution is the name we give to the goddess of creation. Dialectical materialism is the Force or Demiurge driving mankind forward through the cycles of change. But reverse the names and forget the differences in terminology, and there emerges a profound philosophical resemblance. Both put man back into a single, unified, and conditioned universe.

From this fundamental resemblance, certain consequences seem to follow. The role of individual men and women in deterministic societies can only be to conform, for if the whole of reality is expressed in the social process, to fulfill one's part in that process is the only conceivable duty for man. It may be that the process, representing as it did in archaic times the cycle of nature through death to rebirth, may involve the most cruel consequences for individual man. The shedding of blood to insure fertility can include human sacrifice—the savage rituals of Aztec society, the dark worship of Moloch and Baal. Similarly, the dialectical process may demand the liquidation of whole classes of people whose only crime is to be historically redundant. But in neither case can appeal be made against the judgment, for there is nothing outside the system to which to appeal.

The consequences in terms of government seem to follow a similar pattern. It is with modern militant materialism that we have seen the return of totalitarian rule. In archaic society, all civil power was concentrated in a single center. In

Mesopotamia, for instance, the cities were temple-cities, the kings were priest-kings, and the whole ordering of society existed to carry on the single undifferentiated process of a civil rule which was also a religious ritual. In this elaborate hierarchical structure, the individual citizen's task was to fulfill his preordained part in the social pattern. That he should fulfill it is undoubtedly the aspiration of modern totalitarian government. The essence is not simply that Communism exacts total obedience: the forecast that in Communist society the state itself will wither away suggests that citizens will reach so perfect an adaptation of their own wills to the needs of society that a Communist social order will more resemble an ant heap or a beehive than a community of human beings. Though a relapse into purely biological forms is ruled out—and one must believe that man is incapable of such decadence—even so, archaic civilization provides a possible pattern of society in which the whole process of social living is so habitually conditioned and ritualized that men and women are hardly conscious of being governed at all. There is a sense in which ancient Egypt was a "classless society," since all manner of men, whatever their trades and callings, were devoted to one huge social task—the glorification of the Sun-God and his child the God-King. A vast elaborate centralized bureaucracy planned and organized the work of the entire people with the one aim of perpetuating the glories of the state embodied in the God-King and in his kingly ancestors.

One cannot, naturally, press too far the resemblance between modern determinism and the archaic forms. However rigorously a Marxist or a rationalist seeks to accept his own completely fatalistic version of society, he lives today after centuries of belief in liberty and choice and responsibility and in a spiritual order of life. Freedom, like Dr. Johnson's cheerfulness, will keep breaking through, even if it has no place in the system. The determinism of ancient society was more thorough because it was not recognized as determinism at all. The unity of all experience, which has to be proclaimed now as a dogma, was then simply accepted as reality itself.

Yet even if our modern determinism is less certain of itself, more argumentative and insecure, it has enough in common with archaic fatalism to put us on our guard. For, whatever the material advances realized in the earliest civilizations—and they were immense—in those societies the values we hold to be the highest of human existence—freedom, responsibility, the quest of personal goodness, independent law, and representative government—had hardly any place. Nor does it take much reflection to see why. If the whole order of reality is predetermined, then there can be no choice, only fatality. If man's actions are conditioned, then there can be no struggle for goodness, only more or less successful conformity to environment. If all values and all philosophies are included within the social process, then no external judgments can be passed on them. It is no use asking whether they are good or true or just: the only question is whether they exist and whether they survive. Determinism becomes inevitably a system in which staying power is the highest value and whatever is, is right.

III

The insights into man, his nature, and his destiny which make up the fabric of our Western society do not spring from archaic civilization, with its determinism, its pessimism, and its endlessly revolving wheel of history. They must be dated from the next great era in human development—the era of the world religions. It is in this period that the decisive elements in Western thought began to emerge from the old conditioned pattern of society. The starting point was the concept of a God no longer the personification of this or that force of nature nor yet the tutelary spirit of the tribe, rather a God creating and sustaining the entire universe behind and beyond all its physical manifestations. To this sublime concept of a God as the Ground of Being was linked the vision of a just and holy order of society lying beyond the actual physical form of any local social system and representing the ideal toward which all social orders ought to tend. This ideal was not arbitrary. It expressed the will of God for man and was held to embody the laws of social wellbeing almost as the laws of bodily health lay down the conditions of physical wellbeing. This law could not be changed by man's arbitrary fiat. It expressed a divine fitness, a final harmony which it should be the aim of all human societies to attain.

Such a concept of a moral order had far-reaching consequences for man's estimate of his own status and dignity. It involved him in choice and hence in freedom. He became, as it were, the co-worker with God in the building of human society: sharing in the achievements, culpable of the failures, carrying the grandeur and servitude of responsibility. No longer absorbed blindly in the social process, he had reason and conscience to guide his judgments and his actions. Little as he might exercise this freedom, easy as it might prove to fall back into the conditioned life of pure appetite, the godlike spark was in him, the breath of divinity, the terrible yet magnificent vocation of a son of God.

When we ask how this sublime concept of man's vocation began to penetrate human consciousness, one answer at least is clear. The insight was not gained as a result of increasing material wellbeing or because of a growing ability to control the physical environment. The era of the great world religions was, in many respects, less materially advanced than the age of archaic civilization which it succeeded. One can see the contrast most sharply in the case of the two peoples who, more than any others, stamped upon human thought their momentous conception of man. The Jews were a small pastoral people whose history is very largely that of resisting or succumbing to the oppression of more powerful neighbors. It was during their captivity in Egypt, among the splendors of the most highly organized social experiment of the archaic world, that the vision was vouchsafed to Moses of a God who is the Subsistent Ground of all being—"I am who am." The great age of the prophets of Israel was not the time of the brief triumph of Jewish society under Solomon. The sorrowful searching into the meaning of human destiny reached its profoundest thoughts after the Jewish people had been taken once again into captivity and ruined and exiled, had sat down and wept by the waters, the temples, and the gorgeous palaces of Babylon.

A similar contrast between the height of human speculation and a relative harshness of physical environment can be seen in Greek society. The actual material apparatus of Athenian culture compares unfavorably with the complicated luxury unearthed in the palaces of the Minoan kings whose society collapsed a thousand years before the great age of Hellas. The experience of the archaic world suggests that a very high degree of material convenience and technical mastery can be combined with very unadventurous or complacent or inferior levels of human speculation and philosophy. Physical discovery alone is not a spur to an enlarged mental vision. The proliferation of material possessions does not of itself widen the frontiers of human thought. In fact, the experience of archaic Egypt suggests that a highly organized, highly developed material civilization which is not disturbed from without ceases to produce from within any ferment of wider vision or spiritual growth. Egyptian civilization, once alive and vigorous, became transformed into one vast museum of a static and repetitive mode of existence, with little more life in it than in one of its own mummies. To a lesser degree, Chinese civilization, too, appeared for a time to be settling into a fixed, ritual, and unvarying social pattern. And in a striking passage in his essay on history, Lord Macaulay suggests that at the origins of our Western society a similar risk was run. The Roman world ". . . was then in danger of experiencing a calamity far more terrible than any of the quick, inflammatory, destroying maladies to which nations are liable—a tottering, drivelling, paralytic longevity, the immortality of the Struldbrugs, a Chinese civilisation."

Since our modern tendency is to overstress the influence exercised by environment and by physical change, it is salutary to remember that, in what may well have been the greatest revolution and transformation mankind has undergone, the part played by material conditions seems at best secondary and in all probability negligible. In fact, it may even have been the partial destruction of the earlier material achievement that opened the channels to a new communication of wisdom. It is certain that the change from archaic polytheistic religion to worldwide monotheism coincided with a general breakdown of the old societies either under the strain of their wars and rivalries or under the impact of Aryan barbarians pressing down from the North along the entire frontier of the archaic world—through Greece onto the confines of Minoan society, through North Persia into Babylonia, across the Himalayas to the valley of the Indus, and from Mongolia into the ancient imperial society of China.

Yet a physical breakdown is no more a necessary cause of spiritual and intellectual progress than is the opposite state of physical success. Some other factor is needed to explain the enlargement of human vision which occurred in this great era of change; and it is at least possible that the clue should be sought neither at the origins of the world religions nor yet in the preceding millennia of archaic civilization, but far back with the origins of human society in the primitive life of the tribe. It can, in fact, be said that the spiritual intuitions of mankind are as old as the practical, materialist "religion" of totem and spell and magic. The religion and social life of some primitive peoples had elements of a different and less utilitarian kind. It is, for instance, difficult to ascribe to purely physical and environmental causes the gentleness and fraternal cohesion of some primitive groups. The relative smallness of the community and the strength of the collective pattern may be part of the explanation. There was little differentiation between various types of work, and the individual members' sense of separate selfhood was probably very dim. It can be argued, too, that the simple processes of hunting and collecting food in small groups were joint pursuits which fostered the spirit of comradeship. Yet if these preconditions are a sufficient explanation, we are left with the problem why other primitive communities display the opposite characteristics of savagery and aggressiveness.

The difference does not lie in types of pursuit, the hunters showing brutality, the agriculturalists a gentle spirit. The hunting tribes of North America were held together by the mildest of social disciplines. Nor does it lie only in environment—for when Columbus reached the West Indies he found on neighboring islands the gentle Lucayans, mild, gracious, tilling the soil, and the fierce Caribs who actually herded the Lucayans as a modern stockman herds his cattle. The male Lucayans were eaten by their Carib neighbors, and enough females kept for brood stock.

This instance suggests, too, that the peaceful, fraternal organization of primitive society did not recur simply because it had a higher power of survival. Insofar as the processes of food getting are co-operative and in the case of agriculture depend upon a sustained respect for the nature of soil and plant, there is a sense in which "the meek shall inherit the earth"—but only so long as no predatory neighbor is armed and ready to take the spoils.

There is another factor in primitive social life which does not seem to be covered by a purely utilitarian explanation. In primitive religion—behind the little gods of the totem, predecessors of the nature and fertility gods in polytheistic, archaic society—there is sometimes found the idea of a single undifferentiated Unity or Reality or Power upon which all else depends. Among Siberian tribes, this Reality is known as The Master on High; the Indians of North America called it by many names—Orenda among the Iroquois, Wakan among the Sioux. Even more remarkable is the degree to which some primitive peoples seem to have felt their way toward definitions which the highest thought of Greece and the deepest insights of Jewry would not disdain. The Master on High of the primitive Siberians was also known as That Which Exists. The Maoris believed that every substantial thing is what it is because it shows forth a divine form. Thus the wanderers on the steppes reached the revelation of God to Moses—"I am who am," while the Maoris, cut off behind the sea barrier of the Pacific, sought after the Platonic archetypes.

There is one possibility which could help to explain both the ethical superiority—as we should say today—of certain types of primitive society and the more abstract forms of religious speculation sometimes attained by primitive man. It is that in these societies, individual men lived and exercised influence whose insight into the nature of reality was more sustained and penetrating than the habitual thoughts and reactions of people immersed in the task of material survival. There appear to be certain facts imbedded, as it were, in the nature of things which are ultimates in human thinking. To recognize that love is better than hate, peace better than war, co-operation than strife, gentleness than violence, example than coercion, seems to be a direct insight into the nature of reality. Similarly, if a man pauses to reflect upon his complete dependence on powers external to himself and reflects further that all material things appear to bear the same mark of dependence, change, and decay, then he is led insensibly to the insight that beneath all dependence and change and decay there must lie a Ground of Being which is uncaused, unchanging, impassable, and self-subsistent.

Such insights as these have appeared self-evident to sages and contemplatives in all generations. Is there then any reason to suppose that primitive man was barred from a similar vision? There is in fact some evidence to suggest that the wisdom and insight of outstanding men played a vital part in primitive religion and social life. The first figure, for instance, to emerge from the undifferentiated work group of the primitive tribe was the shaman—priest, miracle man, witch doctor —chosen, it seems, because he was believed to possess special psychic powers and a unique ability to penetrate beyond the veil of life. Such men may in many cases have had no more capacity than that of a modern medium. Spiritualist trances play a large part in the practices of the Siberian shamans. They may have included tricksters and impostors. But some of them were the type of high contemplative which all societies have agreed to set apart and protect so that wisdom may be distilled from their experience for the benefit of the whole people. (In our own day, concentrated as we are on material things, it is above all the scientific seer whom we withdraw to laboratories and research institutes where his communion with reality may not be disturbed. The artist has, largely, to fend for himself. The saint is not even recognized.)

Among the North American tribes, we read of one such initiate who beheld in early life a vision of the spirit of peace and devoted the rest of his life to settling tribal disputes and differences. "Blessed are the peacemakers for they shall be called the children of God." Many of the great North American tribal movements were led by men of prophetic stature and noble character. Religious revivals such as the Ghost Dance Religion are linked to the leadership of one man.

Some ethnologists believe that the whole attempt to derive primitive religions and ethical insights solely from antecedent physical conditions is a grave distortion of the way in which the concepts were formed. Dr. Paul Radin, in his *Primitive Man as Philosopher*, argues that "No progress in ethnology will be achieved until scholars rid themselves once and for all of the curious notion that everything possesses a history; until they realize that certain ideas and certain concepts are as ultimate for man, as a social being, as specific physiological reactions are ultimate for him, as a biological being." Among these ideas is the oneness, the truth, the wisdom, and the goodness of God; among them, the concept of His will as the profound law of man's existence; among them, the duty and capacity of man to fulfill or neglect that law and hence to build a human or an inhuman society.

IV

These then are insights which it is reasonable to suppose existed in some human minds from the dawn of man's capacity to think and to question. The problem is to determine why, at some particular point in time, these ideas ceased to be the fruits of private contemplation and entered the general patrimony of mankind. The answer seems to be in the interaction between material conditions at the close of the archaic phase of history and the insights of the contemplatives. The barbarians who burst into the confines of civilization in the second millennium before Christ were men of greater vigor and lower culture than the societies they invaded. Their incursions led to anarchy and collapse and to the breakdown of the traditional ritual order. Men were bewildered and at sea. We can well believe that they began to compare the present confusion with their memories of the old stable order (we begin to hear for the first time of Golden Ages to which mankind looks back with nostalgia) and that they lost their old ability to accept existing conditions as the whole of reality. Dualism crept in, a sense of division between what was current and the happier and better times that had been or could be. From this critical sense there sprang a reaching-out after an ideal or way of life not incorporated in existing conditions but one by which existing conditions could be judged.

Yet if the ideal order no longer existed in the world itself, either it did not exist at all and the current evil times were all the reality men could know, or else it existed in some invisible form, in some higher order of reality, in short, in a divine order which could no longer be confused with the material universe. But this withdrawal of the ideal from earthly life left the responsibility for evildoing, for the wars and the disorders and the destruction, squarely upon the shoulders of men. They were the agents of misery and it was by their actions that the gap had opened between the ideal and the real. The conception of men as independent actors on the stage of good and evil begins to appear.

It may be that conclusions as general and vague as these could have been reached by any reasonably reflective soul living sorrowfully in the "time of troubles" that brought the archaic world to its end. But there is at least a reasonable possibility that mankind owed its new insights to individual men of more than ordinary intellectual and moral power. Like the scattered mystics of primitive society, they reached that primal intuition of a single self-subsistent Ground of Reality and of an order of goodness, love, and peace which at times had pierced through the utilitarian and magical activities of primitive religion.

Whether this primitive insight recurred in individual men during the heyday of archaic society, when a successful materialist religion embraced all human activities, we do not know. There are suggestions from history that such is the case. There are instances of single men setting their face against the massive strength of tradition and attraction contained in the fertility cults. In the fourteenth century before Christ, the Egyptian Pharaoh Ikhnaton attempted to impose pure monotheism and ethical religion on his subjects and to oust ritual polytheism from Egypt. The early chapters of the Bible are full of the anger of prophets denouncing in the Israelites their constant tendency to prefer the fleshpots of nature religion to the austere insights of a single transcendent God worshiped in obedience and lowliness of heart. Moses, coming down the mountain bearing the tables of the Law and finding the people of Israel dancing joyously around the Golden Calf, gives us in a single picture of intense dramatic power the travail undergone by men of spiritual insight in their striving to convey their vision to peoples half submerged in the myths, dreams, and comforts of a materialist religion. There is thus a possibility that the vision of the new world religions was latent throughout the long development of early civilizations and came into its own when the collapse of that civilization brought agony and questioning to the people at large.

One fact, however, is certain. At the origins of virtually all the new world religions stands a man or a group of men who by their wisdom and superior vision became the founders, leaders, prophets, and sages of the new way of life. Anonymity may have been the rule of primitive and archaic religion. Individual personality appears with the beginnings of the world religions. Sometimes these men are known chiefly by their writings, as are the authors of the Indian Upanishads. Sometimes their historical existence is a little blurred by myth, as in the case of Zoroaster, the Persian Magus. But Confucius and Lao-tse in China are men whose lives and personalities are a matter of fact, not conjecture. The Lord Buddha lived in historical times. The prophets of Jewry live for us in overwhelming vitality. We know when most of the Greek philosophers were born and where they taught and died. In the Founder of Christianity we have a man born and registered at a precise date under one Roman emperor and crucified and buried on a certain day under another.

V

There is an immediate link between the ancient societies and the new insights of the world religions. The old order was contained within a ritual order of ceremonial and sacrifice. In every case, the great teachers of the new religions preserve this concept of order but give it a completely new interpretation. It is now a spiritual order of justice and truth and man's fulfilling of its rites is no longer a matter simply of the correct gestures and sequences. It turns on his inner acceptance of truth and justice and his conforming of his life to the ideal pattern. In Confucian thought, the rites "have their origin in Heaven and the movement of them reaches to the earth." In Persian thought, *arta* is the symbol of the new order of justice, in India, it is called *rita*, and the same concept appears in the Greek ideal of *dike*—eternal justice—and in the Jewish Law. When men conform to this, the inner law of their being, then the whole order of the universe flourishes. In the Confucian Li-ki, it is written: "When the Son of Heaven moves in his virtue like a chariot, with music as his driver, while all the Princes conduct their mutual intercourse according to the Rites, the great officers maintain the order between them according to the laws, inferior officers compete with one another by their good faith and the common people guard one another in a spirit of harmony, all under the sky is in good condition. This produces the state that is called the Great Unity." One may consider with this a comparable extract from the Greek writer Hesiod, in his *Works and Days:* "When men follow justice the whole city blooms, the earth bears rich harvests, and children and flocks increase, but to the unjust all nature is hostile, the people waste away from famine and pestilence and a single man's sin may bring ruin upon a whole city."

This central concept of a superhuman order of reality which, if man will know and follow it, brings harmony and peace, was interpreted with different emphasis in different societies. In Confucian China, at one end of the scale, the new religion did not seek to inquire more closely into the nature of the

Reality the fulfilling of whose laws brought the Great Unity. It was simply accepted as the "way of heaven." The main interest in Confucian thought lay with the way of the virtuous man on earth and in society. These ways were not, however, simply ceremonial and exterior. They implied the adherence of the sage's mind and spirit to the inner law of benevolence, justice, and truth by which his behavior could be made part of a universal harmony. The gap left in Confucian thought by its comparative worldliness was filled in China by the Taoists, who were absorbed in studying the Reality which lay behind the world, the Reality whose law the Confucians accepted but whose being they did not explore.

It is in Hindu thought that this concentration of thought upon the Source of all being reaches its highest pitch. Seeing the world as archaic thought had seen it, as a constant order of change, of birth and death, of growth and decay, the Indians sought passionately for the changeless, the undying, the absolute Ground of all being. Earthly things fell away before this search for uncreated Reality, dwelling apart in inaccessible light. Indian religion turned away from the painted tapestry of appearances. Rejection, asceticism, and spiritual detachment became the way of advance. The man who is caught by ambition or greed remains trapped among the transient goods of this world. Only complete purification from all desire and complete stillness of spirit can lead to the goal of all existence—union of man's spiritual essence with the Reality that is Spirit. Indian thought believed that at the base of each man's separate selfhood dwelt the universal Spirit. Atman was at once the soul of man and the Absolute principle of the Universe. If man could disentangle himself from the web of desire and detach himself from the melancholy wheel of existence, he could reach deliverance in merging his soul with the World Soul, Atman returning to Atman, "the flight of the Alone to the Alone."

The other great religion of India and the Far East, Buddhism, is in its original form an apparent combination of the Confucian and the Hindu approach to religion. Like Confucius, Buddha was not concerned with the nature of Reality.

The moral law, *Dharma*—like the Rites of Confucius—is the inner law of man's being and the acquiescence of the whole self to this law is the way of salvation. Nothing further is needed. But from Hindu thought, Buddha took the meaninglessness of life, the weariness of the flesh, the emptiness of earthly existence, and the one aim of life—deliverance from life into the peace of extinction or Nirvana. "One thing only I preach," said Buddha, "sorrow and the ending of sorrow." Later, however, under Greek influence, the concept of God and of Buddha as a redeemer came into Mahayanan Buddhism and it was in this form that it traveled from India into China.

One may speculate what would have been the future of mankind if these religions of the Eastern world had been the only systems of thought to arise at the end of archaic civilization. They seem each to have labored under the handicap of certain one-sidedness and this lack of balance may perhaps be discerned in their later development. Although for Confucius, the Rites were rules of inner morality and purification and demanded the free adhesion of man's spiritual nature, their concentration upon social life and upon man's behavior in society made it all too easy for them to degenerate into exterior rules and ceremonies and thus to repeat the fixed and static pattern from which the spiritual insight of Confucius had rescued them. Chinese society, as Lord Macaulay pointed out, tended to return to the idea of an unchanging ritual order, to return, in a word, to an archaic pattern which threatened to bring with it the fate of ossification undergone by Egypt. The violent incursion of Western traders in the nineteenth century put an end to this danger but we cannot be certain that China, fixed in its ceremonial Confucian world, had the inner power to change and develop within itself.

Indian society seems to have run the same risk of ossification but by a different route. The doctrine of absolute transcendence and the rejection of this world in man's search for Reality proved too austere and remote for the mass of the people. The priests, the seekers, the holy men were honored for their asceticism, and in theory all religion was based upon the transcendent reality of pure Being. But in practice the old rites and rituals of the fertility religions persisted in enormous strength and beneath the serene view of such mystics as Shankara there flourished such dark remnants of archaic rites as the bloodstained worship of the goddess Kali or such crude cults of fertility as may still be seen in village shrines the length and breadth of India. And in spite of repeated invasions from without—by early barbarians, by the Greeks, by the Moslems —it was this nature religion with its crowded pantheon of gods and goddesses that fixed the pattern of Indian life almost unchanged until the full impact of the West began to be felt as the eighteenth century ended.

There is thus at least a chance that in two of the greatest centers of archaic civilization, the change which came over the world in the second and first millennia before Christ was to a certain extent abortive. The new religious insights, great as they were, did not succeed in permeating the old archaic world sufficiently to transform it and set it on a new route. The material gains of the old order survived. In fact, India and China remained in a state of material splendor that could astonish Europe in the Middle Ages. But they tended toward a static magnificence. The growing points of history lay elsewhere.

Law and the Logos

WITH the Greeks and the Jews, we enter into our own heritage. For fifteen hundred years in Western civilization, the two traditions have been at work and between them they have formed the intellectual and moral basis of society. It is only in the last hundred years that they have lost their power. Even when we criticize them and believe that they have been transcended, we do so in the name of principles such as social justice or reason or scientific truth which we have learned from them and which possibly will not survive when the springs that nourished them are dried up.

For those who believe that all history can be reduced to its underlying physical necessities, the Greeks and the Jews must be an extraordinarily unrewarding and irritating field of study. The two peoples possess such a stamp of individuality, such a rich, unpredictable, and idiosyncratic character that they resemble not a local instance of some general scientific rule but the uniqueness and the creative freedom of a work of art. From the moment the Greek world first begins to break in upon our imagination, in the poetry of Homer, we know that we are face to face with a people of intense genius whose intellectual force is matched only by their sense of beauty and whose passionate interest in all things human is balanced by a noble and somber vision of universal destiny and law. Even in translation, the opening of the *Iliad* makes the reader instantly aware of a new power and a new perspective. The story is no long rambling mythological account of the wars of Troy, comparable to other discursive annals thrown up by tribal societies in times of trouble and migration. On the contrary, it is one brief episode in the long desperate war. It concerns the consequences of Agamemnon's intolerable pride and Achilles' destructive wrath, moral evils which, like all violations of the moral law, bring down disaster on the two guilty men but further "brought ten thousand sorrows on the Greeks, sent the souls of many brave heroes down to the world of the dead and left their bodies to be devoured by dogs and birds; and thus was the will of Zeus fulfilled."

In a moment, we are launched in the full flood of the epic; and as it carries us along through the throes of battle, every page illustrates the Greek capacity to concentrate on an essential theme, to illustrate it brilliantly but sparingly, to allow the individual man or woman to appear in full humanity (Who can forget Hector's tender meeting with his wife and little son on the walls of Troy, when the boy starts back and cries with fear at his father's great helmet and horsehair crest?) and yet under the daily flux of fighting and quarreling and deliberating, never to forget the laws of necessity—the will of the gods—by which all human beings are bound.

It is impossible to explain away this first flashing forth of the Greek genius in terms of underlying economic and social pressures. Barbarian peoples of Aryan stock were pressing in from the North on most of the old archaic societies. The languages they brought with them have some elements or even words in common. But in richness and flexibility, in its ability to express the finest shades of meaning and relation, the Greek tongue surpassed them all. Again, the Greek community began, as did the Roman community, in a series of city states. But Rome never evolved a communal democracy, solved few of its constitutional problems without civil war, and in spite of its greater strength and greater wealth, at last adopted the cultural traditions of the Greeks whose territory it had conquered. In the economic field the Phoenicians, like the Greeks, were great traders from their parent city of Tyre and, again like the Greeks, established trading colonies along the Mediterranean, of which Carthage was the most powerful. Yet Carthage remained faithful to the darkest gods of antiquity and evolved no form of government save despotism. Thus neither racial background nor social organization nor economic system can give an adequate explanation of the Greek miracle. Each played a part, no doubt, and Greek life in some degree conforms to general sociological laws and patterns. But in essence it has to be accepted, like the supreme genius of individual men and women, as a unique and irreducible fact.

The power and the proportions of the Greek achievement can best be judged by reflecting on what the Athenians managed to do, to think, and to create between, say, 600 B.C. and 300 B.C. Attica, their territory, was no bigger than Massachusetts or Middlesex. The total number of citizens was never more than 100,000. Athens itself was about the size of Providence or Bristol. Yet this minute community was the home, within a few generations, of great legislators like Solon, Cleisthenes, and Pericles; of poets of the stature of Aeschylus, Sophocles, Euripides, and Aristophanes; of Thucydides, the greatest of all historians; of Phidias and Praxiteles, the first outstanding sculptors of the human body; of architects capable of designing the Acropolis; and of a brilliant line of philosophers crowned by Socrates and Plato. In all these fields, the Greeks of genius had little or no tradition upon which to work. The inheritance from the past was largely of material things such as the remains of the submerged Minoan culture, some practical geometry and engineering learned from Egypt, and the serious astral studies of the Chaldeans. But in the great fields of speculation, of scientific inquiry, of political philosophy and the humanities, the Greeks were doing things for the first time in the history of man. The intense influence they have exercised on all subsequent ages is simply the reflection of supreme genius. It is we who are impoverished if, by ignorance, we can no longer yield to their spell.

II

Early Greek religion does not seem to have been essentially different from the polytheism of other primitive societies except that it was more complex. The original inhabitants of Greece, who were part of the old Minoan culture, were worshipers of the Great Mother and participants in the fertility cults. But the Achaean barbarians who brought the Greek tongue with them followed sterner tribal gods and in the fusion of the two peoples a very large company of gods and goddesses began to jostle for the devotion of the new Greek communities. However, with that spirit of order so characteristic of the Greek mind, the competing deities were sorted out, often married to each other, and an orderly Olympian hierarchy of heaven under Zeus came into being.

But beside this pantheon of deities, representing in vivid dramatic form—a form beloved of the Greeks—the forces of nature or the tutelary collective spirits of towns and clans, the Greek poets had a vision of another, deeper and more sober reality. *Dike* (justice) or *ananke* (necessity) was recognized as the inescapable law of the universe, binding on all created things, binding even on the gods themselves. In one sense, this law was no more than the fatalities of existence, the certainty of sorrow, the inevitability of death. For all his genius and magnificence, the greatest of men dies like the meanest. Homer, contemplating his kings and heroes in all their splendor, wrote: "As is the life of the leaves, so is that of men. The wind scatters the leaves to the ground: the vigorous forest puts forth others, and they grow in the spring season. Soon one generation of men comes and another ceases."

But *ananke* is more than a recognition of inevitability. The law which governs the universe is also a moral law and moral events have their inevitable consequences just as have physical events. An evil act sets in train a sequence of disaster which must work itself out either in sacrifice and expiation or in blind catastrophe. And of all evil acts, none seems to draw disaster upon itself more certainly than *hubris*. *Hubris* is perhaps a particularly Greek temptation, for the Greeks found man so preeminent, "in action how like an angel, in apprehension, how like a god," that they felt little of the Indian contempt for the vitalities and vanities of human existence. They reveled in worldly greatness. But for that reason they knew all the more keenly how disastrous to himself and to his neighbors is the man who succumbs to *hubris*, to overconfidence, to overmastering ambition, to unrelenting pride and self-conceit, to a ruthless overreaching of others in pursuit of his own interests.

This lesson—that immoral acts darken creation and destroy the harmony of nature—is the greatest theme of the Greek poets. Every Greek child to receive a formal education imbibed the idea from Homer and learned from the cradle the grandeur and servitude of earthly life and the supremacy of the moral law. It is no doubt this sober training that prepared the Greeks to become the most serious and cultured mass audience artists have ever had to please. It is not that they did not like fun. The comedies of Aristophanes are full of the most boisterous and unprintable kind. But year after year, the people of Athens crowded into the great amphitheaters, young and old, rich and poor, men, women, and children alike, to watch the dramas of Aeschylus, Euripides, or Sophocles and to listen to the theme of man's moral nature proclaimed in the highest verse. Only one audience in the world has even faintly compared with them—the groundlings of London who made up Shakespeare's box office. When the standard is compared with its modern equivalent—the queues at the movies, the group round the television set, the captive audience at a Communist propaganda play—it is possible that men of our own time will be spared one temptation at least—that of *hubris*.

At first, the primal moral law was held to be supreme over the gods themselves. Later, again in the interests of order, it was seen not as a separate force but as "the will of Zeus." At this point, however, the irreverence and blatant immorality of so many of the myths connected with the gods began to open a breach between the poets and the philosophers. The poets used myth as the stuff of poetry and distilled from it profound discoveries about the nature and destiny of man. The philosophers were concerned with the purity and universality of law— rational law, scientific law, moral law—and could not tolerate the raw material with which the poets worked. Plato even decided that Homer could not be admitted to his ideal Republic. In this dispute, the philosophers erred in believing the poets to be immoral. As we have seen, Greek art was a profoundly moral force. Yet in the development of man's thinking about the universe, the Greek philosophers had the more lasting influence, for they rose above the local limitations of race, geography, or mythology to study reason itself.

The Greek mind could not tolerate the idea of a disorderly, unruly, unpredictable, and therefore lawless universe. The puzzle of creation lay in the apparent flux of material things and the apparent arbitrariness of so much that happens. The Greeks' desire for order led them to search this stream of phenomena to find in it the elements of certainty and of law. In the process, they believed themselves to have discovered certain truths both about their own minds and the universe their minds were exploring; these conclusions represent a new element in the thinking of man.

It is probably most people's experience that once they begin reflecting upon the processes of thought or knowledge, the commonsense view of how we think and know gives way to a sort of bewilderment that processes apparently so straightforward should turn out to be so complicated. We think we see a table. But what we see is a limited number of sense data of color and shape and depth. From them we deduce the existence of other sense data which we cannot see—the back legs, for instance—and we pronounce the picture made up in this way, part seen, part deduced, to be a table. Again, we see a man strike a ball. The ball slides away. We say that the man has caused the ball to roll, but all we have seen is a succession of sense data which would be the same if at the exact moment the man reached out to the ball, a breeze had blown it. In other words, the sense data by themselves do not tell us that the ball moving is the effect of the man's reaching out his hand. Our judgment is in the main based upon our own inner experience of causality, in which our own decisions cause our brain to guide our hand and our hand the ball. Causality is deduced from our inner experience, not given in the external environment. Day follows night with monotonous regularity, but we do not say one causes the other. Heart failure is followed equally regularly by death and we do say that the one causes the other. But sense impressions alone give us no more than sequence. If we can distinguish between a sequence that does represent cause and effect and another that does not, it is because we do so not by direct experience but by a refinement of experience effected by our reasoning powers.

Again, there are some types of knowledge which appear to be independent of any exterior material universe perceived by the senses. That if two things are equal to a third thing, they are equal to each other seems to be such a logical certainty. That something cannot come from nothing is another. In this field of logical necessity, the laws of mathematics are supreme. They can be applied to weighing and measuring and are the final test of scientific accuracy; but even in an abstract universe, in which there were no energies to measure or planetary orbits to plot, numbers would continue to enjoy their certain and symmetrical relations—two and two would forever make four, and the square on the hypotenuse of a right-angled triangle would still be equal to the sum of the squares of the other two sides.

The Greek philosophers were the first people to think systematically about these problems of knowledge—of the knower and the known—and it led them to their belief in the supremacy of reason. Reason, they believed, is the power in man's mind that enables him to make sense of the flood of fleeting phenomena beating on his brain. From the sense data of brownness and woodenness and legginess, reason constructs the idea of a table. Again, it is reason that distinguishes such relations between things as causality or dependence, which are not given by the senses and must be deduced. It is reason therefore that establishes the notion of law behind the flux of phenomena. Reason sees directly and without intermediary sensations the truths of logic and of mathematics. In fact, only reason can give any sense to the notion of truth itself.

Reason, further, can grasp by direct intuition the highest of all realities, which is the idea of the Good. Here we find the concept of a moral order freed from local and mythological entanglements, an order accessible to reason much as are the truths of mathematics. The proposition that I must not pursue my own wellbeing at the expense of my neighbor or—our earlier example—that *hubris* brings destruction is felt to be as di-

rect a rational insight into the nature of reality as that two
plus two equals four. Reason and virtue are one and knowledge leads not only to truth but to goodness.

These intuitions of order in man's knowledge called for a
comparable order in external reality. A rational mind could
hardly make sense of an irrational universe. The Greeks sought
order, unity, and symmetry so unswervingly in their thinking
about the world that they often saw unities where none was
to be found and tried to impose rational patterns which existed
only in their own minds. So intoxicated were they by reason
that they were tempted to think that everything could be deduced from first principles and forgot to go and verify their
deductions by concrete results. But even if some of their theories are wrong—for example that the whole world is made of
water—they managed to reach a surprising number of correct
conclusions. Democritus had an atomic theory not incompatible with Rutherford's. Anaximander deduced from the de-
fenselessness of human infants the evolutionary principle that
they must have descended from animals that can look after
themselves.

The extraordinary results of modern science, in which fact
after fact of human experience is unified and shown to obey
coherent law, would have delighted the Greeks and would certainly have confirmed their greatest thinkers—Socrates, Plato,
or Aristotle—in their belief that the external world is permeated with law, that law implies reason, and that the source of
all reality is Reason itself.

"In the beginning was the word," the Logos, the Idea. Just
as the Indian philosophers by reflecting on the fact of existence
reached the concept of God as the Being behind all being and
the individual soul as a reflection of that almighty Life, so the
Greek philosophers reflecting upon the nature of knowledge
and upon the mind of the knower reached the conclusion that
ultimate reality has its source in divine Reason. Of this intense
light, men's minds are a minute refraction.

III

Since this sense of rationality and law permeated all Greek thinking, it is not surprising to find that it lies at the basis of Greek political thought and that here, as in other spheres of human life, the new ideas the Greeks entertained opened a new phase in human development. Until their time, in recorded history, government had been arbitrary. Tribal societies had perhaps a rudimentary sense of the chieftain's need to secure his people's support. In some of the primitive social groups of West Africa, the king can be deposed—destooled, as it is called—by a dissatisfied people. But in the archaic societies which developed from primitive religion and magic, government was universally despotic, a private matter for king or priest, arbitrary, unpredictable, at the mercy of palace cliques or rival generals—remote, too, and cut off from the subject, whose whole duty seemed to be exhausted in simple obedience. This method of government was distasteful to the Greek mind for two reasons.

The first, we believe, with our modern concept of democracy, that we understand: it is the Greek desire to participate in processes which touch his life at so many points. To be excluded from government is to be deprived of an essential freedom. We, too, argue that a man must have the right to decide by his vote who shall govern him. But participation for the Greeks meant something much more than this. It meant actually joining in the deliberations of government and later in the carrying out of the decisions. This was possible since the *polis*—the Greek city state—was no bigger than a small modern town and could still be governed by the town meeting. The Greeks thus started democracy off in the Athenian *polis* on a level of vitality and achievement which no large state can ever match. But the brilliance of the experiment guaranteed its power to survive as a criticism and condemnation of all despotic forms of government.

The second reason why despotism was anathema to the Greeks is perhaps not so clearly in our minds today when we speak of free government. Despotism, so the Greeks maintained, denies freedom because it denies objective and intelligible law. The whim of an autocrat of whatever kind exposes a man to irrational and unpredictable hazards. He is not free because he does not know where he is. Only if government conforms to law—to *themis* or *dike*—can the citizen be said to be free. In our modern theories of the absolute sovereignty of parliament or nation or people or the General Will we have strayed far from the Greeks' concept of legality. They believed that lawful government could be endangered as much by the majority of the people voting an illegality as by the action of a clique based on birth or wealth and intent on preserving undue privilege. The various constitutions devised by Greek statesmen of genius—by Solon, by Cleisthenes, and by Pericles —were all designed to secure legal government by preventing the domination of any one group. In the darkest day of Athens, when the thirty-year struggle with Sparta had undermined the moral and physical substance of the *polis*, the Athenian assembly did claim complete sovereignty: its members condemned to death their unsuccessful generals, they outraged and lost their maritime dependencies, they crowned their lawlessness by the judicial murder of Socrates. For this reason we find, in Greek philosophers of the stature of Plato or Aristotle, no love for democracy as we use the term today. Indeed, they would agree with the somber warning uttered by Lord Acton: ". . . that government by the whole people, being the government of the most numerous and most powerful class, is an evil of the same nature as unmixed monarchy and requires, for nearly the same reasons, institutions that shall protect it against itself and shall uphold the permanent reign of law against arbitrary revolutions of opinion."

IV

The three great ideas which the genius of the Greeks gave to mankind are the rationality and intelligibility of the universe, the independence of the moral order, and the free and responsible citizen participating in a political community based on law. Law is the central intuition: law above the "arbitrary revolutions of opinion," above the will of men—law, in short, as a divine order showing forth the supreme Reason, the Logos, God Himself. Greek society did not fully realize this exalted vision, though in the age of Pericles, it perhaps came as near to it as transient and fallible mortal man can reach. Slaves were excluded from citizenship—though the most gifted could become free. Statesmanship did not overcome the internecine wars that tore Greece apart. War led to lawless government. And perhaps as a result of these troubles that overcame Hellas, the Greek mind, for all its joy and pride in living, has at last a melancholy tinge. In Plato we find echoes of an almost Indian detachment from the fleeting world of phenomena. In the *Phaedrus*, he says that "if man had eyes to see Divine Beauty, pure and clean and unalloyed, not clogged with the pollutions of mortality and all the colors and vanities of human life," his one aim would be "to fly away from earth to heaven." Even Aristotle, who rejected Platonic idealism and sought truth and knowledge through the study of everyday phenomena observed by the senses, believed that the natural world was involved in a permanent cycle of growth and decay and that all natural things are fixed upon a wheel which, revolving through all the changes of the Great Year, at last brings man back to the beginning to repeat the process. Once again, we hear echoes of Indian pessimism, of life bound to a "melancholy wheel," and of human existence condemned to meaningless repetition. For mankind's break with this form of determinism, we have to look not to the Greeks but to the other unique people of the ancient world, the people of Jewry, who were the first to believe that history itself has meaning and that progress, not repetition, is the law of life.

4

God in the World

IF AN exponent of the materialist explanation of history had been living and teaching by the shores of the eastern Mediterranean in the second millennium before Christ and had been asked to make his forecast about the next stage in human affairs, he would no doubt have examined carefully the great archaic societies around him—Egypt to the south, Babylonia to the east, the rising Assyrian power in the north, the Hittite community of Asia Minor, and the flourishing maritime empire of the Minoans. He would have considered their relative relative economic strength, their differing military abilities, the pressure on them internally of rising population and externally of barbarian encroachment, and out of these calculations, he would have made his guess that in the next phase of history one or other power would exercise the greatest influence—Egypt perhaps because of its high degree of administrative organization, Minoan Crete for its maritime flexibility and commercial wealth, Babylonia for its elaborate economy, or perhaps Assyria for its addiction to naked aggression.

But one thing we can be fairly certain our early Marxist would have overlooked. He would have missed the significance of a small pastoral hill people of Judea whose immediate destiny was to be overrun by the Assyrian conquest of Babylon, to be scattered far from their native Jerusalem, and to endure exile in the very capital of the enemy. Yet in the three thousand years that have followed the Babylonian captivity, history has borne the living imprint of the Jews while the great empires that overshadowed them have vanished into dust. The Jews, like the Greeks, are a unique fact in the development of man. No amount of explanation derived from environment or race or economic pursuits can dissolve their obstinate separateness. There were other pastoral peoples in the Levant. Other tribes had their own single jealous tribal god. Other groups were ground between the upper and nether millstones of war, invasion, and captivity. If material explanations were all, they too should have produced similar insights into man's nature and destiny. But it was this particular race, living in this particular time of history, that became the vehicle of the new ideas. These ideas have the originality and unpredictability of genius. They do not "abide our question." Like the utterance of the great artist or the great thinker, they remind us of the element in man that is free and creative, the element that cannot, by however elaborate a materialist explanation, be reduced to a mere projection of environment and heredity.

Perhaps the most remarkable of the insights contributed by Jewry was the break with the universal archaic idea of a history in endless cycles of repetition. Because the idea of progress in history is still so strong in us in spite of the catastrophes of this century, it is difficult to realize what a startling break with universal thought the Jews made when they saw in history not conditioned recurrence but progressive manifestation of a divine plan for the human race. It was not only that all previous thought on the subject weighed against their new view. The catastrophes in which they were involved and the rise and fall of empires through which they clung with fierce intensity to their national and religious identity ought to have convinced them that meaningless recurrence is, materially speaking, the lot of human societies, and that the growth and decadence of peoples is slower but no less certain than the spring and autumn of each revolving year. Yet with obstinate faith they chose to turn history upside down and to maintain against all experience and all apparent reason that the God of high heaven had chosen them, a single pastoral people of a few thousand souls, to declare to the world the fact that history had a meaning and that the meaning was contained in the destiny of their own race. It is difficult to imagine a claim that would have seemed more laughable to their contemporaries: the priests of Egypt, the scientists of Chaldea, or the merchant princes of Crete. But it was not to these men that the future belonged.

Other tribes, as we have seen, had an original insight into the unity and supremacy of God—the sky god, the master on high. The unique feature of the Jews' development is their preservation of the original vision. It was not that they were never tempted to discard it. The episode of the Golden Calf is a symbol of the pressure exercised on the Jewish people to fuse their worship of their tribal deity Jahweh with devotion to the multitudinous gods of the fertility cults. The Jews were surrounded by peoples more powerful and more cultivated than they, whose totems and titulary deities had entered the pantheon of nature worship, had been provided with female partners, and now presided over a ritual religion whose orgiastic rites drew down the thunderous denunciations of a long line of austere Jewish prophets. These moral leaders clung to the concept of a unique God beside whom there could be no other gods, and they compelled an often reluctant people to accept their fierce, intolerant, but sublime vision.

This God of the Jews was not a nature god. He was something more. He was the God of nature. He did not in some way symbolize the cycle of nature, dying with the harvest and resurrecting at the time of sowing as did the grain-kings of the fertility religions. He made the harvest and He ordained the passing of the seasons and He ordered the movements of the planets. Nature's Cause and Creator, beyond nature, He "formeth the mountains and createth the wind and declareth unto man what is His thought, that maketh the morning darkness and treadeth on the high places of the earth." He is not part of nature. Nature itself is His domain. "The beasts of the field are Mine. Mine are the cattle upon a thousand hills." He it is who "laid the foundations of the earth . . . when the morning stars praised Me together and all the sons of God made a joyful music." Thus the Jews reached a concept of God which differed in vital respects from any other insight achieved by the ancient world. On the one hand, God was

Lord of nature, separate from it and in no way immersed in its fatalities. The Jews had no part in the polytheism of the fertility religions. But since Creation was the work of God's hands, it could not be dismissed as an illusion, as a mere transitory flux of appearances, as the *maya* of Indian philosophers or the recurring and unchanging cycle of Greek thought.

II

This picture gave a peculiar vitality to the Jewish concept of God and a special value to the Jewish idea of the world and of time. The vitality is quite simply the overwhelming impression of a *living* God. His ways might be unsearchable and His wisdom incomprehensible. He might be as remote from human understanding as the pure Being adored by the Brahmans or the ultimate Rationality sought for by the Greeks. But He was never in any danger of becoming an abstraction. Father, Creator, Worker, Judge—He floods the holy books of the Jewish people with an enormous, almost an appalling vitality. The Jews themselves felt it. "It is a terrible thing to fall into the hands of the living God." So often we think of "being"—if we think of it at all—as the last anonymous something left when all recognizable qualities have been abstracted. But the God who declared Himself "I am who am" to Moses represents the fullness of being, its inexhaustible energy (which only in the atomic age can we even faintly grasp), its plenitude of quality, its torrent of life.

The world represents the outpouring of this creative energy. God looked on His handiwork, in the Jewish version of Creation, and "found it good." It was inconceivable that anything made by God should be without value or without meaning. The Jews could not entertain the idea that the sense and purpose of history lay wholly beyond time. God's will had also to be manifested in time since time, too, was His creature. The almost universal ancient belief in revolving cycles of change, in which the end brings back the beginning, was blasphemy to the Jews, for it condemned the works of God to futility and made nonsense of Creation itself.

Yet if the Jews' view of God as Creator and Father necessarily involved the belief that nature is good, it left them with a difficulty which Eastern philosophy could dismiss. If the world of appearances is an illusion, the ills and miseries that arise in it are no problem to the philosopher. They are what one would expect in a world of nightmare unreality. But what were the Jews to make of the apparent botching of God's masterpiece? They were as fully aware of evil as any Indian philosopher or Buddhist sage. The book of Job is probably man's most sublime cry of agony and protest at the insensate disasters which overcome mankind, tragedies which do not spare the good, horrors that are visited on the innocent. Through the later book of Ecclesiastes there runs a note of pessimism almost as extreme as that of the Buddha himself: "I saw the oppressions that are done under the sun and the tears of the innocent. And they had no comforter and they were not able to resist violence, being destitute of help. And I praised the dead rather than the living."

This problem of suffering was particularly poignant to the Jews, for they had more to explain than the general discrepancy between the goodness of God's creation and the terrors that happened in it. They also had to understand how it was that the lot of His chosen people should be so particularly wretched. Uprooted, scattered by their enemies, their holy city invaded, their temple desecrated, they sat by the alien waters of Babylon and pondered the inscrutable judgments of God.

III

In one sense the Jews made the transition we have remarked in other cultures in their times of tribulation—the transition from the idea of an exterior order of ritual law and sacrifice to the idea of an inner righteousness more pleasing to God than the richest material offerings. "Obedience is better than sacrifice and to hearken than the fat of rams." A moral law is perceived in the place of the old ritual law. The Jews, too, believed even more intensely than the Greeks that the disorder in the universe is the inevitable and unalterable consequence of wrongdoing. In their view, man's individual wickedness darkens the world and destroys the harmony of things; moreover, the collective infidelity of the Jewish people is the reason for their disasters and their dispersal. God is a God of righteousness and a God of judgment. The judgments are worked out in time, and if His chosen people dance around the Golden Calf, then sooner or later they will undergo the Babylonian captivity. Disaster is not a sign of God's impotence or of His failure to protect His own people; it is the rod of His anger chastising them for their iniquities. The Assyrian conquerors are the Lord's mysterious instruments in the working out of history, for all things and all peoples are subject to Him and show forth His secret judgments. The Jews as a people may not be aware of this sublime vision. They are as involved as any other nation in the struggle for survival, in wars and disputes and dynastic squabbles, in harvests and in failures of the harvest. It is the great line of Hebrew prophets who interpret to them the meaning of the history in which they are submerged and, like the supreme dramatists of Greece, use the facts of history to illustrate the working out of man's moral destiny.

There is a strong resemblance between the moral order as the Jews perceived it and the moral law lying at the base of the other world religions. In all of them, the root of evil is man's preference for himself and for his own desires and interests. Sin lies in the variety of ways in which he sacrifices others to his own self-love. Thousands of years before Freud set out in our own day "to lance the poisonous bubble of human pride" by his revelation of the heart's hidden motives, the Greeks knew that *hubris* was the most baleful expression of self-love, while the Jews pictured mankind expelled through pretension and pride from the natural felicity of the Garden of Eden. The symbolical temptation offered to man's first parents was that, in eating the forbidden fruit, they should become "as God, knowing good and evil." Pride was the lure baiting the paradisal tree. This original insight appears to have made the Jewish moralists particularly sensitive to the evils which flow from pride—the pride of possession, the pride of power—and to dwell with special tenderness on the lot of the meek and the afflicted and the poverty-stricken whose condition of life seems to hold them aloof from the temptations of authority and wealth. In the song of Anna, mother of Samuel, "the bow of the mighty is overcome and the weak are girt with strength." In the canticle of Mary, the Mother of God, "He hath put down the mighty from their seat and hath exalted the humble. He hath filled the hungry with good things and the rich He hath sent empty away."

The unique development in Jewish thought was the fashion in which these insights common to all the world religions—of a moral order expressing the will of God for men—were caught up in a vast historical drama unfolding both in time and eternity, involving the entire human race and leading human history to a climax and a conclusion. The starting point is the false choice of the first Adam. Pride and self-love began the alienation of man from God; and matching the physical continuity of the human race, the heredity of genes and chromosomes, there is a spiritual continuity derived from the original moral alienation, a bias away from God and toward the self. Generation after generation, man's wounded nature has involved him in more evil, more self-love, more injustice, and has built up institutions and whole societies mirroring his vanities and his greeds. National pride and economic exploitation—the vitality of the tribe and the vitality of survival—these were the recurrent temptations imbedded in the very fabric of human society and leading in remorseless sequence first to triumph and then to catastrophe.

It is not, it must be said, desire and appetite as such that the Jews thought evil. Only a philosophy which rejected the material world—as did Hindu or Buddhist thought—could put the blame on man's very vitality and will to live. For the Jews, the evil lay not in desire itself but in desire directed to false ends—to the love and pursuit of the self, to the hunt for wealth at the risk of exploitation, to the gratification of power at the expense of other men. These were the evils which, century after century, built up the pride and oppression of empires and led, equally inevitably, to their collapse. In the days of their glory, the "sentence of the watchers" could go forth, the writing would appear on the wall, and yet another monument to human vanity would crumble in the dust.

But man's alienation from God is only the beginning of the cosmic drama. He is not to be left to the senseless repetition of rising and falling civilizations. In history another hidden purpose is at work. God Himself, God the Creator and Father, God the living God will end the alienation of humanity. The Jewish people are to be the instruments of this supreme intervention. Their race will bring forth the savior and reconciler. They are the people in whom the mysterious Messiah will be made manifest.

Many Jews doubtless thought of this "far-off, divine event" primarily as a restoration of Israel to the brief eminence it had enjoyed as the secular kingdom of Solomon. The Messiah would crown his people with temporal glories and manifest the power of the Jews to the unrepentant Gentile. Even the disciples of Christ himself were tempted to think of a restoration of physical power to the Jewish race. For centuries after the Babylonian captivity, Jewish leaders were found who attempted to defeat the encroachments first of Hellenic and then of Roman power by seeking violently to restore Israel's temporal kingdom. The last of them, Simon Bar Kokba, declared himself Messiah in 132, and bringing down the full weight of Roman anger upon the Jewish insurgents, perished with them in the total destruction of Jerusalem.

But while the miseries of the Jews made some of their leaders all the more eager to seize on temporal weapons, there were other (and as it proved) more lasting stirrings in Jewish thought. There grew up an apocalyptic literature in which the restoration of the Kingdom came to mean the beginning of a new reign of justice, the ending of oppression, the raising of the poor, and the actual "putting down of the mighty from their seats." Sometimes, this year of jubilee seems to be a new beginning in the actual physical universe. More often it gives the sense that eternity will in some way invade time and that mankind will see a new heaven and a new earth. Nowhere is this vision of a renewed creation more beautiful and more poignant than in the Apocalypse of St. John:

"Behold the tabernacle of God with men: and He will dwell with them and they shall be His people; and God Himself with them shall be their God.

"And God shall wipe away all tears from their eyes and death shall be no more. Nor shall mourning nor crying nor sorrow be any more, for the former things are passed away.

"And He that sat on the throne said, 'Behold, I make all things new.'"

But however obscure the coming of the Kingdom may seem in Jewish apocalyptic writing, there can be no doubt of the tremendous fascination it has exercised since on the imagination of mankind. The vision of injustice made good, of the poor raised to power and the proud brought low, which appears fully for the first time in Jewish thought, has made the Old Testament a revolutionary instrument in Christian and post-Christian society. The Anabaptists of Munster and Cromwell's Diggers were Old Testament men. For all his secularization, Marx himself is a great Jewish apocalyptic prophet. Certainly Communism owes its immense vitality more to its biblical vision of the mighty put down and the poor raised up than to its theories of value or its interpretation of history.

The Second Adam

YET neither the physical restoration of Jewry nor the apocalyptic reign of material justice exhaust the meaning of the restored Kingdom. The great prophets of Israel caught glimpses—"as in a glass darkly"—of some other profounder sense in which a coming Messiah would reconcile mankind to God, bridge the chasm hollowed out by sin, and bring in a new reign of justice. This Messiah would not be a triumphant king nor even a severe judge. He would be a "man of sorrows," a "suffering servant." In some inconceivable sense, he would carry the sufferings of mankind and repair the damage which follows ineluctably upon the breaking of the moral law. "He was wounded for our iniquities," cries the prophet Isaiah, "he was bruised for our sins. The chastisement of our peace was upon him and by his stripes we are healed." The new covenant that He would bring would indeed begin a new phase in the life of Jewry and of mankind, but not necessarily a phase of material triumph nor yet an immediate reversal of the secular weight of sin and suffering. The prophets only foresee obscurely a Messiah totally different from the ordinary expectations of the Jewish race—or indeed of any people ancient or modern waiting for deliverance. And when He came, He came as "a scandal to the Jews and a folly to the Greeks." And a scandal He remains to all who believe (as did some Jews) that man's destiny is fulfilled in the triumph of an earthly kingdom or (as some Greek philosophers taught) that the mastery given by human knowledge is enough to secure the peaceful soul and the good life.

In one sense, Christ belongs to that sublime band of teachers who, in the era of the world religions, taught mankind to turn from the idea of an external ritual order to the concept of an inner moral law, chosen in freedom and fulfilled in spirit and in truth. The rule of life laid down in the Gospels is not greatly different from the teachings of Buddha or Lao-tse or the Stoic philosophers of Greece, just as they in turn recall the spiritual insights of the mystics in primitive society. To love the Good, to practice altruism, to hold one's spirit aloof from the ambitions and desires of the world—these are the staple doctrines of the Golden Rule, common to all great sages and fully revealed for humanity in the millennia before Christ. There are differences in emphasis. In much of Eastern philosophy, the greater stress seems to be on ridding the soul of all desire so that no obstacle may hold it back from absorption into infinite nothingness: the world is a snare from which the spirit must be loosed. In Christ's teaching, the emphasis is not on the absence of desire but on the direction of desire into the right channels—away from self-love and toward God, who alone is the Good, and toward our neighbor whom we love for God's sake. The world is not evil: we are bidden to consider the lilies of the field and to take delight and instruction from homely things—from the shepherd who discovers his lost sheep or the housewife who sweeps up her lost penny. But the natural order is darkened by sin and can be redeemed and used rightly only by those who seek first the kingdom of heaven. St. Augustine's phrase, "Love God and do what you like," expresses the safety of the world for those whose desires are rightly ordered.

There is also in Christ's moral teaching a psychological penetration not always found in other great sages. It is not enough to avoid sin in action. Evil in men begins in the mind and heart, and it is here, at the roots, that the temptation must be cut out. Anger is a kind of murder that has not found its outlet. Lust is adultery waiting for its opportunity. The Jews were particularly tempted to a species of external righteousness, judging virtue by the exactness with which ceremonial prescriptions were obeyed. It was this complacent conformism that Christ denounced as the gravest obstacle to love and virtue. Complacency sends its incense up daily before the inner altar of the self and when the self is served and worshiped there is no room for the worship of God. Once again, in a new form, we find *hubris* as the greatest obstacle to man's true end. The publican who beats his breast and confesses himself a sinner at the threshold of the temple is justified rather than the pharisee who stands before the altar to enumerate his own excellences. It is the humble of heart who see God. All the ordinances of the moral law, all the thunderings of the prophets, all the teachings of the sages amount at last to this— that goodness is from God alone and we can make room for it only by emptying out the nagging, hungry, envious self and letting God work in us. "Not I, but God in me" is the foundation of the Golden Rule.

Yet it was not the pre-eminence of Christ's moral teaching that made His life and death a turning point in human history. We have to remember the character of the times into which He was born to begin to understand the transformation wrought in His name. The long horror of the Hellenic "time of troubles" was coming to an end and after four centuries of carnage Augustus Caesar had established a peace of exhaustion. During those decades of destruction in which every conceivable form of warfare was practiced to the limit, there had been no lack of teachers and sages denouncing the fury and proclaiming the primacy of the moral law. In fact, it is difficult to find a more clear or more moving statement of it than in the writings of the Stoics.

The tragedy of the collapsing Hellenic world was the sense of man's complete inability to practice any moral law and the belief that drift or anarchy or the revolving cycles of a meaningless creation were driving man through a brief bitter-sweet life to the ignoble certainty of dying. Whatever else was uncertain, death was not. The taste of mortality contaminated everything. "The night is single and perpetual through which we must sleep." This was the bitterness at the bottom of every cup, the blight on every flower, the shadow under the bright Mediterranean sunshine. Bread and circuses were not enough to satisfy the restlessness of the urban mob. Nor were

its leaders more at peace. At the height of the Empire's success, in the Indian Summer of the Antonines, Marcus Aurelius,
the nearest approach to Plato's Philosopher-King ever to reign
on any throne, declared, as we have seen, that a man of forty
would have undergone the entire cycle of human experience.

The attraction exercised by Christianity on this vast and
weary Roman world did not lie in the doctrine that man must
love his neighbor. The best of the Romans and of their subject peoples knew this doctrine perfectly well, but they found
they could not do so. They "approved the better but followed
the worse." Hate and cynicism and greed and power, not love,
were the rulers in their society. The "good news" of the Gospel
was quite simply that man was not alone in his heartbreaking
struggle against social and personal evil. God, the remote impersonal Reason, the unconditioned Good of the philosophers,
had taken human form, had lived as a Man among men, and
had by dying and rising again conquered "the last enemy,"
Death itself. The cry of the first apostles was not "Love your
fellow men." It was "He is risen." This was the spring of hope
that first rose in Jerusalem, from there to flow through the
whole Empire.

Naturally, it seemed to many minds a repellent and ludi-
crous belief. The Messiah a Jewish carpenter? A convicted
felon the Lord of life? The doctrine was, as St. Paul very well
knew, a scandal and a folly. When first he preached Christ
crucified to the philosophers of Athens, they laughed so much
they could not listen to him. Yet for the jaded world of the
Empire, the promise that was longed for above all was the
promise that life after all had significance and that a new start
could yet be made, in spite of all the weight of individual sin
and of past sin encrusted in institutions, in slavery, in the exploiting plantation system, in the urban slums or the corrupt
court. This promise—the promise of a new start—was the essence of the Christian hope. The Savior's triumph was essentially a triumph over sin and death. His offer to man was a new
kind of life, His own divine life which would transform man's
human mode of existence even more completely than the ap-

pearance of reason in man's evolution had transformed his animal nature.

It was as if, long before the process of evolution had been grasped—save in the mind of some Greek thinkers of intuitive genius—the next stage of evolution had begun. From inorganic to organic life, from organic to sentient, from sentient to rational life, the creation of man had gone forward. Now a new phase was to begin, a life of grace in communion with the Godhead, a life as far above the purely rational level as the rational is above the purely sentient. Neither individual life nor the whole cosmic drama could be held to be meaningless if this was the tremendous promise held out to humanity. The second Adam, Christ, is the prototype of the new man. The meaning of history is concentrated in this point when the eternal breaks into time, when "death is swallowed up in victory" and under the vast superstructure of material civilization a new society begins to take shape: a spiritual fellowship, a Church with a life both in and out of time, which when the heavy overload of monuments and institutions begins to totter will be found to have laid the foundations of a new society—our own.

II

This sense of a new life and a new hope is nevertheless not altogether sufficient to explain the power of Christianity to permeate Hellenic society in its declining years. Other religions based on personal salvation and on participation in a new life offered themselves to the jaded peoples of the Empire: the followers of Isis had their temples next door to the worshipers of Mithras. The triumph of Christianity lies perhaps in the completeness with which it not only answered the religious needs of the time but also incorporated all the greatest insights of the pre-existent world religions. No Jew could have believed in a more personal deity than the living creative God of Christian faith who so loved the world as to send unto it His only begotten Son. Yet no Buddhist sage could have insisted more finally on the utter transcendence of the Godhead nor have conceived a more remote and mysterious concept of the divine life than that of a three-personed God. The Greeks found in Christianity their own belief in the full rationality of the universe, of its interpenetration at every point by law expressing the will of the Creator. "In the beginning was the Logos." It was God's thought that called creation into being out of formlessness and chaos.

One can even say that some of the insights of archaic religion were not lost in Christianity. One of the central themes of the fertility cults had been that of the god who dies with the sowing of the seed and rises again with the new harvest. In these rites, it was often not only the grain and the grape which were renewed by the god's sacrifice: the desire for personal salvation drew followers and devotees to participate in the mysterious ceremonies of the cult. They partook of the sacrifices offered and through this sacramental meal shared in the power of the dying and rising god. Christ, to the horror of most of his Jewish hearers and to the scandal even of his closest friends, told his hearers that they, too, must partake of the sacrifice he would offer—which was His own body—for the salvation of man. He took bread and wine and gave them to his apostles, saying, "This is my body. This is my blood." By sharing the sacramental meal, they could become sharers in His death and resurrection.

This resemblance between the sacramental core of Christianity and the mystery religions which preceded it has led many historians to dismiss Christianity as one more projection of man's early dependence upon soil and harvest, the last of the religious systems springing from an inadequate mastery of science and technique. But the identification is not so simple. In the first place, the God who dies in Christianity is not a vague mythological figure, spouse or son of an equally mythological earth-mother. He is a Jew of known parentage, born under one Roman emperor, dying under another, at dates which can approximately be fixed. Nor is His death and resurrection an endlessly repeated symbolical rite. It happens once in stark historical reality, witnessed to by hundreds of men who considered their witness to the physical fact of resurrection to be the most important contribution they had to make to their neighbors' moral wellbeing.

Nor is Christ the wan victim of fatality—an Adonis or an Osiris who has no choice and no function save to die and rise. This God-man, whose superhuman personality has continued to exercise a shattering influence on men and women through two millennia since His death, chose His own immolation with perfect freedom and announced it as the culmination not of an archaic rite but rather of the whole cosmic drama divined and foretold by the prophets of Jewry. By an apparently inexplicable twist, the one dying and resurrecting leader of whom history has concrete evidence was the child of the one ancient religion which had rejected all fertility cults and set its face against what it believed to be the shams and illusions of earth-mothers and corn-kings—for the Jews believed that it was their especial role to serve God Himself and not all the semblances of God which the peoples around them in their ignorance and longing had fabricated.

There is one possible explanation which might cover both the uniqueness of Christ's death and resurrection and the resemblances between it and the old fertility cults and mystery religions. It is that they, for all their vague mythology and their frequent degeneration into orgy and delirium, represented a deep and inescapable need in the human heart—a need to express man's dependence and a need to seek external aid amid the weariness and evil of life. When, therefore, in the fullness of time the true God they sought by false roads came to give that strength from beyond nature which they had so anxiously sought, He was born among the Jews—the one people who had not compromised with His unique Divinity. But He enacted a drama of sacrifice and triumph of which the archaic rites had been in some sense reflections. Christianity recalls the ancient religions not because it is yet another of them but because it is the original of which they are faint, botched copies.

III

With the concept of God incarnate in history and the institution of a sacramental system, we are at the core of Christianity. It is revealed as a religion which accepts the meaning and value of material creation and bids man—as in the revelation to St. Peter—to "call no things unclean." Modern man, whose view of reality tends to be consciously or unconsciously materialist, is not likely to see anything remarkable in the Christian defense of the value and reality of created material things. But in the first centuries of the Christian era, oriental influences were pouring into the decadent Roman empire and bringing with them ideas and influences derived from the oriental world religions with all their contempt for a supposedly illusory universe. The early Christian heresies were attempts to "spiritualize" Christianity by decrying the reality and value of created things. The Gnostics taught that the material world and man's animal nature are evil and illusory. They sought to introduce the idea of a purely spiritual redemption of man's spirit by an emanation of the Timeless One whose manhood was that of an apparition or a ghost. St. Irenaeus wrote in protest: "Since men are real, theirs must be a real establishment. They do not vanish into non-existence, but progress among existent things." These early doctors of the Church placed man and his redemption in time at the center of their teaching. Eusebius calls man "the dear child of the Divine Word," St. Gregory of Nyssa, "the godlike image of archetypal beauty." Greek humanism was fused with the Jewish sense of history to produce a religion whose ambition it was to renew all things—time, space, material forces, animal nature, social organization—by the action of God working together with man's own spark of unconditioned spirit. Men were to be the earthly instruments of this transformation—men who, again in the words of St. Gregory of Nyssa, were created both body and spirit: ". . . in order that the earthly element might be raised by union with the Divine and so the Divine grace in one even course . . . might uniformly extend through all creation, the lower nature being mingled with that which is above the world."

Even while this debate continued, history began to illustrate the supreme importance of maintaining the balance between time and timelessness, between supernatural destiny and natural vocation, which is the essence of Christianity. In the first centuries after Christ, the Eastern half of the Roman empire had become, with the building of Byzantium, the seat of the emperor. It was also the part of the crumbling Empire most exposed to oriental influences—not only to the religions of pure spirit which denied the value of creation but also to the older traditions of absolute government that had prevailed in archaic society. The concept of the priest-king of Sumerian and Babylonian origin had remained an active principle of government among the Persians and had prevailed against the Hellenizing influence of Alexander the Great. Now its influence percolated into Byzantium. Even though the Eastern Roman emperors had accepted Christianity as a state religion, their version of it was, in the words of Lord Acton, "to make the Church serve as a gilded crutch of absolutism." The head of the Orthodox Church, its Patriarch, was subordinate to the quasi-divine emperor, and the oriental otherworldliness of Eastern or Orthodox Christianity undoubtedly made more complete the control exercised by the state over the Church. If material things were of no immediate concern to the Christian, it could not matter much if the religious community was materially controlled by the state—even though the risk might be run of becoming no more than an arm of government, the ecclesiastical wing of the state bureaucracy. Absolutism remained the Orthodox principle of government, with consequences that are still fateful for us today.

When pagan Russia entered the society of Christian civilization, the missionary task was accomplished by the monks and priests of Eastern Orthodoxy. Absolutist traditions of government were transmitted to the new society at the same time. The Russian state, which began to be re-formed in Muscovy after the interregnum of Tartar invasion, grew from the fusion of two tyrannical traditions of government—Orthodox absolutism and Tartar despotism. Thus a direct link seems to run back from the modernized tyranny of Soviet Russia by way of Muscovy and Byzantium and the Persian empire to the archaic society of Sumer and Akkad. So ancient a cultural tradition is a reminder not only that the uprooting of tyranny in Russia must necessarily be slow but also that the Soviet government, which claims to have evolved the most modern type of society, is in great measure a throwback to the most archaic form of rule of which the world has record.

In the Western half of the old Roman empire, the development of society took another route. In part, the total collapse of the Roman authority was responsible for this difference. In Byzantium, the imperial court and bureaucracy remained intact, with enough strength and prestige to succeed in its aim of subordinating religion to the state. But in the West the barbarians broke up the old order, and in Rome itself the only authority able to exercise an influence in the debacles of the fourth century was the Roman pontiff. The Papacy could not be subordinated to the state, for there was virtually no state to which it could become subordinate.

At the same time, the classical and humanist tradition of the Greeks was strong enough to counter oriental and Gnostic influences. The ideal of a religion remaking heaven and earth and responsible to God for both man's earthly and heavenly destinies was elaborated in the writings of the Fathers and in the doctrinal definitions of the Church. St. Augustine, who more than any other man set his stamp upon the development of Western Christianity, saw the whole of human history in the dynamic and dramatic form of a struggle to remake earthly society in the image of a divine order. Two loves, he wrote, built two cities. The love of self builds up Babylon to the contempt of God; the love of God builds up Jerusalem to the contempt of self. The whole purpose of creation is to build the city of God. Earth is the seed ground of the new life of the spirit. With this tremendous ambition of remolding the whole of reality, the Christian experiment in the West was launched.

TWO

GROWTH

6

The Building of Europe

EUROPEAN society begins in another of those reversals of probability which seem to mark the development of history in the Mediterranean cradle of the West. Just as no contemporary historian could have foretold in the days of the glory of Babylon or of Knossos that the shape of the future would be molded by the Achaean invaders in Greece or the hill people of Judea, so no cautious observer, watching the convulsions of the Roman empire in the fifth or sixth centuries after Christ, would have foretold that Rome, not Byzantine Constantinople, held the keys of man's further development. Every material advantage lay with Byzantium. It had an intact bureaucracy, armies in being, a statesman of genius in Justinian, a subservient church, and, stored up in its libraries and centers of learning, the mighty works of the classical tradition—the philosophers and scientists of Greece and Rome. Civilization's next advance seemed certain to remain under Byzantine control.

In the West, on the contrary, all was collapse and confusion. Even if the nascent Christian Church had wished to lean upon the Empire and exercise authority as its spiritual arm, the hope was vain—for under the waves of invasion from the North the imperial structure of government crumbled in Italy, Spain, and France. War bands set up principalities under their tribal leaders. Cities, roads, country estates, communications disintegrated. Even today, in the rich mosaic floors of ruined Roman villas one can see the crude holes driven by the Goths to support tent poles holding up rough coverings of skin. The new masters squatted on the polished pavements of the old.

Nor was it a question merely of one engulfing tide: for nearly a thousand years, the area which was to take final form as Europe had to withstand repeated waves of invasion. No sooner had a local work of recivilization begun than a new flood of invaders swept in to pillage, massacre, and settle, and the task had to be taken up again from the beginning. From the North, after the Goths and the Saxons, came the Jutes and the Danes, behind the Danes the Normans. To the East, the Saxons and the Avars pressed on the frontiers of the Rhineland; and when these were conquered and converted by Charlemagne they gave place to the pressure of the Wends. In the South, the invaders were Moslem Arabs.

The Moslems were not only alien but also prophets of what could be called the first triumphant Christian heresy. In all the early disputes on Christian doctrine, there had been that Oriental element suspicious of Christianity's humanism. The idea of an Incarnation, of a bridge between God and man, and of a progressive transformation of humanity and the material universe, was alien to the otherworldly philosophies of the East. At the end of the sixth century this ideological dispute, combined with the grievances and miseries of the subject peoples of the Byzantine empire, gave the Arab war bands under Mohammed the battering ram of Islam with which, sweeping along North Africa, they assailed the Spanish frontiers of Europe and spread northward to be defeated only in the heart of France at Poitiers in 732.

The perpetual warfare of these centuries left its mark on the social substance of the new civilization. The Northern invaders brought with them from their dismal forests a type of kingship in which the tribal leader exercised complete authority only in time of war, could be deposed, was often elected, and was bound by the advice of the elders of the tribe. In establishing the new kingdoms the first necessity was effective fighting leadership, and the perpetual recurrence of invasion put the highest premium on military skill: warriors were inevitably the kings' closest associates. And since, with the collapse of Roman order and Roman roads, commerce had vanished and subsistence farming was once more the basis of the economy, the military magnates took their reward and upheld their status with grants of land to which laborers were inalienably attached—for without workers the land was useless to men dedicated to the pursuit of arms. It is therefore arguable that in Europe the social order known as the feudal system had its origins not in economic necessity, as Marxists must believe, but rather in military pressure.

The distinction, however, is more or less irrelevant. Whether the institutions of feudalism sprang from economic or from military necessity, they belong, as it were, to the physical substratum of society, to the brute raw materials with which the men of the Middle Ages had to work to create a social order and a civilization. In fact, the more one compares the great divergences between the various civilizations the world has known—above all, the differences in their dynamism and growth and achievement—the more remarkable it is to consider the extent to which, over the millennia, their basic economic conditions have been alike. The dependence of peasant upon landlord in a subsistence agriculture was, until the Industrial Revolution of the nineteenth century, the greatest single fact in the world economy. It can even be argued that some of the supposed ancient and modern exceptions to this rule are more apparent than real. The serf on the feudal estate worked for two masters. He owed labor to the fields of his lord and he paid the tithe to the Church. For himself, he worked on his own strips and shared with his neighbors such joint rights as grazing or fuel collecting on the village's common land. Is this in essence so totally different from, say, the communal organization of the Incas, whose laborers divided their produce between the state, the state religion, and the tribal group? Is it even fundamentally different from modern collectivized agriculture, apart from the suppression of Church receipts? The Russian kolkhoznik who divides his work between his private garden and the public domain labors partly for himself and partly for his master. True, the superstructure of ideas and institutions based on this simple economic fact has changed, but the economic foundation is markedly similar. It seems, therefore, that if we wish to understand the meaning of a civilization and of its laws of growth and development, we shall find the beliefs it fosters and the ideals at which it aims a better guide than any one-sided study of economic conditions.

This is not to fall into the error of dismissing the physical factors in a society. Long before Marx and Freud denounced the sublimations and rationalizations with which men cover their grosser motives, it was common knowledge that men would seek their own interests under the plea of the public weal. As Sir Thomas More wrote in his *Utopia:* "When I consider all these commonwealths which nowadays everywhere do flourish, so God help me, I can perceive nothing but a conspiracy of rich men, procuring their own commodities under the name and title of the commonwealth." Men's ambitions and desires and hungers enter into every relationship and every institution. The raw material from which social institutions are fashioned is always more or less recalcitrant and any human society will tend to produce a caricature of itself. But beside the hunger for gain and the hunger for power there is a hunger for creation, for justice, for the realization of an ideal—in a word, St. Augustine's two cities coexist in every civilization and neither Europe nor any other society can be understood unless the opposite energies of the human heart are allowed their play.

II

The raw materials for the building of Europe were the invading war bands and their military and later feudal organization. The forces which molded them into a single civilization lay on the side of the Church. In the West, the great traditions of Roman order and Greek humanism, insofar as they survived at all, survived with the clergy. The attraction and prestige of Rome's past greatness was sufficiently strong to draw the leaders of the invading tribes toward an ideal of social organization and justice; and since the clerics alone possessed literacy and a tradition, they became the organizers and the administrators of the new kingdoms. Clovis, King of the Franks, was baptized a Christian in 496. Gregory the

Great, whose vast labors of reform and reconstruction made the Papacy the master institution of Europe by the end of the sixth century, prepared for the conversion of the Gothic kingdoms in Italy from the widespread Arian heresy to Catholic Christianity by baptizing the Lombard queen, Theodolinda. His despatch of missionaries to Saxon England secured the conversion of the kings of Kent, and from that center, Christianity spread to all England. Saxon England in its turn, in the great age of monks and missionaries, the age of Boniface and Alcuin and Willibrord, sent out the men who converted the heathens in Germany, reformed the Frankish church founded by Clovis, and prepared for the revival of order and learning under Charlemagne.

The popes could not have directed this immense missionary effort if they had not been supported by the other great institution of early Christianity—the Benedictine monastery. Monks were not unknown in the primitive Church, but (as in Oriental monasticism) they were men who had turned their backs on all worldly concerns. Fasting in the deserts of Egypt, withdrawn to the tops of pillars in Asia Minor, they gave mankind a supreme yet remote commentary upon the transitoriness of the flesh and the single reality of Divine transcendence. But the peoples of the West—their cities sacked, their farms in ruins, a splendid civilization disintegrating all round them —did not need to be reminded that "all flesh is as the grass and all the glory of man as the flower of the grass." They needed, on the contrary, some breathing space in the whirlwind of disaster and some example toward the rebuilding of their shattered physical environment. This they received in the new Benedictine dispensation. St. Benedict conceived his rule essentially in social terms. His communities would labor and study as well as fast and pray. In fact, labor would be prayer. They would seek out the wilderness left by invasion and warfare and make it blossom again. They would preserve the documents and traditions of ancient learning and set up schools to transmit it to the coming generations. The great missionaries were all great monks, and wherever in those dark centuries we begin to see flickering once again the light of learning and culture, its hearth is always a monastery.

The bare record of the Church's work between 400 and 900 A.D.—the conversion of kings, the setting up of bishoprics, the founding of monasteries—gives not the faintest idea of the travail of the times. Until the outward missionary movement of the West met the confines of Orthodox Christianity in the East, and until in the North it completed the conversion of the Norsemen—in other words, until well into the tenth century—the task of laying even the foundations of a civilized community had to be taken up again and again. Nor was the pressure from without the only danger. So rough and primitive were the new communities and so recent the civilizing effort that they tended to fall away under their own inefficiency and violence. The kingdom of Clovis, the successors to Charlemagne, the Papacy itself, all fell into evil ways and had to be renewed by the laborious efforts of new reformers and missionaries. One of the great saints of the early Frankish church, St. Martin of Tours, said on his death bed: "Lord God, if I am necessary to the wellbeing of Thy people, I will not refuse the labor." Only if we count the martyrdoms, the monasteries rebuilt, the churches restored, the ravaged monastic fields replanted and replowed not once or twice but time and time again—only then can we realize the scale of the work rendered over the centuries by men of the stamp of St. Martin or St. Boniface, St. Gregory or St. Bede.

III

At the beginning of the eleventh century, the stage was largely set for the expansion of a Christian civilization. The long cruel years on the defensive were over. Frontiers had been given to Christendom, a measure of peace established within. After the heavy frost, life and energy—the sap of a new culture—began to rise again. In Rome, the Tuscan Hildebrand sat on the papal throne as Gregory VII and by his reforms of the clergy, banishing concubinage and simony, by his foundation of schools and universities and his encouragement of monastic development, he helped to create in men's minds the ideal of a Christian commonwealth, of which the anarchic feudal principalities were but a part and in which men would owe two loyalties—to God and Caesar.

With the new insight into despotism which the totalitarian experiments of the last thirty years have given us in the Western world, we may well be inclined to see in this fundamental division of power in European society the key to all later development in the direction of freedom. In the wide arena of Christendom, the Papacy faced a rival claimant to universal power. When Charlemagne took up the task of conquering paganism in Germany, he evoked the memory of the old Roman empire and had himself crowned emperor of a new Holy Roman empire, of a new temporal Christian society whose frontiers he was pledged to defend. When the struggle against paganism moved to the East, the imperial crown passed to the new guardians of the marches, the Saxon kings, until the last frontier was pacified. Thereafter, about 1024, Saxon power diminished and the crown passed back to the feudal leaders of Central Europe. Of these, the Hohenstaufen dynasty interpreted their imperial power as implying suzerainty over the Lombard and Tuscan states of Italy, a claim which brought them to the frontiers of the principalities now ruled directly by the Pope in Rome. For a time, in the early stages of the Hildebrandine reform, the two powers worked together to secure the correction of abuses, but an open struggle broke out between them over the question of investitures. This contest was fundamentally a dispute over power, for the Pope claimed the right to name clerics to ecclesiastical posts without securing the concurrence of the emperor or of the feudal monarch within whose territory the appointment might be made. The emperors and monarchs, in their turn, sought to uphold their own sovereignty against the establishment within their lands of authorities owing allegiance only to Rome.

This open conflict not only made men conscious that power was divided at the very apex of authority; it also gave a number of subordinate institutions new opportunities to assert their own autonomy. As one side or the other bid for support in the great struggle, the price had to be paid in terms of political concessions. Charters for free cities, representative institutions —the Parliament in Britain, the Estates General of France— were secured in part by the need of monarch or Pope to enlist new energies on his side. It is significant that this flowering of independence occurred first where the fiercest battle between Pope and emperor had been fought—in Lombardy and Tuscany. Milan, Bologna, Florence, and Venice bartered their support in return for charters and freedoms, and it was in these cities that the first full experiments in self-government were made since the collapse of freedom in Greece nearly two thousand years before.

This link with ancient Greece is no coincidence. Contact with the Orthodox empire at Constantinople had been reestablished by the Crusades and by the trade which the opening up of the Levant made possible. The documents of classical learning preserved in the Byzantine world returned to Italy to induce an intoxication with the learning and splendor of antiquity. The Italian city states, like the Greek city states before them, became dynamic centers of thought, art, and technology. In the thirteenth and fourteenth centuries, they began to surpass the still semibarbarian feudal world around them as Athens had once surpassed the ancient Mediterranean civilization.

IV

The development had its economic roots. With the pacification of Europe the opportunity for trade revived, but the great stimulus to it came not from the subsistence farming of the interior but from Europe's new contact with the East. The Crusaders established their ephemeral kingdoms along the Eastern Mediterranean and found themselves in contact with the greatest trading people of the age—the Arabs who sailed down the Persian Gulf and across the Indian Ocean to bring back the silks and precious stones and perfumes of the Orient or sent their caravans northward along the Silk Road to China. To the semibarbarian knights of Europe, whose cloth was coarse and whose castles were carpeted with rushes, the robes and carpets of the materially resplendent Orient were a revelation of beauty and convenience. Accustomed as we are today to the material superiority of the West, it is difficult to imagine the impact on the nascent civilization of Western Europe of trade with China, which by the ninth century had already discovered printing, or with the luxurious Arab Caliphate, which had united the territories of the Levant into a single Moslem theocratic state. Here the material inheritance of Persia's Hellenized civilization and the wealth of the Arabs' worldwide trading activities produced a way of life whose prosperity seemed prodigious to the rude Crusaders. This story is told of the Caliph Aziz, who lived in Cairo in the ninth century, when Europe's princes still ate rough bread and meat. He wished for some of the fresh cherries of Baalbek for his table. Hearing this, the wazir of Baalbek collected six hundred carrier pigeons, attached a cherry to the leg of each bird, and sent them flying across the four hundred miles of desert between Baalbek and Cairo. The cherries arrived in time for dinner on the same day and in perfect condition. The ingenuity of the wazir's method and the refinement of the caliph's taste would have seemed alike fabulous to a contemporary European.

It is therefore not surprising that one of the great byproducts of the Crusades was an immense stimulus to trade, particularly in the Italian ports which lay most conveniently athwart the trade routes to the Orient. Venice and Genoa began to grow up as prosperous, independent rivals. Growth stimulated growth and all north and central Italy began to expand and prosper with the spread of commerce.

The movement spread northward through the Empire, to Regensburg and Augsburg and Frankfurt, great merchant cities of South Germany. But in the high Middle Ages—from the eleventh to the fourteenth centuries—the life of Europe beat with the steadiest and strongest pulse in the Italian city states. The new communities, with their wealthy merchants, their busy artisans and young apprentices, broke away from the old feudal pattern of landlord and peasant and claimed the right to evade the mesh of feudal government. As the cities grew, the territorial magnate fought a losing battle to maintain political control, and the burghers of the trading cities wrested their charters and their constitutions from Pope or emperor in return for financial or military support. Elective representative government, an extended franchise, and control of taxation were the privileges they succeeded in turning into rights.

For the student who sees history in terms of economic determinism, the link between trade with the East, the growing prosperity of Italy, and the rise of a merchant class is enough to explain the emergence of medieval democracy in the city states. If it is true, as Marx wrote, that "human beings, developing material production and material intercourse, and thus altering the real world that environs them, alter therewith their thoughts and the products of their thoughts," what could be more significant than that the feudal order of economy produced the supremacy of baron and bishop while the growth of trade brought the free merchant into authority? The physical world alters. The ideas and institutions follow suit. In short, as Marx would put it, "assume a particular state of development in the productive forces and you will get a corresponding society."

Yet the supposed medieval illustration of this point suggests formidable difficulties. The spark given to the expansion of Europe's commerce came from the great hearths of Arab trade, infinitely wealthier, infinitely further flung, and more highly organized. If the democracy of the cities expresses no more than the economic substratum of merchant enterprise, we should expect to find in Cairo or Baghdad or Aleppo a strong structure of civic self-government, with free elections, a wide franchise, and a firm control over taxation. In fact, the Arab Caliphate gave its people a form of despotic rule made all the more absolute by the union of spiritual and temporal authority in the caliph. This is not to decry the influence and prestige of the merchants. But nothing in their wide commercial enterprise seems to have been enough, of itself, to create a ferment of freedom or to lay the foundations of more liberal rule.

The reasons may have more to do with philosophy than is

comfortable for the determinist. The element in Christianity which Mohammed had rejected was its insistence upon the central fact of the Incarnation, God Himself deeming human nature worthy to be His dwelling place. The early doctors of the Church had defined this essential humanism in a hundred debates against the Oriental heresiarchs who sought a religion of pure spirit and pure transcendence. Islam represented the triumph of the Eastern tradition. The Godhead withdrew to utter transcendence, the image of man was banished from sacred art. This reversal of interest and value had profound effects on Moslem society. Although in its libraries and universities it preserved much of Greek learning and, in science in particular, had a far greater basis of knowledge than was available to Europe (in medicine and mathematics the Arabs were the instructors of medieval Europe), nevertheless the rigid transcendence of Moslem theology and the little weight laid upon the position of man in the world or upon the study of the material universe led to stagnation of thought and to an unchanging form of authoritarian government. Great Moslem thinkers such as Ghazali believed that Greek philosophy, based as it was upon an intelligible universe and upon man's rational nature as a reflection of the Logos, could not be combined with Moslem theology. Rather than dilute the central Moslem belief in an omnipotent, incomprehensible, and utterly transcendent Deity, Ghazali entitled his greatest work *The Destruction of the Philosophers.*

v

The possibility is therefore at least worth examining that the development of free government in Europe in the Middle Ages resulted as much from the spirit and the philosophy of Christianity as from the growth of wealth and the diversification of society introduced by commercial expansion. The transforming activity of Christianity had been apparent from the origins of the new society. Military necessity and primitive economic conditions had produced the feudal state, but the Church's social teaching sought to soften and idealize what

were, in origin, brutal and barbaric institutions. Its first insistence was upon the mutual obligations of each man to his
neighbor, whatever their respective place in the social scale.
The most frequent analogy for social relations in medieval
thought is the organic constitution of the human body, in
which each member has a different function but is utterly dependent upon all the rest. Therefore each, whether king or
baron or serf or priest, must exercise his calling in such a way
that he contributes to the good of the whole Christian commonwealth. The effort was made to balance rights by duties
and to mitigate power and property by the ideal of responsibility and trusteeship. True, the chief defense lay in the good
conscience of men reinforced by the threat of spiritual penal-
ties. Yet before such barriers are dismissed for their frailty, it
is salutary to remember the degree to which the tolerableness
of any system—whether its officers are barons, businessmen,
bureaucrats, or commissars—depends upon the decency of individual men and women. Moreover, there were other sanctions, some explicit, some implicit in the divided power of
Church and state and in the very nature of Christian thinking.

Among the explicit sanctions was the Church's attempt to
bring the vitalities of economic life under some sort of moral
control. The conception of economic life was at first that of
the static agricultural community in which commerce, credit,
and the expansion of wealth play almost no part. In such a
community, the amount of wealth to be shared tended to be,
year in, year out, an amount fixed by the harvests. If any man
engrossed too much of such wealth for himself, he was liable
to do direct personal injury to his neighbors, who as a result
of his action would go short. Hence cornering the market,
holding back supplies, setting up monopolies, and selling at
more than "fair" prices were economic malpractices of which
the ecclesiastical courts could take cognizance and for which
they could impose fines, restitution, and even imprisonment.

In the rural community, the chief need for credit was to
carry a man over a period of real need. To charge interest on
any loan was virtually the equivalent of taking advantage of
someone else's misfortunes. Hence usury, the crime of charging

interest on a loan of money designed to relieve want, was very generally denounced and punished. As commerce grew, and as the provision of credit became the essential condition of bringing distant cargoes to Europe or of starting up local enterprises, the rules on usury were modified. The creditor could expect a share in profits made as a result of his loan, for instance, provided he shared the risks. The fifteenth-century teachings of St. Antonino upon usury and the just price are subtle and rational and bear the marks of dealing with existing commercial conditions, not with the fading world of subsistence agriculture. But the aim is the same: to lay down conditions which put a check upon avarice and prevent men from using their economic power to prey on other men. Property, like the other privileges of feudalism, is a trust. It may be privately owned but it must be social in its use. To exploit the advantages of ownership in order to amass, speculate, and impoverish is an abuse which society has the right to check.

The same desire to set limits to power is apparent in medieval political theory. The existence of Church and state, neither able to absorb the other, was a primary barrier against the concentration of all power in a single center; and, as we have seen, the rivalries of Pope and emperor gave other subordinate interests the possibility of growth and autonomy. But it is not likely that such a flowering of free association could have been possible in Europe unless on the one hand the temper of theology and philosophy had been favorable to it and unless on the other the desires and beliefs of the people had pressed forward in that direction. The teaching of the Church was undoubtedly favorable to the idea of hedging political power around with constitutional limitations. In the very first principalities established under the influence of the Church this view is apparent. The clerics who provided the primitive Gothic kingdoms of Spain in the fifth and sixth centuries with an administrative apparatus established the principle that royal power is elective. Kings, moreover, were subject to the law—"under God and the law," as the great medieval jurist Bracton put it—and the Church supported the English barons in their revolt against John and their drawing

up of the Magna Carta of rights. The greatest theologian of
the Middle Ages, St. Thomas Aquinas, thus summed up the
balance of power that should prevail within a Christian kingdom: "A king who is unfaithful to his duty forfeits his claim
to obedience. It is not rebellion to depose him, for he is himself
a rebel whom the nation has the right to put down. But it is
better to abridge his power, that he may be unable to abuse
it. For this purpose, the whole nation ought to have a share
in governing itself, the Constitution ought to combine a
limited and elective monarchy, with an aristocracy of merit
and such an admixture of democracy as shall admit all classes
to office by popular election. No government has a right to levy
taxes beyond the limit determined by the people. All political
authority is derived from popular suffrage and all laws must
be made by the people and their representatives."

In medieval teaching, moreover, the checks from below on
absolute power were reinforced by checks from above. The
king should not override the rights and privileges of the
various "estates" of his realm. Equally, as a member of a
wider Christian commonwealth, he owed respect to the rights
of neighboring sovereigns and was urged to accept the arbitra-
tion of the popes in case of dispute. Sovereignty was thus at
every level conceived of as a limited authority, hedged in by
law, by traditional right, and by pious respect for the ideal of
Christian brotherhood. How far below the ideal fell the reality
we shall presently see. But it is difficult to quarrel with Lord
Acton's judgment: "The issue of ancient politics was an absolute state planted on slavery. The political produce of the
Middle Ages was a system of states in which authority was
restricted by the representation of powerful classes, by privi-
ledged associations and by the acknowledgement of duties
superior to those which are imposed by man."

VI

Yet institutions, laws, and traditions tending toward greater
freedom would have had little effect if the peoples of Europe
themselves had not received some profound instinct for free-

dom from their education and from its theories about the
nature and destiny of man. However much the Church might
seek to soften and make acceptable the inequalities of feudalism by trying to induce the spirit of trusteeship—of wealth with
a social duty, of property private in ownership but social in
use—there was in Christianity a strongly egalitarian undercurrent. Christ had been born a poor man and worked with
his hands as a carpenter. All over Europe, monastic houses
cared for the poor and the sick; and once a year, the monarch
himself washed the feet of poor men on Maundy Thursday.
The mendicant friars made a glory of poverty—the Lady
Poverty loved with ardor by St. Francis of Assisi. In spite of
the arrogance and brutality of feudal rule, the serfs and villeins
were men with immortal souls to save. As St. Ivo of Chartres
wrote: "Before Christ, there is neither free man nor serf, all
who participate in the same sacraments are equal." On the
very walls of the churches and in the paintings of such Christian painters as Fra Angelico, this fundamental equality of
men before God found vivid expression, in the unending
scenes of medieval "dooms"—flaming presentations of the Last
Judgment in which princes, barons, bishops, or cardinals could
be seen going down for their ill doings into everlasting fire.

The very helplessness of the poor and the unfortunate gave
them an especial claim on their neighbors. The phrase "the
weak to the wall," which in modern terms suggests the very
slight chance any but an able-bodied man has of escaping
when a crowd panics or a building burns down, had in the
Middle Ages an exactly opposite sense. Often the only seating
in the great monastic churches was a stone bench around the
wall, and to this bench were carried the feeble, the sick, and
the lame. The queen who placed the leper in her own bed,
the friar embracing and washing the ulcerous beggar were
symbols of a humanity and a compassion before which the
arrogance of power and wealth was perpetually arraigned.

This underlying respect for men, which sprang not from a
sense of status and position but from the sheer fact of their
humanity, made it possible for Europe, alone of contemporary
civilizations, to break from the traditional world of autocratic

rule and fixed feudal relationships. Even before the merchant class began to press for self-government in the cities and the country squires to demand representation on the central councils that would tax them, Europe was covered with a network of small associations in which men met together to carry on common purposes—the brotherhoods of the highway, for instance, into which men banded themselves to ward off brigandage on their journeys, or the "charities"—small societies, meeting under the patronage of a popular saint, to carry on works of mercy. And behind these local activities stood the universal organization of the Church, the ladder of advance for lowborn men of fine intellect, the exit opened to piety and learning from the closed society of feudalism. Since the Church was the organizer and guardian not only of the secular clergy and the monastic orders but of the schools and universities as well, and since in many communities the Church was the only source of educated civil servants, the arena of advancement open to talent divorced from birth was considerable and the progress from apprentice to abbot, bishop, or even chancellor was not unknown.

The Church's teaching of an organic social system in which the various orders had a different but an honorable role to play might have degenerated into a practical caste system, for how could a child born of a laboring family, representing the calloused hands of the body politic, aspire to the organic enormity of becoming society's eye or ear or brain? This stratification was avoided because the implications of equality, in the Christian view of immortal souls all equally valuable in the sight of God, made a caste system unthinkable. Between the Brahman refusing food because the shadow of an untouchable has crossed it and the Christian king setting aside his crown to kneel and wash the beggar's feet is a gulf so vast that no superficial resemblance of class or social or economic structure can bridge it.

The fundamental difference lies in the different philosophers' estimate of the nature and the destiny of man. Christian thought at the foundation of Western civilization derived its beliefs from the humanism of the Greeks and from the mercy of God to man made manifest in Jewish and Christian teaching. The great synthesis of these two traditions of thought lies in the Scholastic philosophy of St. Thomas Aquinas, who, unlike the Moslem philosopher Ghazali, found that the humanism of the Greeks and the humanism of Christianity were perfectly reconcilable. There was place not only for the transcendent philosophy of Plato—who had long been popular among Christian teachers—but also for the teaching of the practical and materialist Aristotle, who had sought not only to reflect upon phenomena but actually to go out and examine them and to lay the basis for a science of observation and classification. This interest in the real nature of the external world, which otherworldly religions tended to dismiss as belonging to the world of illusion, could find a place in Christian philosophy since God had looked on His creation and found it good. For all Scholasticism's errors in material fact, it is a false perspective to dismiss Scholastic philosophy as dogmatic obscurantism. The popular myth about Scholasticism is full of angels dancing on the points of needles. In fact, the Schoolmen were the first thinkers since the Greeks to attempt to submit the whole of reality to the severe and disinterested scrutiny of human reason. Habits of thought and of concentrated study were formed which, as Professor Whitehead has pointed out, became the basis of all future scientific advance.

None of this immense labor would have been possible without the particular insights of Christian thought. Scholastic philosophy saw the whole of creation as an intelligible order, a reflection of the divine Logos, universally subject to law and revealing in its very structure its divine origin. At the core of Scholasticism stands the figure of man, who insofar as he has an animal nature is deeply imbedded in the material universe and subject to all its vitalities and irrational forces. Yet in man is also implanted reason, the reflection of the Logos, and a spiritual life through which, at the point of the soul, he is already mysteriously at one with the eternal, immutable Godhead.

Man is thus the crown of material nature and the bridge to another order of reality. Sharing something of the freedom, creativeness, and spontaneity of the Uncaused First Cause, his task is to remake the material universe in the image of the divine order, to penetrate its materiality by the light of reason and the exercise of science, and to transform its irrationality by the power of wisdom and love. This, no less, is the destiny of man. No system of thought has ever placed him on a higher pinnacle. Scholastic philosophy sought to work out with all the objectivity and sustained inquiry of the logical method the full implications of the Psalmist's triumphant cry:

"What is man that thou art mindful of him? Or the son of man that thou visitest him?

"Thou hast made him a little lower than the angels: thou hast crowned him with glory and honor and hast set him over the works of thy hands."

7

The Loss of Unity

IF ONE were to seek to sum up in a single sentence the great change that came over Europe in the sixteenth century, one might say that a vast growth in the vitalities of European society—in nationalism, in economic power, and in overseas trade and discovery—coincided with a great weakening and falling away in the ecclesiastical instruments whose task it had been to mold the raw forces of social life into the semblance of an ordered culture. National governments and new economic classes grew in strength and self-confidence. The wider European institutions of Papacy, supernational clergy, and monastic orders grew weaker and their international influence dwindled. True, this changing balance was beginning to become apparent by the fourteenth century. In a sense, the Reformation, beginning in 1517, only confirmed tendencies which had long been in movement. Yet it is a decisive date, for the success of Luther in dividing Christendom meant that the only supernational institution expressing European unity was broken. Thereafter Western culture grew under the star of division.

This is not to say that the medieval world did not know war. The struggles of kings and great magnates for fiefs and dowries were perpetual; and if the Crusades drained off some of this feudal cantankerousness into a century of skirmishing in the Levant, they nevertheless perpetuated the ideal of a warrior caste. Some of the most bitter quarrels in Europe had their origins in the disputes which flared up between Crusaders before the walls of Jerusalem and Acre. And the rare achievement of the Fourth Crusade was not to liberate the Holy Places but to sack the Christian city of Constantinople.

Yet the continuing sense of unity was a restraint. On occasion, the arbiter's role of the Papacy had its effect. And beneath the struggles, the life of Europe, knit together by the movement of merchants and scholars and monks, speaking a common tongue and accepting, even while they often betrayed, common standards and ideals—this life went on. It was, moreover, something greater than a physical unity. The various aspects of life—economic, social, moral—bore some relation to each other. Even if existence was oppressive and brutal, it was not entirely discordant and men had the sense of belonging to a larger and a familiar whole. It is true that with the growing material strength of Europe, this wider framework was ceasing to feel like a home and began to impress the bolder spirits as a prison. But the choice was still possible between building a more commodious house on the tried foundations or tearing down the fabric. In fact, the two possibilities seemed to become, as it were, physically incorporated in two great antagonists during the early sixteenth century—in Erasmus who looked to the way of reform and organic growth, and in Luther who wanted to simplify but helped to destroy.

A welling up of national feeling underneath the loosely knit feudal society was apparent throughout the Middle Ages. England, under the rule of a series of energetic kings, Henry II and the first and third Edwards, received something resembling centralized and unitary rule before the close of the thirteenth century. England's Hundred Years War with France, which was climaxed by the triumph and martyrdom of Joan of Arc, sharpened nationalist feeling on both sides to such a pitch that a struggle which began in largely feudal terms—as a contest for the English king's hereditary suzerainty over the Crown's Norman fiefs—ended as a patriotic conflict between nation states.

The transformation of France from a feudal kingdom to a nation owes as much to the influence of Italian politics as to the struggle with England. In Italy, the growth of commerce and the political maturity of the city states introduced new levels of efficiency into the conduct of affairs. Not only in every manner of fine art—in literature, painting, sculpture, and architecture—but also in the art of government the cities and principalities of Italy became the models of Europe in the high Middle Ages.

It was a centralizing model, tending, by way of efficiency, to the concentration of power. Moreover, the perpetual struggles between a score of sovereign states in the narrow Italian peninsula brought a steady refinement to the art of fighting. The old feudal levies gave place to the trained professional bands of the condottieri—half brigand, half prince—who in turn set the keenest Italian minds to experiment boldly with arms and fortifications. As an outcome of these struggles, the various city states began by the fourteenth century to be concentrated into larger units by the more successful of the condottieri. In these new principalities and dukedoms, united by the sword, the pattern of government no longer reflected the democracy of Athens but had reverted to another Greek pattern, that of the *tyrannis*. The new despots—the Visconti, the Sforza, the Este—were men of absolute power, ruling by army and police, spies and assassins; the checks which medieval theory had placed on sovereignty were swept away in the new centralized states whose efficiency, ruthlessness, brilliance, and artistry mesmerized the Transalpine feudal kingdoms.

After the capture of Constantinople by the Turks in 1453, many of the Greek scholars of Byzantium took refuge in Italy, bringing their greater knowledge of classical culture with them. The passion with which Italy went to school with these new masters gave a new impetus to the Renaissance of learning and a new luster to the Italian people. Italian fashions, Italian models, Italian ideas became the rage of Europe.

Imitation of Italy was not content with clothes and manners and art. It went naturally to the heart of the matter, to political and military organization. At the beginning of the fifteenth century, Europe might have developed its future political institutions largely within a framework of city states. Free cities were scattered along all the great trade routes—

through South Germany, along the Baltic coasts where the Hansa merchants held the monopoly of trade. The development of industry in the Burgundian lands—woolen goods at Tournai, tapestries at Brussels, iron at Namur, and munitions from the environs of Liège—led to the growth of proud and independent cities (Ghent, Bruges, Brussels, Antwerp) whose burghers defended their liberties with little respect for their Burgundian feudal overlord. Their sense of independence grew as new sources of trade were opened up in the fifteenth century. The advance of the Turks in the East, which closed the old trade routes, together with other merchants' resentment at the Italians' monopoly of Eastern trade, had encouraged Portuguese mariners in the fourteenth and fifteenth centuries to go coasting far down the bulge of Africa and in doing so to discover the sea route to India. Thus they prepared the way for Christopher Columbus who, in the name of Spain, discovered the Americas in 1492. For Portugal and Spain, linked with the Netherlands by a network of dynastic marriages, the Low Countries became the great center and entrepôt for the new trade. By the beginning of the sixteenth century this trade was bringing in, without Arab intermediaries, the spices and silks of the Orient; soon it would begin to flood Europe with the bullion of the Aztecs and the Incas. For vigor, for free institutions, for life and growth, the Netherlands seemed to match the Italian city states of two centuries before. It would not have been unreasonable, at that time, to see Europe's future in terms of a federation of city states.

But in Europe in the sixteenth century the web of city states was shattered by a mighty engine of politics which, more than any other force, has given its character to the modern world. It is with the end of the Middle Ages that we meet in first consciousness and growth the modern nation state. The idea that the political sovereignty of a community should coincide exactly with the frontiers of a national group was barely apprehended in the Middle Ages. For one thing, feudal power—suzerainty—could extend over many different duchies and principalities with inhabitants speaking different tongues and descended, however distantly, from different tribal groups.

For another, the concept of nationhood was still very dim. A man was a citizen of Touraine or Anjou, of Bologna or Ravenna, even though he might share a common language with a much wider community. (An educated man in any case put chief store by his Latin, which gave him access to every European state.)

The master institution of the modern world arose in the West—in England, France, and Spain. The invention of the nation state by these communities springs in part from the fact that within them language and frontiers do in fact coincide. The seas around England, the Pyrenees for Spain, were natural limits. Mountains and rivers served France nearly as well, save in the North East where the Burgundian fief, half-French, half-Flemish, gave no place for a clear ethnic frontier and as a result has been the scene of virtually every European war from the fifteenth century to our own day.

Yet the coincidence of frontiers and languages was the opportunity rather than the cause of modern nationalism. The decisive steps to inaugurate it were taken by a number of vigorous sovereigns who were determined to turn their ramshackle feudal domains into modernized centralized states on the efficient model of the Italian despots. Separate fiefs had to be consolidated, power drawn to the center, armies of mercenaries established, and finance gathered in to underpin the wholesale effort of modernization. Ferdinand of Aragon in Spain, Louis XI in France, Henry VII of England, all contemporaries, were fervent centralizers on the Italian model. In a generation they overrode the old feudal checks and balances and brought all power into their own hands. It seemed to them that they were consolidating an absolute monarchy as the single source of sovereignty. In fact they were laying the foundations for the absolute sovereignty of the nation state.

II

While these new despotisms were in the making, Europe went through a profound economic revolution. The early commercial development of Italy and South Germany had been its springboard. Further stimulus came from the discovery of silver mines in Germany and the Tyrol. In addition, the static subsistence agriculture of the Middle Ages was disturbed by the attempts (of lords of the manor and also of wealthier peasants and of merchants from neighboring cities) to encroach upon the villagers' common lands and to introduce the highly profitable production of sheep for the new woolen industry. Each accumulation of capital encouraged the adventurous to new action. Enterprising men broke through the old guild organization of industry—with its protection for all members, its avenues of promotion from apprentice to master, its funds held in reserve for charity and for the pious remembering of the dead. A new class of banker and financier arose at the end of the fifteenth century. Financial houses—the Welsers, the Hochstetters, the Meutings, the Fuggers—controlled enterprises in every part of Western Europe and had trading interests all over the world. Antwerp, the center of the new commercialism, had a banking system almost indistinguishable from modern banking. By the beginning of the sixteenth century the framework was ready to receive the vast increase in wealth flowing in from Portugal's direct trade with the Indies and the Spanish looting of South America.

The new wealth undermined the old relationships. Rural society was disrupted by the pretensions of the new rich and collapsed in the awful convulsions of the Peasants' Wars. Floods of bullion forced prices up and shattered the old attempts to establish and enforce a "just" price. Even if the laws against usury were still sometimes put into effect, the new enterprises were, as the best ecclesiastical minds of the fifteenth century realized, more than simple loans for bare necessities. They were expressions of the risks taken on distant ventures and of the time and "abstinence" needed to accumulate capital instead of spending it at once on consumption or display. However, even without these fine distinctions, the new financial houses were safeguarded by the extent to which, by the early sixteenth century, every prince of Europe, lay and ecclesiastical alike, was in their debt.

A prudent Henry VII of England, a Louis XI of France, or

an Emperor Frederick III might hoard the nation's wealth. But the next generation of despots were without exception fantastic spenders. The English Henry VIII, Maximilian of Austria, Francis I of France all were drunk with splendor. Clad in satin and sables, caps fringed with ostrich feathers, jewels glowing at neck and wrist, they rode in cavalcade from palace to palace, banqueting on the most delicate food and wine, throwing fortunes to their mistresses, and patronizing in lavish extravagance any art that could adorn their kingdom.

Their political extravagance was no less. It was nothing for a French king to invade Italy to reclaim some dubious feudal privilege or for Henry VIII to fight in France for the English sovereign's long-lost title to the French throne. There was hardly a dream of European glory that Maximilian did not at one time or another entertain. But it was at the election of the Holy Roman emperor in 1520 that the fading visions of the feudal world blazed most fantastically with the new wealth of the Fuggers and the Welsers.

There were three claimants to the office—the English Henry VIII, France's King Francis I, and Maximilian's solemn grandson, the Habsburg Charles V, who, as heir to the Burgundian Low Countries, to Austria, to Spain, and to the Spanish empire in the New World, seemed to his worried neighbors a menacing colossus of power. The office itself lay in the gift of seven electors and Charles V received the promise of the votes of five of them only by an outlay of gold which in terms of modern money was probably the equivalent of fifteen million dollars. Yet this was only for the promise. To keep the Elector of Brandenburg, the Count Palatine, and the Archbishops of Mainz, Trier, and Cologne to their pledge when the actual election came, another fifteen million dollars had to change hands.

Probably half the figure went into the treasuries of the Archbishops. (Half the share allotted to the Archbishop of Mainz was earmarked to repay the house of Fugger for the money advanced to the Archbishop to enable him to purchase his archbishopric, with its spiritual and temporal authority, from the Pope in Rome.) The other half was destined for the building of St. Peter's. Not only into the secular authority of the old medieval world had the new wealth penetrated—the Church, too, had caught the intoxication of gold.

III

While the large vitalities of human existence—nationalism and the amassing of wealth—were growing into ever greater importance throughout the late Middle Ages, the forces which had molded European society into form and cohesion lost their creative power. Every institution which grapples with the problem of molding recalcitrant material into a fairer shape —and nothing is more recalcitrant than the passions and interests of men—runs the risk of being defeated by its material. And since the institution which proposes the ideal is itself served by fallible human beings, the danger is not only that the experiment may fail but that the artists themselves, wrestling with such insidious substances as power, responsibility, and material goods, may themselves be caught by these powerful instincts, may appropriate to themselves the power they sought to tame or the riches they had hoped to divert to a nobler cause.

The popes of the Middle Ages were not only the spiritual heads of a great society in which, ideally, political power and material wealth would be directed toward the common good. They were also secular princes of some of the small states in Italy which had fallen to them unsought, as a responsibility, in the sorrowful interregnum after the final collapse of Roman authority. Many of their spiritual officers, the bishops, were in the same ambiguous position. In times of confusion and distress, they had not refused to provide their Christian people with secular order as well as spiritual guidance. Bishops were also rulers, feudal overlords as well as fathers in God. The medieval Church was thus in a position of very delicate balance between the things of God and the things of Caesar and it would have required a perpetual and indeed holy discrimination between the two spheres to hold the balance steady. As the Middle Ages advanced, it was clear that the necessary wisdom was lacking.

In part, the failure came from the normal human reaction to the temptations of power. Beside many saintly bishops whose personal austerity and devotion to the poor raised them later to the altars of the Church—St. Thomas of Canterbury, St. Thomas of Valencia, St. Antonino of Florence, St. Lawrence Justinian of Venice—there were others whose names became a byword for luxury and display—false clerics whom the great poet Langland laments in *Piers Plowman* and whom unknown artists assigned to hell in their paintings of the Last Judgment. In the fifteenth century, the worst examples of this personal surrender to luxury were to be found on the papal throne itself. Intoxicated by the splendors of the Renaissance, the Borgia and Medici popes spent the revenues of the Church on beautifying their palaces as well as their churches and on living in the style of corrupt imperial Rome.

Yet possibly the greatest single cause of the decline in the Church's spiritual power was the ambiguity of the Pope's position as at once head of Christendom and ruler of an Italian principality. To maintain his secular kingdom in the jostling, greedy world of feudal power entailed the maintenance of armies and the manipulation of alliances. The former need plunged the Church back into the simony which the great Hildebrand had tried to drive out. The Archbishop of Mainz, whom we saw in debt to the Fuggers for the price of his see, was only one among a long line of clerics who had purchased their spiritual authority with money destined to be spent on the secular diplomacy of the Pope.

The network of alliances had, perhaps, an even more damaging effect. It brought the Papacy into collision with one after another of the secular princes. At one stage in the fourteenth century, a Pope was physically kidnaped by the French king. In the early fifteenth century, different kings supported rival popes in the Great Schism. The breakdown grew graver as the princes outside Italy, attracted by the riches and splendors of the Renaissance, began to look greedily across the Alps and to seek allies and pawns among the various Italian principalities. By the beginning of the sixteenth century, the struggle for power had grown so vicious that hardly a year passed without a new war in which last year's enemies were reconciled in order to fight last year's friends.

For two decades after 1508, the Papacy and the rival states of France, England, the Italian principalities, and the Habsburg Empire fought, made friends, and fought again. Only when every treasury was empty and all the peoples of Western Europe were in revolt at the perpetual misery of taxation and expropriation did a peace of exhaustion temporarily break the struggle. But by that time the unity of Christendom was lost between Catholic and Protestant, and when the battle was next engaged it was to be rendered even more ferocious by being fought with the passions and slogans of rival faiths.

In one sense the wars of the early sixteenth century are a classic example of the anarchy that follows when a group of states of more or less equal power fear that the expansion of any one of them will upset the security of all the rest. The World Wars of the early twentieth century represent much the same phenomenon: after the Second World War, we have seen a reversal of alliances no less startling than those of four hundred years ago—Germany and Japan, the enemies of 1945, becoming in the 1950's the potential friends of the West in the effort to contain the ally of 1945, the Soviet Union. But the sixteenth-century example is cited not so much to illustrate the workings of the balance of power as to demonstrate the fatal inability of the Papacy to fulfill its role as the one supernational guide, arbiter, and spiritual authority of Europe. It could not fulfill this role when its popes, either greedy for more territory or fearful of losing what they possessed, joined in all the shifting alliances of the princes, spent the money collected from benefices and indulgences upon warlike preparations, and even used—as did Julius II in his war on Venice—their spiritual weapons of ban and excommunication for military ends. In 1517, between the first and second bout in the European struggle, Martin Luther nailed his theses to the church door at Wittenberg and the unity of Christendom was lost.

IV

The weakening of spiritual power and integrity at the center of the Church naturally spread throughout the structure. It was felt, for example, in the monastic network of what we should now call "social services" that had spread all over Europe and thanks to which the sick and the poor and the vagrant were certain of an asylum. The monastic system was itself involved in the changing economic life of Europe. The monasteries were great business enterprises as well as charitable institutions. Business responsibilities could understandably tempt an abbot to care more for his rent rolls than for the needs of the poor. In the Peasants' Wars, both the ecclesiastical estates and the feudal lands of secular lords were attacked by the angry serfs. Moreover, the monastic system was weakened by the decimation of the clergy during the terrible plague of the Black Death in the middle of the fourteenth century.

One has the impression in reading of these times that the holiness of the Church was being compelled to work not with but against the institutional pressures. We can measure the strain in the lives of such saints as St. Catherine of Siena, a girl of such renowned sanctity that she became the counsellor of popes but had to use her main influence to persuade Gregory XI to end the papal captivity in Avignon. Vincent Ferrer is another example of a saint of eminent holiness whose life was caught up in diplomatic efforts to end the Great Schism. In the Hildebrandine reform, the Papacy had been the instigator of sanctity, the patron of learning, the innovator in thought, the hopeful, courageous guardian of a new Christian order. As the years passed, care for its own territory and its political status among other princes transformed it little by little into a force of growing conservatism, conserving good and faulty alike. One symptom of this loss of resilience was the setting up of the Inquisition and the use of force and even torture to repress unorthodox thinking. Another was the stultification of learning in the Christian universities and the rise of scholarship divorced from religious influences.

The medieval world, unlike the modern Soviet world, left a man great license to think what he liked provided he was reasonably discreet and did not attempt to preach to great crowds and disturb the peace—"seditious" heresy, active proselytizing heresy, was the quarry of Church and state. But the Church, whose Master had preached mercy and compassion and had chastised His followers when they had asked Him to "bring down fire" upon a city which had refused to listen to Him, now handed men on to the stake and used torture to secure confession of heresy.

One should not, it is true, forget the role of the state in this context. The Inquisition was established by governments before the popes took action. Its revival by Ferdinand and Isabella in Spain was not so much a religious move as one more part of the centralizing policy of the monarch who was determined to have a single kingdom unified in frontiers and thought. Once the tragic division of Europe into rival interpretations of Christianity had come about, the new absolute monarchs were all the more anxious to secure uniformity of belief within their boundaries, and the fires were stoked horribly with Catholics and Protestants alike. But whatever the encroachments of secular power, the Church whose belief it was that "truth is great and will prevail" exhibited the decline in its spiritual vitality and in its power to mold material things to spiritual ends when it reversed its own order of values and used physical force to accomplish a supposedly spiritual purpose.

A decline in intellectual mastery occurred at the same period. The synthesis achieved by St. Thomas Aquinas in the thirteenth century gave full weight to the importance of created things. They enjoyed their own position below the supreme sphere of uncreated spirit. The duty of man, as the head of nature and the link between the world and supernature, was to understand and master the material universe and to bring it under the rule of reason and law. Thus a framework was provided within which the study of the real world might have been carried on side by side with the contemplation of the nature and mystery of God. But the later Schoolmen did not follow up the new possibilities. They simply continued their intellectually vigorous but increasingly arid disputations drawn *a priori* from first principles, or they commented with increasing refinement on known classical and Christian texts.

The first men to follow St. Thomas's clue to the study of nature—the liberating observation of fact—were therefore not the Schoolmen, but the artists of the Renaissance whose starting point was not *a priori* argument or rational induction but the vision of beauty that assailed their senses and inspired their pens. It is no coincidence that the first man of genius in Europe who began to grasp the possibilities of modern science was also the greatest artist of the fifteenth century, Leonardo da Vinci. It is clear from his notebooks that he was led to minute study of rocks, trees, plants, movements of water, and human physiology by his artistic desire to portray them and reproduce their splendor. But this artistic interest changed into a detached study of things in themselves and a desire to understand, by experiment, their reactions and behavior. "Experiment," wrote Leonardo, "is the true interpreter between nature and man"; and, "Thou, O God, dost sell us all things at the price of labor."

It must not be thought that Leonardo was breaking with all metaphysical thinking in order to base a new science on pure deduction from what he found in nature. He believed with the Schoolmen that the universe was an orderly system of law and with the Greeks that mathematics were the key to the pattern of creation. But he no longer wished to consider mathematics in timeless abstraction. He wished to discover mathematics, as it were, physically at work in created things. "Mechanics," he said, "is the paradise of the mathematical sciences, for in it the fruits of the latter are reaped." There was thus no inherent or necessary cleavage between religious metaphysics and the new science. Both rested upon the vision of an orderly and intelligible creation. But religious thought was too cluttered with allegorical irrelevancies and perhaps still too tinged with Gnostic undercurrents, condemning the world and the flesh, to remain the great philosophical framework within which science could develop. The divorce between them began.

V

In the early sixteenth century, these forces of change and growth and decay were clearly working towards a crisis. Rising nationalism, a flood of new wealth, the new curiosity of science, all faced a Church that was weakened by the secular policy of the Papacy and the general decline in spiritual vigor that followed from it. There were two routes ahead: on the one hand, division, head-on-collision, and lasting conflict; on the other, reconciliation, the regeneration of spiritual power, and the continuance in Europe of a growing but still organic culture. This second choice was the burning hope of a band of men who count among their number some of the noblest of human spirits. The Christian Humanists—Erasmus, Budé, Vives, Thomas More, Colet, Linacre, to name the greatest—attempted at the beginning of the sixteenth century to bring a distracted Europe and a disintegrating Church back to the paths of peace. It was not of necessity a vain hope. Before them, Europe's powers of recuperation had proved to be very strong. The Papacy of Gregory the Great had fallen low in the Dark Ages before the reforms of Hildebrand had recreated its lost greatness. The Benedictine order, declining in Italy, had been reformed from Cluny and the Cluniac reform had been revived at Cîteaux. If spiritual regeneration had been possible in the past, why not now?

The Humanists believed that the new invention of printing could be used to carry the Gospel to the people, and that if learned men were provided with clear, accurate translations in Greek and Latin of the sacred Scripture, they would drop the universal habit of allegorizing—which, as St. Thomas More put it, was "as useful as milking a he-goat into a sieve"—and turn to the glorious, unadulterated word of God and of the early Fathers. The English scholar, Colet, was the leader in this movement to persuade people to read the Gospels and the Epistles historically as actual events or as real letters written by a real man. He did not exclude all allegory. In fact, with a freedom that would have shocked many Victorian Christians, Colet suggested that the whole account of Creation in Genesis should be taken as an allegory. But the Humanists' supreme aim was to restore theology by restoring the unabridged study of the texts. Erasmus's greatest work was a Greek translation of the New Testament.

In the secular field, the reformers saw some hope of achieving their greatest aim—the restoration of international peace and order. There is no greater source of unity than the existence of a common enemy, and in sixteenth-century Europe an external pressure became yearly more menacing. While the princes of the West quarreled among themselves and the popes pursued their territorial ambitions, a new danger had arisen in the rear of Europe. For two centuries the Turks had been encroaching on the old Orthodox empire of Byzantium. In 1453, Constantinople had fallen. The Moslem troops drove into the Balkans and were narrowly defeated by John Hunyadi. By the end of the century, the pressure had been renewed. The Balkans were overrun and, while the Western kings completed the shameful wars and betrayals of the new century, the Turks entered Hungary and shattered the Christian armies at Mohacs in 1526. The Humanists pleaded on every side for the unity of Christian princes and prelates against the inroads of the infidel. They received their most agonizing setback when in 1513, with the Turks at the gate, Pope Julius II summoned his secret allies to war against another Christian power, the republic of Venice.

Yet the Humanists continued their work, pleading for peace, for conciliation, and a settlement of disputes. St. Thomas More, more keen-sighted than his master Henry VIII, distinguished clearly between the spiritual authority of the Pope and his territorial pretensions. He implored Henry not to follow the Pope blindly in his European conflicts, for "the Pope is . . . a prince as you are and in league with all other Christian princes. It may hereafter, so fall out that your Grace and he may vary upon some points of the league, whereupon may grow war and breach of amity between you." Indeed, when the breach came, over the Pope's refusal to grant Henry VIII a divorce, it cost England its link with Catholic Christendom and it cost St. Thomas More his head.

The Humanists sought, too, to mitigate the evils of the economic revolution. Vives wrote a treatise on the state of the poor in Europe, and all Humanists urged that the peasants and poor townspeople be protected against the rage for wealth that had fallen upon the West. They watched with pain and anxiety the obvious eagerness of the new capitalists to seize the wealth stored in the monasteries; and they sought the reform rather than the dissolution of the monastic foundations. In a word, their efforts were aimed at a reconciliation between the old faith and the new vitalities. They wished to preserve from the Middle Ages the sense of the common life, of social obligation, of the duties as well as the rights of property, and they wished to reinvigorate the old faith by new learning and by science. We, looking back from a new watershed of trouble and anguish, may well be startled by the extent to which their problems resemble our own. International peace, control over national sovereignty, the proper use of wealth and property, the conflicts between the apparent claims of science and faith— these are the riddles neither we nor they have resolved. Thomas More, dying on the scaffold for the last liberty—the liberty to think his own thoughts—or Erasmus, pleading for wisdom in the midst of the strident folly of perpetual aggression, seem closer to us than do many more complacent leaders and thinkers who have lived between our two ages of confusion, questioning, and change.

8

Machiavelli's Disciples

EUROPE, even at the height of the Middle Ages, had not possessed a uniform culture such as underlay the great societies of India or China. It was a tip of the world peopled by different races with different traditions and histories and held together for a time in a dynamic unity-in-diversity by the institutions of the Church. At the Reformation, the older traditions reasserted themselves. The Renaissance and its successor, the Counter-Reformation, were an expression of Latin Europe's return to its classical roots—to the humanism and sense of law and administration once embodied in Greece and Rome. In Germany the Reformation—which some have called the Renaissance of the North—expressed in some measure the deep instinct of the old, untamed, tribal peoples to throw off the rules and complications of an alien Latin civilization.

It is not surprising, therefore, that the new lines of division between Catholic and Protestant Europe tended to follow the old lines of the Roman Empire. The German and Scandinavian lands which had lived beyond Roman rule came under Lutheran influence while Latin Europe remained Catholic. Along the old frontiers of the Empire—in Scotland, the Lowlands, and Switzerland—the distinction between the two traditions was a little blurred. There the form of Protestantism most akin to Catholicism—the Calvinist Church—exercised its strongest influence. In England, Calvinism was so diluted with traditional Catholicism that the Anglican Church developed as a *via media* of its own unique kind. In France, Catholicism remained the religion of the state but evinced in Jansenism a strongly Calvinist trend and, in its spirit of independence from

Rome—its so-called Gallicanism—a continuing undercurrent of the mood of the Reformation.

This division of Europe between rival Christianities did not at once weaken the influence of religion upon men's thinking. On the contrary, division for a time intensified it to a pitch of fanaticism and violence which found expression in more than a century of wars. These wars, however much their origins lay in nascent nationalism, were in the popular estimate wars about religion, and were thus to be fought with all the tragic bitterness that men exhibit when they feel that their entire way of living and believing is at stake. But if the Reformation did not at once weaken religion, it introduced new directions into men's thinking. These new trends had the effect of very greatly strengthening the national and economic forces which, even before the Reformation, were struggling against the restraints, such as they were, of medieval society. If the fiercest arguments of the sixteenth century turned on how man should worship and serve the one true God, the outcome of the arguments was to divert men more and more to the pursuit of secular divinities—to what Bacon called "the idols of the market and the idols of the tribe."

"The idol of the tribe," in other words the emerging nation state, was clearly and directly served by the abolition of the Pope's universal authority. However much the influence of the Papacy had waxed and waned, it expressed in institutional form the existence of laws, interests, and ideals lying beyond the reach of state government. St. Thomas More chose to go to the scaffold rather than recognize in Henry VIII the supreme head of the Church in England. He feared the concentration of authority which the gathering of civil and religious power in a single hand would entail. He foresaw the weakening of Christendom and the growth of tyranny. He died, he said, "the King's good servant, but God's first." His distinction was to be made largely meaningless in the century after his execution, for the secular princes who actually fought the wars of religion compelled their subjects to adopt the religion of the prince and used religion as an instrument of national control and national aggrandizement. There is some reason to believe that the German princes actually precipitated the Reformation in order to weaken the influence exercised by the emperor—a Catholic, an Austrian, and a Habsburg. The German bishops were anxious, after Luther had thrown down his challenge to the Pope, to reach a conciliatory outcome. Rome, alarmed at the split in Germany, elected to the Papacy, after a series of notorious Italians, a pious and ascetic Dutchman, Adrian VI. But Luther's cause was espoused by the German princes and the open breach was used to reinforce their national and secular authority.

Elements in Luther's teaching made it all the more possible for them to do so. There were many strands in this passionate and complex soul. He expressed the revolt of German sensibility and German simplicity against the Latin legalism and administrative structure of the Church. In some measure, his protest resembled that of the Humanists against the corruption of the Papacy and the laxity of monastic life. The sale of indulgences was the occasion of his outburst and there is a sense in which, as a great Catholic saint, Klemens Maria Hofbauer, later wrote, "the Germans brought about the Reformation because they wished to be pious." This measuring of sin against money, this traffic and business of forgiveness had become profoundly offensive to all sensitive souls.

If Luther had carried his protest no further, he would have been denouncing evils against which Erasmus, Thomas More, and Budé had raised a Catholic voice. But it is significant that Luther called Erasmus "the greatest of scoundrels" and detested the desire of the Humanists to reconcile the new learning with the old theology. To Luther, the whole Latin heritage—classical or Christian—was anathema. It spelled worldliness and corruption. It diverted men from the simple word of God. It laid down rules and regulations to trap the soul. Its good works had become measured in terms of reward and punishment and, behind the idea of indulgences, there lay almost a penny-in-the-slot concept of salvation. For Luther, therefore, works were of no account. They might be the consequence of salvation but they were not its measure. Salvation would lie in simple abandonment of the self to Christ, in a deep emotional and personal experience of conversion: "As the soul needs the Word alone for life and is justified by faith alone and not by any works . . . Therefore the first care of every Christian ought to be to lay aside all reliance on works and to strengthen his faith alone more and more."

This sense of salvation depending entirely upon an internal experience of the human heart had profound social and political consequences which Luther only dimly realized. It struck at the idea of the Church as an independent institution, for what were organization, hierarchy, monastic order, or corporate charity but "works" in the grossest sense? It went further. It undermined the power of religion to seek to control the vitalities of human life. Luther denounced with medieval vigor the iniquity of avarice and covetousness, but when he was asked by some German magistrates whether they ought to take action against usurers, Luther's answer was disquietingly vague. "The preacher shall preach only the Gospel rule and leave it to each man to follow his own conscience." Above all, the Luther view opened a chasm between the inner life of the soul where salvation might be achieved and the outer secular world in which, since no religious restraints or institutional checks were to be allowed to work, men would be left to the temptations and violence of their own desires.

Luther, having divorced social ethics from religion, believed that the secular state, another external and worldly force, must take over the task of restraining worldliness. Thus the Christian would not be contaminated by secular concerns and the dead would be left to bury the dead: "You see it is as I said, that Christians are rare people on earth. Therefore, stern, hard civil rule is necessary in the world, lest the world become wild, peace vanish and commerce and common interests be destroyed . . . No one need think that the world can be ruled without blood. The civil sword shall and must be red and bloody."

Luther's belief in the necessity of order was greatly increased by the disorders of the times. The peasants began to believe that the Reformation meant the removal of all oppressive authority: the baron would go with the prelate. The

Peasants' Wars seemed to Luther to take the whole spiritual content out of his gospel. "This article," he protested, "would make all men equal and so change the spiritual kingdom of Christ into an external worldly one. Impossible!" He looked all the more eagerly to the German princes to reimpose social discipline. They in their turn were only too ready to accept the alliance of a religion which taught that their own authority was absolute and that their "civil sword" could and should be "red and bloody." Luther's social teaching thus set a part of the German nation on the road of passive citizenship and state absolutism. It was one strand in the eighteenth-century *tour de force* whereby Frederick the Great of Prussia transformed his barren northern principality into an armed camp and built a state to support an army. The Prussian state itself exercised a mystical fascination upon later German philosophers bred in the Lutheran tradition. For Fichte and Treitschke it came close to being the embodiment of the Absolute in history. In our own day, the tradition of passive acceptance of state authority undoubtedly assisted Hitler in the securing of totalitarian control over the German people.

II

Yet Luther was not the only nor even the main force in freeing the state from all external restraints and inhibitions. It was the successful despotism of the Italian principalities which set the fashion for despotism in the new nation states of sixteenth-century Europe. Equally, it was a brilliant Italian thinker of the same epoch, Niccolo Machiavelli, who stamped upon European thinking an essentially absolutist concept of the state which still has its influence today. The state, it is true, may be absolute in two different senses. It may be an internal dictatorship overriding all the rights of its citizens. Absolutism in this sense has not entirely reconquered the Western world. But a state may also be absolute in an external sense. It may recognize no laws beyond its own sovereignty, admit of no obligations which it does not itself accept, and hold no genuine belief in its membership of any wider community. In this sense, absolutism has been the universal rule in the Western world since the disappearance of our society's first weak and embryonic experiment in international order, the medieval Church.

The advocacy of both forms of absolutism is to be found in Machiavelli's political writings, *Il Principe* and the *Discorsi*. He was himself writing for a particular purpose and against a particular background. As the servant of the Florentine Republic and later of that typical Italian despot Cesare Borgia, he saw at first hand, at the close of the fifteenth century, the ravages caused in Italy by the anarchy of competing states and by the growing tendency of foreign powers to intervene in the anarchy. His deepest desire seems to have been to achieve a union of Italian states and in Cesare Borgia he thought he had found a leader vigorous and determined enough to launch the movement. His writings are therefore in some measure a practical guide to action in the unstable Renaissance world of Italian feuds and alliances. Since, however, they are virtually the first modern systematic study of power politics, they have exercised a far wider and more lasting influence than their writer intended.

There was nothing new in power politics in Machiavelli's day. In fact, the first thirty years of the sixteenth century covered some of the rawest and most cynical contests of Western history. What was new was the entirely objective analysis of power which Machiavelli achieved, with his underlying assumption that power is the normal and rational aim of states and the contest for power the normal condition of relations between states. Medieval theory—like the highest thinking of the classical world—had taught that the aim of civil society is the common good, to which each would contribute according to his status, rulers and magistrates seeking to maintain justice in both the internal and external relations of society. Medieval practice, on the other hand, had displayed all mankind's capacity for allowing passion, not reason, to be its guide. Avarice, bad faith, ambition, and aggression had marred the lives of medieval rulers, lay and clerical alike. An ugly gap existed between the pretensions of a Christian civilization and the savage conduct of its supposed upholders.

In one sense, Machiavelli is simply another expression of the sort of disgust felt by Luther at the shams and hypocrisies of a social order which pretends to be good but is bad. Luther's solution was to withdraw morality into the private world of the soul and to leave the state to take care of itself. Machiavelli's reaction was to do away with morality altogether. Since moral precepts were invariably flouted by most rulers, it was better to deal with the state not as an instrument of the common good but "realistically" as an engine of power: power is the end of the state, and the aim of the ruler—the prince—must be to preserve power. To do so, he must recognize that any means are permissible—good faith, bad faith, the making or the breaking of alliances. Machiavelli admits that this principle—that the government is not bound by any previous undertaking, however solemn—is not particularly ennobling. "If men were all good, this precept would not be a good one, but as they are bad and could not observe their faith with you, so you are not bound to keep your faith with them." For Machiavelli, it is thus realism to act on the belief that all men are bad; and a ruler who accepts this axiom is more likely to make a success of maintaining his power than one who is held back by scruples or weakened by principle: "How we live is so far removed from how we ought to live that he who abandons what is done for what ought to be done will rather learn to bring about his own ruin than his own preservation." The prince must learn to be both fox and lion and use force and cunning to rule men who are themselves little more than beasts of prey.

The statesmen of Machiavelli's day no doubt read *Il Principe* with a considerable sense of relief and reassurance. The realization that most people's practice is far below most people's ideals can produce, in the short run, a sense of liberation and a sloughing off of impractical prohibitions and restraints. Yet the abandonment of the Christian ideals of statecraft in theory as well as in practice led not to an improvement in the conduct of the state's affairs but to a further cynical slide into despotism. The greatest statesman of the Renaissance, St. Thomas More, who, as we can read in his *Utopia*, was no less aware than Machiavelli of the actual malpractices of kings and princes, nevertheless gave this advice to the man who succeeded him as Chancellor of England: "Master Cromwell, you are now entered into the service of a most noble wise and liberal prince; if you will follow my poor advice you shall, in your counsel-giving unto his Grace ever tell him what he ought to do but never what he is able to do. . . . For if a lion knew his own strength, hard were it for any man to rule him."

Machiavellianism as a state of mind spread far beyond the select number of men who had actually read *Il Principe*. As a general attitude toward politics, it must be held to have contributed considerably to the extinction in post-Reformation Europe of the medieval experiment of constitutional government. With few—though vital—exceptions, Western government in the sixteenth century took on an arbitrary stamp. The will of the prince became, as Machiavelli would have wished, supreme law. All over the Continent, the old Estates and Councils and free city governments either disbanded themselves or were dissolved from above. France, the dominant Continental power of the seventeenth and eighteenth centuries, was a centralized despotic monarchy whose most renowned king could say *"L'état, c'est moi."* While all life and all activity revolved around the remote and megalomaniac splendors of Versailles, the people starved on grass and six million died of hardship in a single generation.

The divided authority of the Middle Ages had vanished. Baron and bishop upheld the throne whose influence they had once held in check. With their peoples held down in dire subjection and the insurrections of the late Middle Ages forgotten, the princes could devote themselves to another chapter in the Machiavellian gospel, the maintenance and extension of state power at the expense of other nation states.

The long wars which ravaged the mainland of Europe intermittently from 1523 to the Treaty of Westphalia in 1648 are called the wars of religion, but differences of faith were the excuse and national rivalries the substance of the battle. Religion was employed in a strictly Machiavellian sense, to rouse ardor, to cloak ambition, and to turn an enemy's flank. Machiavelli had written in the *Discorsi* that the religion of a people was a matter of vital importance to the ruler but not in the sense that it made for the common good or for the maintenance of brotherhood. He meant simply that religion was a most useful instrument for controlling the people and for using them as pawns in the real business of the state— the maintenance and expansion of power.

Cardinal Richelieu, more than any other statesman, was responsible for the horrors of the Thirty Years War—a war during which one-eighth of Germany's population was slaughtered and large stretches of fertile land went out of cultivation for a generation. He, in name a Prince of the Catholic Church, in fact a complete Machiavellian, made a cynical use of religion in his shifting alliances and worked with Catholic, Lutheran, and other Protestant princes in his persistent efforts to strengthen France and weaken the Habsburgs. His Catholic Majesty of France fighting "for true religion" in close alliance with the Protestant Gustavus Adolphus would have gained Machiavelli's entire approval. The credulity of the masses, in his view, had no other purpose than to forward the enterprises of Kings.

The "wars of religion" so sickened Europe of religion—if not of war—that the power politics of the eighteenth century, though still concerned with precisely the same objects, were conducted with less fanaticism and hence less wholesale slaughter. The cynicism, however, had not diminished. In fact, it reached a new pitch in Frederick the Great, who wrote a book denouncing Machiavelli while preparing with Russia and Austria to partition Poland. Napoleon, who used the new religion of nationalism and revolution to conquer Europe, was a perfect Machiavellian and his statement "I judge men only by results" is in the true spirit of the master.

The twists and turns used in Bismarck's diplomacy to secure the one overriding aim of German unification illustrate the further development of nineteenth-century Machiavellianism, but it would be wrong to see in Bismarck's policy more than the most realistic working out of a general nineteenth-century attitude which fully accepted state supremacy and tolerated all types of diplomacy provided they subserved the power of the state. It was the English writer Walpole who made the comment: "No great country was ever saved by good men because good men will not go to the lengths that may be necessary." And it was a liberal and respectable English statesman, Lord Grey, who remarked to Princess Lieven: "I am a great lover of morality, public and private, but the intercourse of nations cannot be strictly regulated by that rule."

Yet in the eighteenth century, rational principles and in the nineteenth the strength of evangelical respectability still laid some limits upon the general Machiavellianism of international politics. Diplomacy was conducted under a sort of umbrella of decency. There were degrees of lying and treachery that lay beyond the accepted limit. Bismarck himself reverted to conservative diplomacy once his objective of German unification had been secured. It was not until the coming of the totalitarian state in the twentieth century that the world began to see the implications for international society of boundless lying and limitless bad faith. Then the moderate Machiavellians of the type of Mr. Neville Chamberlain (who, after sending a government mission to mediate in Czechoslovakia, could still refer to it as "this far-off country about which we know so little") were completely bewildered and defeated by the total Machiavellian Hitler, who announced the end of his territorial ambitions in one breath and his new claims in the next. And even after a decade of Soviet diplomacy, Western would-be practitioners of "psychological warfare" cannot—mercifully—emulate the cynicism of Russian propaganda in which to invade is to "liberate," to exploit is to "reconstruct," and to "seek peace" is to arm to the teeth.

It is possible that the Machiavellian perversions of diplomacy would not have reached their twentieth-century pitch had it not been for one more general consequence of the modes of thought which we trace back to Machiavelli. His writing, since its whole aim is to direct the attention of the ruler away from an ideal world of truth and justice to the "real" world of power, aggression, and untruth, is a complete break with the greatest single tradition of classical and Christian thought. That tradition was based on the recognition that a moral order underlies the changes and vicissitudes of temporal society and that the lasting good of men and women and the final good of states can be secured only if the moral order is not too grossly outraged. To the Greeks, Machiavelli's suggestions to the prince that he should lay aside principle and pursue power would have seemed the height of impiety and the ultimate instance of *hubris*. In the lonely end of Napoleon on St. Helena, in Bismarck's rejection by Wilhelm II, in Mussolini's corpse swinging by the feet at a filling station, in Hitler's sordid end underground in a Berlin bunker, the Greeks would have seen the visitation of a nemesis which, sooner or later, strikes down all those who pit their will against the moral laws of the universe.

Under Machiavelli's influence this distrust of arrogance and this sense of its moral consequences tended to fade from modern Europe, and in their place grew up the opposite concept —that what succeeds is right and that the only yardstick of judgment offered by history is whether an enterprise has staying power. German thinkers such as Treitschke believed that the state did not belong to the order of morality at all but to the order of power. This is metaphysically not a hairbreadth from the claim that "God is on the side of the big battalions" and from Stalin's cynical query, "How many divisions has the Pope?" Success is virtue, might is right, and any aggression, however despicable, can be justified by simple duration. Such a philosophy inevitably empties political life of all moral content and returns it to the condition Machiavelli believed it never left: that of life in the jungle in primitive animal aggressiveness.

9

Constitutional Victory

HAPPILY for the Western world, the relapse into despotism, almost universal in the sixteenth century, was arrested in the seventeenth century by new political developments in the British Isles. Many influences worked together to weaken the Tudor dictatorship. England was spared by its island isolation from involvement in the century of wars of religion. The navy which Henry VIII had strengthened protected its shores from invasion and the English part in resisting Spain's hegemony was played out very largely at sea. This withdrawal from Europe, which has been compared to the relative isolation of Italy in the high Middle Ages—and could also be related to the isolation of the United States in the nineteenth century— gave the English a breathing space in which to adjust their institutions. The perpetual harrying of war reinforced despotism on the Continent. In England, there was a chance for second thoughts.

In part, this rethinking brought with it a sense of having lost earlier freedoms. Medieval constitutionalism and the medieval rule of law, which had established such rights as that of trial by jury and of no imprisonment without due trial, were alike violated by the centralizing Tudor monarchy. Yet the tradition of independent justice was maintained in the Inns of Court, where the Common Law was defended against the encroachments of Roman law, a system which, the lawyers argued, was devised for and derived from a servile empire. Parliament, too, although it was summoned irregularly and remained a compliant tool in the hands of Henry VIII and his formidable daughter Elizabeth, continued its corporate existence and made occasional feeble shows of maintaining such rights as that of "no taxation without representation" upon which medieval Parliamentary influence had been based. When the popular Tudor dynasty died out and was succeeded by the alien Stuarts, the traditional constitutional forces gathered strength. The great jurist Coke fought the usurpation of the ordinary courts' jurisdiction by such royally appointed and controlled bodies as the Court of Star Chamber, which the monarchs found very convenient for extra-legal trials and punishments. The determination of Parliament to restore its own authority, meeting the equal conviction of Charles I that kings ruled by divine right, finally precipitated the English Civil War.

It was not, however, only the memory of former privileges that led the burgesses of Parliament to risk rebellion. A new force had entered English politics with the Reformation in the shape of Calvinism. And it was the Puritan, Presbyterian, and Congregational groups of Calvinist Protestants who provided the driving power behind the revolt of Parliament and the leadership of the Parliamentary forces. Calvin, like Luther, had broken with the medieval Church in disgust at the luxury of bishops and popes and at the corruption of men who borrowed money from successful usurers and sold indulgences in order, in Calvin's view, to live lives of vanity and idleness, the while preaching poverty and condemning avarice. Like Luther, too, Calvin disbelieved in the efficacy of works: men would be saved not by good works, not even by faith, but by the direct election of God who "by a just and irreprehensible, but incomprehensible judgment," predestined some to eternal bliss and the majority to damnation. Yet a man might know that he was among the elect by the experience of conversion and, as the chosen of God, it was then his duty by his way of life to manifest God's power and majesty to man. In this sense, works were not the cause of salvation but its consequence. The elect of God could not leave one moment of their earthly life unconsecrated: everything belonged to the mighty Power who had chosen them.

Such an ideal might have seemed to encourage a revival of

the dedicated life of the monastic orders. But for the men of the Reformation, the monasteries seemed the very core of idleness and uselessness. Moreover, Calvin was brought up in Geneva, one of Europe's vigorous commercial cities, and before his mind was the contrast between the industry of the merchants and the uselessness—as he saw it—of nobles, clerics, and monks. The consecration taught by Calvin was therefore a gospel of work: each man in his "calling" should by his industry, his sobriety, his utter disregard of worldly pleasure manifest God in his daily life and convert the world from luxury and laziness to the pursuit of useful activity, glorifying God in the counting house and at the bench, creating wealth, not for display or self-indulgence, but to the greater honor of the Creator. This gospel of work distinguished Calvin's teaching from Luther's belief in passive citizenship. If the world was to be remade by godly men, no part of it could be left uninfluenced. Civil government, like every other department of life, must come under the control of the elect. Calvinism, like Catholicism, contained a social as well as a personal gospel.

The economic consequences of this new glorification of work must be considered separately. Here it is only necessary to point out what a new driving force of individual self-confidence and dedicated striving was injected by Calvinism into the world of politics. The claim of the medieval cities to self-government was renewed with a more iron determination. In fact, wherever Calvinism became the dominant faith—as in Geneva or in the New England settlements—the force and vigor of the new faith and its claim to dedicate everything to the service of God led to the establishment of theocratic dictatorships under the iron rule of Calvinist ministers and merchants. In England, the religious situation was too confused for any Calvinist hegemony. The Anglican Church, in spite of Edward VI's Calvinizing reforms, was still Catholic in feeling. But Calvinism was the militant creed of the business communities, above all of London, and its adherents made up the element of unshakable resistance in Parliament which led to the breach with the King. In the brief interregnum of the

Cromwellian Commonwealth, Calvinism provided the leadership.

Its disciplines, however, were too rigid for the English, who thought they had been fighting for liberty. Moreover, one wing of Cromwell's followers, looking behind the merchant class to the old communal life of the Middle Ages, began to put forward notions about equality and the sharing of property which split respectable Puritan opinion. The Calvinists were not "levelers." They believed in wealth provided a man had worked hard to create it. In the disappointed reaction of the people and the divisions of the leaders the Commonwealth came to an end, to be followed by a restoration of the Monarchy. Yet the blow delivered to the divine right of kings by Charles I's decapitation prevented the return to royal despotism. The outcome of a century of struggle between the king and Parliament was to leave Parliament supreme after the settlement of 1688 and to establish beyond the reach of royal (or indeed Parliamentary) interference a number of basic liberties of the citizen which, first worked out and protected by law in the Middle Ages, were now enshrined in a Bill of Rights and safeguarded by an independent judiciary.

The system was very far from being democratic. The Revolution of 1688 transformed the divine right of kings into the divine right of property holders. But it was nevertheless an effective transfer of power from despotic to parliamentary institutions and it contrived to adapt the constitutional traditions of the Middle Ages to a growing mercantile community. This element of continuity and legality gave the system an unusual strength and resilience. And its relative freedom, compared with the winter blight of royal despotism in Europe, earned it in the eighteenth century the wonder and admiration which Italy had earned four centuries before when the Italian city states had been the education of Europe. Now constitutional rule had, it seemed, been achieved on a national as opposed to a city scale. Frenchmen traveled to England to understand the phenomenon and returned to France to write in unstinted admiration of constitutional monarchy. This *Anglomanie* became a political force in France itself, undermining the emotional hold of absolutism and preparing for the cataclysm of the French Revolution.

II

Yet it was not from England that the strongest revolutionary influences reached the shores of France. They radiated from a new community beyond the Atlantic where a combination of new land, wide resources, and the Calvinist doctrine of self-reliance and work had created, in the course of the eighteenth century, a degree of liberty under government and responsibility in citizenship that transferred the admiration of free men from England to the new lands of America. Nor was it simply a matter of the extension of freedom in the life of the citizen. The United States, isolated by two oceans from the stresses and pressures of older civilizations, set to work to achieve the physical extension of free government over an entire continent. First the city state in Italy, then the nation state in England, and now the continental state in America had achieved a form of free government. The growth in extension was, for Western civilization, as significant as the growth in depth.

Two political strands run through the colonial phase of American history. One was, to some degree, a projection of English society; the other was a considerable contrast. Wealthy men purchased estates in Virginia and the Carolinas, merchant groups financed plantations and sent out settlers, indentured servants were imported to work on the estates of the established gentlemen, Negro slaves were brought in from Africa for the same purpose. A similar development in Latin America was, however, accompanied by the rigid imposition of government control and the subordination of the political life of the settlers to the despotic rule of governors sent out by the equally despotic rulers of Spain. In the English colonies, on the contrary, the new settlers were expected to set up local assemblies on the model of the British Parliament. Property and religious qualifications limited the vote to a privileged few —as in England. Yet the rule of law and the rights of citizens to independent justice accompanied the establishment of traditional parliamentary institutions.

However, the nature of the new lands made it impossible to build up an exact replica of English seventeenth- and eighteenth-century society. Indentured servants would work out their two years under contract and then those with a taste for hard work and independence could move inland, carve out their own farms from the wilderness, and become within a generation substantial citizen-farmers with a stake in the community and the right to vote. It was hard to keep a man a peasant or a tenant in the new America. There was too much land available simply by moving on.

In America, too, as in contemporary England, the disciplined will and austere industry of the Calvinist congregations heightened the pressure for free government. In the inhospitable lands of the north, English magnates did not buy estates and merchant-adventurers did not finance colonization. The first settlement at Plymouth of the tiny group of Calvinist exiles from England was a symbol of the new forces which would create the distinctive pattern of American society. A mixed group of artisans and clerks, with the little money they could borrow from some London merchants, sailed in the *Mayflower* in 1620, in part to better their economic lot, in part to escape religious repression. Arriving in Massachusetts with the onset of winter, they hastily set up some political authority among themselves—a "civil body politic" empowered to make laws and elect officials—and then settled down to endure the horrors of a winter of darkness, cold, famine, and pestilence, with savage Indians lurking in every thicket and the hostile forest engulfing them on every side. Those who survived were men who had endured, with no outside assistance, the worst that nature could do to them. Their leaders were Calvinists inbred with the gospel of dedicated work and personal election. In this spirit they attacked the wilderness, built towns, established a fishing industry—and they were but precursors of the men who would, for the next century and a half, leave the safety of known society and set out with rifle and axe to tame the wilderness and work their way to wealth and independence. It was not surprising that men trained in such a rigorous school, pitting their will against nature and seeing in their success the proof of God's choice of them as His elect, would be impatient of government by any traditional or hereditary class.

As their experience developed during the eighteenth century, many of them came to believe that English influence would inevitably support the landowners and the wealthier merchants and underpin the authority of the old limited assemblies. Such men as Samuel Adams in Boston, Alexander McDougall in New York, Charles Thomson in Philadelphia, and Samuel Chase in Baltimore, who organized "committees of correspondence" and kept popular agitation alive, fought to prevent any reconciliation with England because they believed that independence for America and the achieving of a wider democracy were synonymous. Their task was made the easier for them since the English link could be fought on strictly legal grounds. The English conception of colonialism was still the traditional attitude of a mother country which protects its settlements in return for securing a monopoly of their trade, a lien on their raw materials, and a secure market for metropolitan manufactures. To tax the colonies seemed merely a normal working out of these rights. But in America, these taxes, however mild, could be made to seem an invasion of the English medieval constitutional right not to be taxed without representation. The radical elements led the fight against all forms of taxation imposed from London, knowing that it was an issue upon which conservative American opinion, also jealous of its rights of self-government, would stand with them. At the same time they hoped and worked for a breach. When the English Coercive Acts followed the radicals' Boston Tea Party the issue was decided, and in 1775 the War of Independence began.

Although the link with England was broken, neither the radical nor the conservative element secured a clear victory in the framing of the United States Constitution. It was a democratic constitution, but its framers, most of them men of conservative temper, sought to include in it safeguards against "mob rule." They divided powers carefully to reduce the influence of the directly elected legislative assembly, provided for the indirect election of the president, and guarded the Supreme Court against coercion by either. The radicals, strongly represented in the state legislatures, accepted the Constitution grudgingly and added to it a Bill of Rights.

The compromise was possible because in fact the differences between the two sides were by no means so great as they must have seemed to the protagonists. The conservative element had no long feudal background. Its members were men imbued with the classical and Christian ideals of responsible constitutional government. They were not perhaps irrational in sharing the Greeks' distrust of government by sheer weight of numbers. They were wrong only in mistaking their fellow American citizen for the demoralized urban proletariat of ancient Athens or contemporary Europe. In fact, the radicals were almost as much "men of property" as the conservatives themselves. Their ideal was, by intense effort and single-minded endeavor, to cultivate a farm or build a business which would bring them self-respect and economic independence. The American Revolution was made in the main by God-fearing, law-abiding, and hard-working men, and their very radicalism had a conservative, religious, and traditional stamp.

Conservative or no, their success was too revolutionary for the *ancien régime* in Europe. The French monarchy, to spike England's guns, had spent men and treasure fighting beside the Americans to secure their independence. The achievement of self-government in America, however, coupled with the cost to France of the war, was an ultimate provocation to the victims of French despotism. The American victory in 1782 was followed within seven years by the French Revolution.

Yet the most revolutionary achievement of the American Constitution may well be felt by future ages to lie not in any of its internal arrangements but in its creation of a federal framework for an entire continent. Here was a solution to the problem which had baffled and brought down earlier democracies in Greece and Italy, in spite of all the brilliance of their civilization. In some ways, it is true, the American task was easier. The thirteen colonies, speaking a common tongue and sharing the same culture, had been united under one rule from

London. They had fought a war together to throw off that rule. They were still menaced by British power in Canada and by the presence of the French along the Mississippi. They had learned in the War of Independence how very nearly the struggle had been lost by the lack of co-ordination between the various colonies and by the lack of central government.

Yet similar pressures had not saved other communities from the consequences of division. Common tongue and culture had not drawn fourteenth-century Italy together, nor had the threat of the Turks. Persian pressure did not create a united Greece. In the America of the Confederation, tariff barriers were already going up between the states and disputes were brewing as they stretched their frontiers westward to claim the unsettled lands. It took the hard and sustained advocacy of a small group of men—the Federalists—to convince opinion in the new independent states that the Confederation (a simple grouping of sovereign states delegating some powers to a central authority) was too nearly like a mere alliance to create firm government or external security or to give the central power any real authority within the states. When their work was done, some of the more visionary of the architects of the new American system—Jefferson among them—believed that they had given the world a pattern and set in being a movement which would spread to all mankind.

Yet their Union, broad as it was and including as it came to do all the races of mankind, did not transcend all the old limited ideas of national sovereignty. A common tariff against the rest of the world was one of the baits which the Federalists offered to the thirteen states and by the time the United States came of age, it had adopted as uncompromising a belief in absolute unrestricted national sovereignty as Machiavelli himself would have demanded for his prince. In spite of its internal federal constitution, in spite of its multinational origins, it had conformed by the twentieth century to the traditional Western pattern of the nation state.

10

Work and Wealth

IT WAS not only in the field of nationalism that the Reformation unleashed vast and unpredictable forces whose effects still determine the political scene in our own day. The economic revolution was no less far reaching. Nationalism and property—government and economic power—were each as profoundly affected as the other, and twentieth-century society bears the marks of the great development. The essence of the economic revolution was the extinction of the medieval philosophy of property and the development of a totally new concept of the working of economic forces. The Schoolmen regarded the right to private property as primarily a matter of social convenience. Property, St. Thomas believed, would be better cared for and administered if under someone's private care. Even so, according to some Fathers, it was a consequence of sin and the communism of the monasteries represented a more perfect way of life. Yet even if private ownership was admissible, its precondition was social use. The man of property held his wealth as a trust and was obliged to see to the wellbeing of those who depended upon him and particularly of the needy who could not care for themselves. That property was heady stuff the Church was perfectly aware. Its sustained attack on avarice and cupidity was an attempt to use moral force as a check on abuse. The weakness lay in the accumulation of property in a few hands under feudalism and the lack of institutional checks to prevent exploitation. The Church's discipline had a better chance in the cities, where property came to be more widely distributed. Yet throughout Europe the charities of the monastic foundations mitigated the avarice of bad landlords and bad masters.

After the Reformation, the three main principles of medieval economic and social theory were totally undermined. Over wide areas, the social services of the monasteries were destroyed and nothing took their place. Avarice and cupidity as vices disappeared and the concept of men accomplishing the public good by pursuing private gain took its place. As a corollary, property lost its social responsibility and was turned over to the absolute discretion of the owner.

First in time came the dissolution of the monastic orders in Protestant lands. The reformers pointed to the abuses of the monks—which such Humanists as Thomas More or Erasmus did not deny. In such pamphlets as Simon Fish's *Supplication of Beggars*, the king was urged to expropriate all the orders and charitable institutions as the only road to social reform. (Who then, More asked, would care for the beggars? Fish seemed to believe that to be rid of the clergy was reform enough.) But Henry VIII and his power-hungry courtiers desired not so much the reform of the monasteries as the spending of the great monastic endowments. So, after 1532, all over England the plunder began. It did not stop short at the religious foundations. The common lands of the peasants, now required for sheep or for more intensive agriculture, were enclosed, and cottages were pulled down. The lord who had taken over a Sussex manor of the Monastery of Sion answered thus the peasants who protested at his enclosing of their land: "Do ye not know that the King's Grace hath put down all the houses of Monks, Friars and Nuns? Therefore now is the time come that we gentlemen will pull down the houses of such poor Knaves as ye be."

This revolution did not go by without protest, once the full implications of the extinction of general education and of the social services became clear. Anglican divines of the sixteenth and early seventeenth centuries were as fierce in their denunciations of the greed and avarice of the new magnates as any of their medieval predecessors. Archbishop Laud gave his entire support to the royal policy of checking enclosures and fining heavily those who pressed on with them. Between 1635 and 1638, something like £50,000 was extracted in fines and six hundred offenders appeared before the Council. During these last years of medieval thinking, the attempt was also still being made to define and punish usury. The decisive break came with the triumph of Calvinist social thought.

This is not to suggest that Calvin approved of usury or exploitation. On the contrary, Geneva and Massachusetts imposed a fanatically austere standard of life and work. But just as Calvinist insistence on individual election and the dedication of all activities to the glory of God prepared for the growth of political democracy, so its glorification of work and its tendency to see in economic success the judgment of God approving the work of man's hands began to take the sting out of such words as avarice and cupidity. If a man worked with deathly concentration, abjuring all luxury and using his thrift to extend the range of his economic activities, how could this be called avarice? If his concentrated energies and sustained abstinence from luxurious spending raised the general wealth of the community, was not his pursuit of gain in the common interest?

Before one dwells on the obvious weaknesses in the argument, it is as well to remember the element of truth. Industrialism is potentially mankind's most useful servant. Its creation from prescientific agricultural foundations demanded a titanic effort of thought and will. If men had sought no more than gain and luxury, it may be doubted whether the vast expansion of industry could ever have come about. The Calvinist belief that work glorified God and that the creation of wealth by thrift and driving activity served the good of mankind was anything but an ignoble one. In communities where this religious sense of work and of thrift has been lacking the building up of an industrial system by independent entrepreneurs is exceedingly difficult. The otherworldly religion of India, for instance, has put little emphasis on creative work and given no framework either to canalize or control man's capacity to build wealth. The communal tradition and the climate of Africa give little weight or prestige to sustained effort.

Mere desire for money is no substitute. Any community can produce speculators, cheats, tricksters, men who treat the economic process as an easy path to quick fortune. But the building of industry—particularly in its early stages—demands a sustained effort, a long vision, and a readiness to postpone the immediate advantage for the slower, sounder gain. The Calvinist dedication of work to the greater glory of God gave to the Puritan industrialists—to the wool manufacturers of England and Massachusetts, to the tool makers of Switzerland and the Low Countries—a seriousness, an abstinence, and an unremitting self-dedication to work which provided the dynamic energy needed for the early experiments in industrialization.

Yet the cult of work and the cult of economic success as a sign of God's blessing demands a discrimination as delicate as the medieval ideal that property is a sacred trust. The desire to dominate other men by means of economic or political power is a constant strand in human conduct and the step is not great between the creation of wealth as an honorable calling before God and the pursuit of wealth as a gratifying aggrandizement of the self. Moreover, not all wealth is acquired by hard unremitting toil. The speculators flourish beside the new industrialists, and behind them stand the magnates whose wealth came from simple expropriation. How are all these wealths to be distinguished? Are all to be granted the reward and blessing of God? Do the honest merchant and the usurer, the hard-working ironmaster and the absentee landlord, equally enjoy the right to appeal to their wealth as a sign that their ways of life are in conformity with the will of the Almighty? Yet can the wealth of one be attacked without endangering the security of the others? In the seventeenth century, the doctrine that wealth is beneficent and its pursuit serves the common good eventually blotted out all distinctions between the various sources of wealth and at last drove out the traditional distrust of riches and distaste for cupidity.

This change was reinforced by another more secular trend

of thought. The passion for science, and in particular for the mathematical and mechanical sciences which Leonardo da Vinci and the men of the Renaissance had introduced into Europe, went strongly forward beyond and behind the divisions introduced by the wars of religion. The first realization—springing from the works of Copernicus, Galileo, Kepler, or Newton—of the vast orderly laws revealed in the universe intoxicated men with the notion of design in nature. God, they believed, had set the first mechanism in motion like a clock and established its parts in harmony so that it could tick on for ever. Human instincts, since they were part of nature, must share in nature's harmony and it was therefore entirely rational to suppose that man's acquisitive instincts worked, like everything else, for the general good. As Pope wrote, in verse as smooth as the harmony he was extolling:

> "Thus God and Nature formed the general frame
> And bade self love and social be the same."

There could be no talk now of avarice and greed. The acquisitive instinct was set in man for the benefit of society and, indulging it, he would only serve the common good. A "hidden hand" brought all separate cupidities into a harmonious system. To quote Pope once more, this time with a positively Machiavellian undertone:

> "All nature is but art, unknown to thee;
> All chance, direction, which thou canst not see;
> All discord, harmony not understood
> All partial evil, universal good;
> And, spite of pride, in erring reason's spite,
> One truth is clear, Whatever is, is Right."

From this premise it was not difficult to draw the further conclusion that any outside interference with the acquisitive instinct would upset the harmony of nature and thwart the economic wellbeing of the community. The "hidden hand" could order these things more smoothly than a bungling government or a dogmatic church. Property must become an absolute, for only if men controlled it completely could they harmoniously follow their natural instincts. In the seventeenth century, therefore, we can follow the total disappearance of the social obligations of property. In the philosophy of John Locke, property is an absolute, unchangeable right antecedent to the setting up of civil government and therefore should be inviolate from all forms of government interference and regulation. Indeed, the chief purpose of government is to protect private property, which now enjoys the divine right once claimed by kings.

It is true that Locke, like Calvin, thinks of property in terms of a man's own efforts. Man's right to private property, he writes, springs from the work that he has himself put into it: "Whatsoever he removes out of the state that nature has provided and left it in, he hath mixed his labor with it and joined to it something that is his own and thereby makes it his property. It being by him removed from the common state nature placed it in, it hath by this labor something annexed to it that excludes the common right of other men. . . ." Such a doctrine, applied, shall we say, to the opening up of a new continent like America, could provide the free settler with a secure doctrine of ownership and protect him against the land speculator or the wealthy migrant who simply sought to buy up land without setting an axe to a tree or a plow to the land. But applied to conditions in Europe in the eighteenth century, it belonged to the realm of pure fantasy. Scientific farmers such as Coke of Norfolk or "Turnip" Townshend, who thought out and introduced the rotation of crops, could justly claim their rights under Locke's philosophy. So, too, could the creative industrialists who in the eighteenth century were diversifying the economy widely by their own efforts. But most landed gentry had received their wealth not out of "the state that nature had provided" but out of the state the monks and peasants had provided. And beside the working industrialists and the enterprising merchants were such men as the organizers of the South Sea Bubble, that orgy of speculation in the 1720's in which fortunes were made and thousands of investors ruined by the systematic circulation of false information. Could a man claim that his lies had added "something

that is his own" to the state of nature? Apparently, for speculation continued to be an inevitable adjunct of property and
in its turn acquired the Lockean sanction of inviolable private
ownership and control.

II

The breaking away of property from all restraints had, as
one would expect, some appalling consequences. The plight
of the poor deteriorated as they lost their traditional claim to
pity as the chosen companions of the incarnate Christ. Since
economic success was now the proof of righteousness, economic failure must be the proof of turpitude: the poor were
poor, not because there was too little wealth available and the
powerful engrossed so much of it, but because they were lazy,
shiftless, and dishonest. To give them alms would only encourage their idleness further; they should be compelled to
work and if they would not, whipped, or preferably both—
and this in a century when a new movement of enclosures
increased the number of pauper men and women with no
means or hope of subsistence. Higher wages would only lead
to more idleness, willfulness, and dumbness. Arthur Young
seems to sum up the general opinion of the eighteenth century
when he says "everyone but an idiot knows that the lower
classes must be kept poor or they will never be industrious."

More grievous still was the attitude of the wealthy toward
crimes against property. By the eighteenth century, property
had acquired an almost sacred character. Justified by the
Puritan conscience, extolled by the new scientific thinking, and
clung to by all who possessed it, it dominated society like a
pagan fetish. To the idol of the tribe the idol of the market had
now been added, and like earlier idols it demanded sacrifice
in blood. Savage man traps protected the squire's estates.
Hanging and deportation were the punishment for trivial
larceny. In England, a woman who tried to pass a bad shilling
was strangled and burned. Young mothers were hanged at
Tyburn for stealing coarse cloth to cover their naked children.
The death sentence covered two hundred different offenses

and, as late as 1815, could be applied for a theft of five shillings. The hulks around the coasts of England were full of screaming, starving prisoners rotting in their chains. Yet deportation, first to America and later to Australia, involved comparable horrors. Dr. White, colonial surgeon to the first governor of the convict settlement of New South Wales, thus describes the arrival of a shipload of convicts: "A great number of them were lying, some half and the others quite naked, without bed or bedding, unable to turn or help themselves. The smell was so offensive that I could not bear it. Some of these unhappy people died after the ship came into the harbour and their dead bodies, cast upon the shore, were seen lying naked upon the rocks." Such Belsen-like scenes called forth from one officer the comment: "The slave trade is merciful to what I have seen in this fleet."

The slave trade was another product of the unlimited play of economic interest. The horrors of the Middle Passage, in which Negroes kidnaped from their native Africa were stowed together below decks and crossed the ocean to a strange land chained, the living and the dying together—these horrors, too, were perpetrated in the sacred name of economic interest: the interests of British and New England slave traders and of the planters in the Southern states. Sometimes, as one looks at accounts of such inhumanities, the question arises whether the guilt and bitterness stored up in those outwardly rational and optimistic years can ever be fully discharged from Western civilization. It is the thought that haunted Abraham Lincoln, the West's sublimest statesman, when he contemplated the bloodshed of the American Civil War and said in his Second Inaugural Address: "Fondly do we hope—fervently do we pray —that this mighty scourge of war may speedily pass away. Yet if God wills that it continue, until all the wealth piled up by the bond-man's two hundred and fifty years of unrequited toil shall be sunk and until every drop of blood drawn with the lash shall be paid by another drawn with the sword, as was said three thousand years ago, so still it must be said, 'The judgements of the Lord are true and righteous altogether.'"

11

A Western World

BY THE eighteenth century, the two greatest forces in society—
the tribe and the market, nationalism and property—had
passed beyond even the theory of moral control. The Greek
concept of a moral order, the Christian idea of God's judgment in time, were ceasing to have any hold on men's minds
in any matter relating to national ambition or economic interest. For the long run no serious classical or Christian thinker
could have failed to predict disaster. But in the short run the
growing area of lawlessness was not apparent. Christian or
classical standards of personal ethics still gave form to people's
private lives. Christian or scientific rationalizations provided a
sanction to the pursuit of interest. In any case, the removal of
restraints can give such strong and immediate sense of liberation and release that the first effect of throwing off inhibitions was to give Western Europe an unparalleled dynamism.
The success of this physical expansion was startling enough
to still questions about the final consequences. They could be
left to the future—and they were.

National ambition and economic enterprise were the two
forces which drove Europe between the beginning of the sixteenth century and the end of the nineteenth to take control
of almost the entire world. In the process every element of
the population took part. While rich families and wealthy
groups of merchants planned settlements on a major scale,
simple artisans and clerks, peasants who saw no future for
their children under feudalism, adventurers and confidence
men, uprooted themselves to the New World to begin life
again in the Anglo-Saxon North and the Latin South. While

the early settlers made their bridgehead in the Americas, British colonists arrived in the temperate lands of South Africa. A century later, the transportation of British convicts to Australia began the settlement of Australia and New Zealand. Nor was colonization confined to movements across the ocean. The covered wagons, the prairie schooners, which carried the Americans across their continent were fully as much a colonizing fleet as the immigrant ships which sailed over the Atlantic. In the harsher climate of Asia, the Russians pressed to the East across Siberia and brought Russian settlement to lands grazed by Mongol nomads.

This vast movement of colonization by the white races had consequences which can be fully realized only in our own day. Commonly, when a European or an American thinks about the distribution of world population, he pictures the white races jostled by the ever increasing millions of the colored peoples. What he fails to realize is that, if there is any question of jostling in the last four hundred years, the white races have been the chief offenders. It is estimated that in 1650 Asia and Africa between them contained eighty per cent of the world's population. Europe and the Americas together had a population of only 113 million compared with 100 million in Africa and 330 million in Asia. By 1940, the share of Asia and Africa together had fallen to sixty per cent. The population of Europe had nearly sextupled, that of the Americas multiplied by over twenty times. Africa had not risen by even fifty per cent and Asia had only about tripled its population. True, in absolute terms, Asia's peoples were still denser—1,155 millions compared with about 800 millions in Europe and the Americas—but during the four centuries of Western expansion, all encroachments of population could in the main be laid at the Western door.

Figures and percentages are, moreover, misleading. They mask the fact that the Western peoples were expanding into what were without exception the best lands of the earth. No doubt, as the millennial work of clearing and cultivating Europe went forward, the peasants and the monks who cut the forests and created arable farming land and safe sheep-runs found the face of nature stern enough. Their descendants, the men who worked their way, farm by farm, and settlement by settlement, through the forests and across the prairies of the United States, thought themselves pitted against the most stubborn and inhospitable elements. But today, with our deeper knowledge of climate and topography and ecology, we realize that the temperate lands of dependable rain, mild sunshine, and secular deposits of uneroded topsoil are mankind's richest inheritance. Beneath them, too, were a great part of the world's mineral resources. Moreover, the steady temperatures and reliable alternation of warmth and frost create a climate in which man and beast are favored and pests and parasites are not.

Between Capricorn and Cancer, on the other hand, lie the world's "underprivileged areas." Here the violence of flood and heat, the scorching sun, the torrential downpours leach and wash away the soil and breed noisome diseases in the steaming rivers and forests. Or else perpetual sun dries out the land and leaves it empty desert. When, in the last four centuries, the vast *Voelkerwanderung* of the Western peoples took place, they moved without exception into the temperate lands, even filtering into pockets of temperate climate concealed in the tropics, such as the highlands of Kenya. Destroying or overlaying the scattered local population, they established a monopoly of the areas in which the greatest concentrations of wealth could be built up and in which even today the greatest increases in the production of food could be achieved. If the United States, for instance, practiced the intensive farming of Denmark, the American population could rise to between 500 and 700 million. The Soviet Union could probably support the same figure.

In short, in the last four hundred years, the Western peoples have engrossed a very large part of the actual and potential resources of mankind. Capitalist and commissar, businessman or day laborer, farmer or kolkhoznik, they make up, compared with the Indian peasant or the African sharecropper, the privileged half of mankind.

Before the invention of modern transport and communications in the nineteenth century, there was little physical basis for the concept—primarily a religious concept—of a single humanity and a unity of mankind. Before the twentieth century, the resources available for the maintenance of human life appeared unlimited and were used with spendthrift carelessness in the new continents. The conditions did not therefore exist in which men could formulate the moral problem offered to the Western peoples by their privileged possession of the earth's best resources—by the concrete fact that today, perhaps seventy per cent of the world's income is enjoyed by eighteen per cent of the world's people, the bulk of them living around the North Atlantic. It is only now that this particular aspect of the expansion of the West is beginning to press on the outer fringes of the Western conscience. Hitherto, the feature of Western expansion that has held the world's attention has been not colonization, but colonialization, not Western settlement in more or less empty lands but Western rule established over lands already full.

The bringing of virtually the whole of the world under the sovereignty of one or other Western nation had its roots in the desire for trade. The Portuguese discovery of the sea route to India, to the Spice Islands, and on to China and Japan began the eastward movement of Europe's merchants who could, in the seventeenth century, hope to make a thousand per cent clear profit on a shipload of nutmegs brought back to European ports. Fortunes little less fabulous were to be had from pepper, silk, jewels, and later from tea. These first ventures of Portuguese, Dutch, French, and British merchants did no more than establish trading points along the coasts of India and establish contact with the courts of China and Japan. These pioneers had to trade with the advanced civilizations of the Orient on terms of complete equality, or indeed of European inferiority.

Toward the end of the eighteenth century, the collapse of all central authority in India after the disintegration of the Mogul empire left a local condition of anarchy in which no Indian ruler had the means or the will to exclude the foreigner. On the contrary, princes sought to attract either the French or the British to gain support in their own territorial and dynastic disputes. They in turn were used, equally unscrupulously and more effectively, by the British and French traders in their efforts to oust their competitors from India altogether. In this struggle, the British East India Company outwitted the French and found itself in the process the sole governmental authority in large areas around the trading stations of Madras, Bombay, and Calcutta. The continuance of trade demanded a measure of local order, and gradually—by direct administration, by agreements with local rulers, and by backing one pretender against another—the effective authority of "John Company" was spread through the whole continent, a British order substituted for the anarchy that had prevailed after the passing of the Akbar dynasty.

Internal Indian anarchy, rather than overwhelming European force, thus gave the West its first control of India. But in the eighteenth and nineteenth centuries, the growth of industry and the development of scientific technique in Europe introduced a decisive change in the world's balance of power. European armies, equipped with an armament steadily improving in range and firepower, were superior to any Asiatic force. The Chinese were compelled, by military pressure, to open their ports to foreign trade. In 1854 a United States expedition to Japan forced the Japanese out of their seclusion. Perhaps the most dramatic reversal of pressure occurred in the Middle East. There, intermittently for a thousand years, the thrust of expansion had run from the East toward the West. The first wave of Arab expansion had robbed Europe of its North African hinterland. The second engulfed the orthodox Christian Empire of Byzantium, poured into the Balkans, and, while the Western states of Europe continued their insensate religious wars, twice reached the gates of Vienna. The Habsburg dynasty, with little help from any other Christian prince, held the Turks at bay and thus consolidated the Habsburg empire in Central Europe, a multinational dynastic state largely held together by the pressure of the Moslem power on the Danubian frontiers. As the eighteenth century advanced, however, the former technical superiority of the Turks and their trained, disciplined armies of Janissaries gave way before the new inventions in warfare perfected by the West in its constantly renewed hostilities. As industry advanced in Europe, the disparity increased and throughout the whole nineteenth century the chancelleries of Europe were perpetually preoccupied by the diplomatic problems caused by the steady waning of Turkish power. At last, for a few brief years after the First World War, the whole Turkish empire was occupied and administered by Western powers.

The African continent was the last to fall to the expanding West. To some extent, political administration was a by-product of the search for trade and markets. The small tribal societies in Africa disintegrated or fought fruitlessly against the pressure of white men with cloth and spirits to sell and a gunboat waiting at the mouth of the river. Thus, as in India, the collapse of internal order led to an extension of European authority. But in the circumstances of the late nineteenth century, it may be doubted whether the most stable local African government could have resisted the white invasion. The industrialization of Europe behind narrow national boundaries was beginning to make acute the need for markets and the search for new materials. Africa, the unknown continent, seemed—deceptively as it turned out—to offer unlimited opportunities for both. The result after 1880 was a species of blackguard rush for the remaining unattached African lands. By 1900 practically the entire world was under one form or another of Western control.

II

It was a world order—of a sort. The driving impulse behind Western expansion had been economic pressure and national rivalry—the two great irrational powers of the age. It is, therefore, not surprising that their main export to Asia and the Far East was the spirit of nationalism and the techniques of economic development. Where settlement occurred, a profounder force of Westernization followed, for a people do not leave their deepest beliefs and aspirations behind when they set out for new homes. Although beliefs may suffer a sea change, the new community is something richer than a mere reflection of economic interest or of the national group. The Americans and Australasians are Western in their roots as well as on the surface of their national life. But the all-embracing world order of steamships and railways and telegrams, of markets, factories, and spot prices, of cargoes moved from the ends of the earth and materials grown to be processed in factories thousands of miles away—this world order had no foundations other than the web of commercial interest and, for a time, the fact of Western political control.

This failure of Western culture to communicate itself in depth arose in part from a narrowness of vision among Christians themselves, in part from the decline of religion as a force in Western life. In India and the Far East, the Westerners were brought into contact with civilizations more ancient and continuous than their own and with a religious and social outlook of immense traditional force. To suggest in such a situation that faith in Christ could be achieved only by those who were prepared to renounce totally five thousand years of Hindu or two thousand years of Buddhist or Confucian experience was the equivalent of rendering certain the rejection of Christ. In a similar debate, at the origins of the Christian Church, some of Christ's first followers believed that unless Christianity was presented in the ritual form of Jewish religion —with circumcision and all the minutiae of the Law—it would not be the true and saving word of God. But the force of St. Paul's conviction that a Hellenic world would not receive the truth wrapped in a Jewish envelope decided the issue. Paul was free to express the Christian gospel of redemption in terms by which the prophet and the philosopher, Isaiah and Socrates, the worshipers of the Messiah and of the Logos, could give their differing yet complementary witness to the same salvation.

Jesuit missionaries reaching India and China for the first time were aware that only a comparable effort of conversion and reconciliation from within would make Christ comprehensible to the children of Krishna and the pupils of Confucius.

They set themselves to learn the Hindu Upanishads and the Chinese Book of Rites. They sought out the teachers and priests. They began the task of translating the Christian Scriptures into the local tongues. Only, they realized, if Christ could appear to the East as the Savior of mankind and not as the tribal deity of Western national religion, could His teaching, life, death, and resurrection be seen as the completion not of a single religious stream of thought but of all mankind's insights into the nature of God and His creation.

The Jesuits failed. They lost the support of the central authorities in Rome. At the same time the Far Eastern powers decided to expel them, suspecting—from the behavior of the traders and soldiers who followed in the missionaries' wake—that Christ might be only the national God of Portugal and Spain. But the failure of the Jesuits had deeper causes than decisions taken in Rome or Peking. The Western nations failed to transmit their religious concept of life because, by the seventeenth century, they were beginning to lose faith themselves.

While the force of nationalism and the power and claims of property grew steadily during the three centuries after the Reformation, and these great vitalities asserted more and more vigorously their freedom from all constraint, the moral ideals and institutions which should have checked them lost much of their old influence. The wars of religion hastened the process. Even if the substance of the struggle centered on the rival nationalisms of Europe's emerging nation states, the fighting was conducted in the name of competing faiths. The falling apart of the old European synthesis into its Northern-Gothic and Southern-Latin elements seemed to be crystallized in the problem whether faith alone or faith and work together could save a man. Like all great heresiarchs, Luther had sought only to restress an element of Catholic truth—in this case, the necessity of grace—which had been overlaid in the late Middle Ages with the mechanical, mathematical concept of so many good works adding up to so much salvation. Within a framework of charity and the will to agree, the loss of balance could have been righted and the unity of Christendom maintained. This had been the hope of the Humanists.

But in Luther's powerful soul, the disgust of Rome, the flame of German nationalism, and the anticlassical sentiment of the Gothic temperament were all at work. The bond of charity was broken. The bond of common faith did not long survive the breach. Indeed, it may well be that all heresies and divisions spring first from the loss of love and fellowship and compassion, and that dogmatic rationalizations only follow later. Certainly, the break between Orthodox and Catholic Christianity had more to do with the rivalry between Rome and Constantinople, the clash of culture, and the behavior of the Crusaders than with the exact definition of the "procession" of the Holy Spirit in the Creed. But one fateful consequence of the rationalization of deep resentments and divisions into a dogmatic quarrel is, after a time, to sicken men not only with the quarrel but with the dogma as well. If men have cut each other's throats long enough on the apparent issue whether faith or works are necessary to salvation, the reaction tends to be to dismiss the dispute as meaningless. It has indeed become meaningless when measured in so much blood.

It is true that the wars of religion were in fact fought over "dogmas" which mankind still accepts—that one Frenchman is better than one German and that the interests of any nation state can be made to prevail by killing any number of citizens in the attempt to crush the interests of another nation state. It is also true that the definition of the way of man's salvation is very far from irrelevant, for a right definition can exclude such false definitions as that only the proletarian can achieve salvation and that salvation itself consists in liquidating all other forms of society. But after the wars of religion, the rival interpretations of religious truth became repugnant to thousands of educated men and women. Like Montaigne, they abandoned fanaticism and abandoned the taste for definition as well. Many wanted to find attitudes and outlooks which would unite men after so much division and they believed they could find them in the new mathematical and mechanical sciences with their objective physical tests. As one of the first apologists of the Royal Society, Bishop Sprat, put it, the aim of the new institution was not "to lay the Foundation of an English, Scotch, Irish, Popish or Protestant Philosophy, but a Philosophy of Mankind."

The desire to be rid of fanaticism was fed from another source. Whether as a result of the horrors of the Black Death or of the violent disintegration of rural society, the late Middle Ages had been haunted and terrorized by the vision of judgment, death, and damnation. One sees it in the macabre Dances of Death which appear all over Europe in the fifteenth century, or in the lurid landscapes lit from Hell of Hieronymus Bosch. The concept of judgment is inseparable from Christianity and, although it is a mystery, a soul which is given freedom can choose to reject as well as adhere to Divine Reality. Yet if one compares the serene contemplation of death, typical of thirteenth-century Christianity, with the dull glare of everlasting fire which flickers through that of the fifteenth, it is clear that a loss of balance and sanity has occurred. It was not mended by the activities of the Inquisition. It was further fed by the terror of witches and witchcraft that swept Europe at that time. By the seventeenth century, men longed to breathe a less sulphurous air. Once again, they believed they had found it in the contemplation of God as the great Mechanic of a passionless universe, in the cult of reason, and in the suppression of "enthusiasm." "Above all," as Talleyrand was to say, "let there be no zeal."

Perhaps the greatest weakening of the Church followed from the loss of its old medieval independence. The identification of religion with the prince, the struggle between Catholic and Protestant powers, reduced all state churches—Catholic and Lutheran—to the role of subordinates to the new power in Europe, the despotic king. God and Caesar were no longer separate. God had become the head of Caesar's ecclesiastical bureaucracy. Everything that Caesar chose to do, in national aggrandizement or in perpetuation of his despotism, the Church was called to bless. French armies invaded Germany in the name of religion. The French people starved to feed the armies and the bishops had to celebrate the fruitless victories. The union of altar and throne had for two centuries increasingly deplorable results for the altar—which found itself, as an international institution, tied to the war chariot of the nation state and, as the supposed friend and guardian of the poor, condoning the gross inequalities and concentrations of wealth of the centralized monarchy.

Yet the influence of Christianity, even in these centuries, should not be minimized. The sap of life might have sunk in the Church but it had not ebbed entirely. In the hard winter of European despotism, thousands of Christian souls still cared for Europe's sick and orphaned. Indeed, in the heyday of Louis XIV's luxury and imperialism, St. Vincent de Paul founded his immense works of charity and a great lady of the court, St. Louise de Marillac, joined him to serve the most wretched of the King's subjects as a Sister of Charity. The deep root of sanctity remained and sent up its flowers of love and compassion, strange flowers some of them, a scandal and a folly to the unzealous men of that rational age. St. Peter Claver, vomiting at the stench as he nursed the dying Negro slaves unloaded at Cartagena, hardly belongs to the world of Newton and the Royal Society. Even more strange is that beggar and vagrant wandering over the eighteenth-century roads of France and Italy, ragged, verminous, sharing his bread and his pity with poor wanderers as wretched and as destitute as himself and protesting in his very flesh against the luxury and the pitilessness of the age. St. Benedict Joseph Labre, who accepted as a vocation the unrelieved misery of the vagrant poor, is a figure of poetry and terror, a Rimbaud of religion, in the age of Diderot and Voltaire.

The influence of the Calvinist independent Protestant Churches has been described already in the development of the idea of responsible self-government and in the more equivocal drive toward industrialization and the creation of wealth. To these groups—and to the Quakers—we also owe the idea of religious toleration, not simply as an eighteenth-century reaction against religion—a tolerance based on indifference—but as a positive toleration springing from the insistence that God is worshiped "in spirit and in truth" and that coercing the body cannot bind or release the soul. In the eighteenth century, too, there began the Wesleyan revival on both sides of the Atlantic—the Great Awakening in America, the growth of Methodism in Britain—which had profound consequences in the following century. Underneath the skeptical triumph of the age, the power of religion as a molder of men's lives and of their social customs was still exceedingly strong.

III

Indeed, this power is perhaps nowhere more apparent than among the philosophers and rationalists themselves. Because the temper of the eighteenth century has been called critical and skeptical, one tends to forget how much these men took for granted and how much of what they took for granted implied a profoundly Christian view of life. It was, for instance, from a thousand years of Christianity that they took the concept of a beneficent Providence, ordering all things for the good of mankind and making Himself accessible to human reason through the working of His laws. It was from Christianity that they took not only their ethics of personal behavior and family life, but even their whole concept of man. Man is the center of eighteenth-century optimism—man, the rational force, the crown of creation, the manipulator of nature. His intelligence, penetrating the wonders and harmonies of the universe, is to bring all things under order and prepare a rational Kingdom of Heaven on earth by the exercise of his God-given faculties. Such a view is direct inheritance from the Greeks' confidence in reason and the Scholastic estimate of man as the link between God and nature. To the eighteenth-century rationalists, the proposition seemed self-evident. They did not realize how much it depended upon the continuing belief in the existence of God. Once the rational temper inclined to reject supernature altogether—to banish the great Mechanic from His vast machine—then Bacon's prophetic warning began to have effect: "They that deny a God destroy man's nobility, for certainly man is of kin to the beasts by his body and, if he be not kin to God by his spirit, he is a base and ignoble creature."

Belief in Providence was likewise the foundation of what is perhaps the most typical of all eighteenth-century beliefs, and certainly the most influential in the following century—the belief in progress. If there were no limits to man's reason or to the beneficence of the Almighty, then rational inquiry, experimental science, and extended education must lead to a steady expansion of knowledge and control over nature, to a "perpetual and unlimited augmentation of the universal human reason" as the Abbé St. Pierre put it, and to a steady improvement of man's condition until a veritable paradise on earth would come into sight. But such a vision of progress, which would have seemed incomprehensible to the ancients, could only spring from minds fundamentally accustomed to the idea of a progressive unfolding of God's plan in the world and of the basic meaningfulness of history.

There is, however, one point at which eighteenth-century thought breaks away entirely from the classical and Christian tradition. Its doctrine of unlimited progress depended on a totally optimistic view of man. The Greeks' sense of tragedy, their belief that *hubris*—man's pride—inevitably invited nemesis, had faded with the fading of fanaticism and zeal. The Christian sense of sin and retribution had been rejected as a mere by-product of superstition and dogmatism. The eighteenth-century mind was inclined, simply by what it had rejected, to think well of man's reason. The triumphs of the new mechanical sciences pointed in the same direction. But the belief received an almost religious sanction from a new source, itself very remote from eighteenth-century rationalism.

Jean Jacques Rousseau believed with passionate and mystic intensity in the original, unalloyed goodness of man. He believed there were no limits to the degree to which men, entering into society for their mutual benefit—by a species of "social contract"—could improve their condition. Their uncorrupted hearts, expressed through the "General Will" of society, would bring about the earthly Jerusalem. Such was the glorious prospect, if only the return could be made to that original purity. How then had men left it? At this point, Rousseau's sociology and his belief in progress appear to become somewhat confused, for he believes that civilization with its institutions and classes and societies is the root cause of the evil in mankind. Clear away the pride and arrogance of Church and state and the original goodness of man will reappear. Human freedom and human happiness will begin, as one of Rousseau's successors crudely expressed it, "when the last king is strangled in the entrails of the last priest." The question of how good men ever came to create bad institutions is shirked. So is the problem of how progress can be achieved by returning to the beginning. But these inconsistencies were as nothing in the burning faith inspired by this new gospel according to Rousseau. It had the effect of another Reformation. The Providence of the rationalists had been too reasonable a deity to move men's hearts. It was the doctrine of the good man, corrupted by bad institutions, that blazed up in Europe in the middle of the eighteenth century with the force of revolution.

The American experiment fed the flames, for here were men, unfettered by feudalism and privilege, forging their own independence and creating a new society very much as Rousseau might have pictured it—by entering, as free men, into a new social contract. The frank simplicity and easy freedom of such visitors to Europe as Benjamin Franklin stirred men's hearts as a portent of a new humanity. He in turn pictured an America in which human capacity, not wealth or pretension, was truly valued. Thus it seemed that Rousseau's dream of a natural man, honorable and incorrupt in a society without inhibitions and institutions inherited from the past, was not a myth but a fact being realized in the new society across the ocean. Dream and reality came together and the power they generated thrust the *ancien régime* into the vortex of the French Revolution.

THREE

CRISIS

12

Ambiguous Revolution

FRENCHMEN believed that in their Revolution they were about "to make all things new." The belief was shared by men all over Europe. Wordsworth thus described the general reaction to the fall of the Bastille:

> "Europe at that time was thrilled with joy,
> France standing on the top of golden hours,
> And human nature seeming born again."

The men who made the Revolution and the sympathizers who watched them saw in it far more than a simple revolt against misery and misgovernment. Past history had been full of such revulsions. But this was something unique and new, the rebirth of humanity, a dawn in which it was "bliss to be alive" and "to be young was very heaven."

This estimate of the French Revolution as the beginning of a new phase in history is, on the whole, unquestionable. Its contribution to economic development may have been largely a matter of clearing away the old obstacles to industrialism, thrown up by obsolete feudalism—feudal dues for instance, or internal tariffs—rather than the evolving of new methods of production, but in the sphere of national life and political thinking a new chapter opened in the West. The Revolution did not invent the nation state, but it poured into the existing mold a new molten flood of mass energies, hopes, and hatreds. When the neighboring kingdoms formed an alliance with the purpose of invading France to restore the monarchical order, the response of the revolutionary leaders was to summon the whole people to arms. The *levée en masse*, the first instance of modern conscription, brought the nation as a whole, a single embattled will, into the field. The old armies of professionals and mercenaries could not resist the armed battering ram of the General Will. Valmy, the first decisive victory of the Republicans over the Royalists, is also the first battle of the modern era. Nor could a whole people, roused in revolutionary energy, be contained by eighteenth-century concepts of limited objectives and national diplomacy. The French armies, led by Napoleon, took the offensive and marched on to the conquest of Europe.

The immediate consequence of this expansion was to repeat in the rest of Europe the pattern of the French upheaval. Everywhere, dynasties and institutions which had survived unchanged from feudal times were destroyed or undermined and the way laid open for the idea of sovereignty vested in the people's will. But once "the people" began to reflect upon the new philosophy of nationalism, they realized that whatever else it might entail it could not mean, for German-speaking or Italian-speaking peoples, government by the French. Napoleon thus spread the ideas with which to undermine his own hegemony.

This spirit of democratic nationalism was not the only new element in the French Revolution. Its political innovations were as great. At first glance, however, the originality is not apparent. After all, the French were only doing what the British had done more than a century before—putting an end to the concept of despotic monarchy. They were only following the American example of setting up representative institutions founded in the consent of the governed and designed to safeguard their rights and liberties. In this sense surely the French Revolution, like the British and the American Revolutions, marks the end of feudal and semifeudal conditions and the opening of middle-class rule. Its greater violence only reflects the delays in bringing about the change, not any fundamental difference in aim and essence.

Yet this obvious comparison is misleading. True, each revolution had in common a revolt against an earlier monarchical and absolutist tendency. In each, a part of the protest came from new and unsatisfied social groups, striving for a role in politics. But the fundamental difference lies in the fact that both the English and the American Revolutions were limited in aim, conservative in tone, and, if such a term can be used of a revolution, in essence legal. The French Revolution was something totally different. It was a new heaven and a new earth, a new dispensation for humanity, the revelation of the first secular religion.

The men of the English Revolution believed that Stuart despotism had deprived them of liberties, of legal safeguards and of Parliamentary rights which had been established during the constitutional struggles of the Middle Ages. They saw their revolutionary effort in conservative terms and believed they were re-establishing a continuity of national tradition which the absolute monarchy had sought to break. Moreover, the men of the English Revolution, however much they believed in the need to transform society by their work and thrift, were still laying up their treasure in Heaven and did not see their political and terrestrial activities in a Messianic light. This essential conservatism, this concrete interest in well-defined "liberties," not Liberty as an abstract concept, this sober estimate of this world's rewards, appear all the more clearly in contrast to the small group of Levelers and "Fifth Monarchy Men" who held a more prophetic view of the downfall of the king and saw in it the coming of a new spiritual monarchy, in which property, the source of all evil, would have been abolished and the apocalyptic vision of the lion lying down with the lamb would be realized in the world of time.

In the American Revolution, the sense of continuity and legality is all the more remarkable when one considers the new and unfettered environment in which the leaders of the movement were working and the extent to which they or their forefathers had already, in the decision to come to America, broken the continuity of the past. Yet they had been trained in a great tradition. The Common Law, the constitutional legacies of Bracton, Coke, and Blackstone molded the minds of such New England lawyers as John Adams. The country gentlemen of Virginia were versed in the classical tradition and

derived from it their sense of law. Some of the leading spirit
in the drafting of the Declaration of Independence were keer
students of the idea of natural law, which was in part a hark
ing back to the ancient traditions of the Greeks, to the idea o:
dike—eternal law—lying at the foundation of the universe. The
idea of natural law was also, in part, a more modern tradition
formulated by the Schoolmen, of a law of God for man ac
cessible to human reason and corresponding, in a sense, to the
physical laws controlling the behavior of material things. The
reason why the principle of "no taxation without representation" became the central dispute in the struggle with England
lay in the desire of most of the American leaders to conduct
their affairs with the fullest legality and to avoid any sugges-
tion of a break with the past in which, they believed, so many
of the constitutional rights and liberties they sought were incorporated and enshrined.

This distinction between the mood and outlook of the revolutions in Britain and America on the one hand and of the
French revolutionaries on the other may seem, at first glance,
a little academic. A century has passed and in all three countries today, in spite of the vicissitudes of war and social upheaval, the forms of parliamentary democracy persist and free
government has been preserved. The basis of the system is
popular suffrage—"the consent of the governed"—and the rule
of law has not been lost. If the results of the revolutions have
proved so similar, are differences in original outlook of anything more than marginal historical interest?

The significance lies in the fact that the seventeenth-century
revolution in Britain, the eighteenth-century revolution in
America, and the revolution in France on the threshold of the
nineteenth century have not been the last in the series of convulsions to shake the Western body politic. In the twentieth
century, the Russian Revolution and the German Counter-
Revolution have carried on the tale—and the debate which, in
a confused and only partially formulated manner, accompanied the French Revolution has since been proved to be central
and decisive by the revolutions of our own day. The Russian
and German Revolutions—like the French—have claimed to

bring into being at one violent stroke a new social society, based on new principles and ruled by new men. The vision is essentially religious and apocalyptic, even though the framework is secular. The questions which the French Revolution first raised, and which the twentieth-century revolutions have repeated, are whether the determination to remake the whole of society in one upheaval does not inevitably lead to despotism and whether abstractions—either "the dictatorship of the proletariat" or "blood and soil," or even "liberty, equality, and fraternity"—must not always tend ruthlessly to destroy the concrete and historical substance of men's lives and communities and to erect nothing in their place but the inorganic unity, imposed from above, of terror and the police state.

The English and American Revolutions had turned upon the defense of constitutional liberties inherited from medieval times. To these liberties were added, as the eighteenth century developed, various guarantees of the right to speak, meet and —apart from certain disabilities—worship freely. In fact, while John and Samuel Adams were preparing, in Massachusetts, their defiance of arbitrary government, liberal politicians in England were equally perturbed at the attempt of George III to recover a measure of the old kingly prerogative and to interfere directly in politics. Edmund Burke supported the demand of the Americans for self-government for exactly the same reasons he put forward to attack the growth of royal power in England. He saw in arbitrary government the chief danger to the citizen's constitutional rights and liberties, guaranteed and maintained by the rule of law. There is no inconsistency in the fact that, for such thinkers as he, the test of the French Revolution was whether or not it put an end to despotic government.

The men who made the French Revolution were so obsessed with the royal tyranny they hoped to pull down that they had no thought to spare for the general hazards of government and for the risk inherent in all political power: that it will become too strong and swallow up the individual citizen. They knew only one kind of despotism—hereditary monarchical despotism—and this they would abolish. Yet even without this obsession, the eighteenth-century reformers—Diderot, Mably, Condillac, Condorcet—would hardly have foreseen the risk of a new type of despotism, since all of them were inspired with Rousseau's confidence in man's original goodness. It was the institutions of monarchy and feudal privilege that had corrupted him. Remove them and his original unspoiled humanity would reappear. This was the whole sense of the new dawn of a restored mankind. This was the fundamental hope of a new age based not upon tyranny, privilege, and oppression but upon liberty, equality, and fraternity—the three great passions of the uncorrupted human heart.

But conservative philosophers of the stamp of Burke had no faith in these abstractions. "Abstract liberty," he said, "like other mere abstractions, is not to be found." What he meant by "abstract liberty," in concrete terms, was the rule of the many instead of the rule of the few. Was there any innate guarantee that the rule of the many would safeguard the liberties and legal rights of the citizen? The Greeks had not thought so. Burke did not think so either. On the contrary, he believed that the idea of the General Will as absolute sovereignty, unrestrained either by tradition or by any independent system of law, might prove the very recipe of tyranny.

In the intoxication of the new revolutionary ideas, the French masses realized all the worst fears of the conservative philosophers. The idealists and rationalists who had unleashed the revolutionary flood were swept away. First violent tribunes of the people—Danton, Robespierre—and then corrupt, self-seeking, political manipulators such as Barras and Rewbell took their place. Condorcet, the prophet of progress, himself perished under the Terror. The abstraction "liberty" was seen to be wearing the awful mask of the Committee of Public Safety, under whose jurisdiction the most elementary of "liberties"—the right to life—was at the mercy of the private informer and the neighbor with a grudge. Europe was given its first taste of absolute dictatorship exercised not in the name of a man or a dynasty, but of the nation itself.

The other abstractions—equality and fraternity—proved no less ambiguous. The idea of equality had entered Europe at its very birth in the metaphysical concept of souls equal in value and in responsibility before God, "neither male nor female, neither Jew nor Gentile, neither bond nor free." Medieval constitutional thinkers had formulated, but not realized, the concept that all men had a right to join in governing themselves. After the winter of royal despotism, Britain and America had achieved the first practical realizations of the principle. As a result, the aspirations of the idealists and reformers on the eve of the French Revolution were drawn up very largely in terms of political equality—manhood suffrage, annual parliaments, elective offices, and so forth. Indeed, until the "Year of Revolutions"—1848—radicals and revolutionaries continued to put their emphasis on the right to political equality as the gateway to the new society. Yet popular sovereignty and political equality determine only the instruments of policy. They give no guide to its content. On this point, opinion at the time of the French Revolution was uncertain—as it is to a very large extent still uncertain today.

The medieval concept of society as an organic whole, each class fulfilling different functions, had faded. Absolute property rights had dominated the seventeenth and eighteenth centuries. What would follow—what form of social philosophy—was still unclear. The men of the French Revolution had theoretically no quarrel with property. In fact, the right to property was among the rights they were prepared to guarantee to man. Many of the leaders saw the Revolution as their chance to confirm their access to lucrative government posts and to consolidate the middle class in property and influence. But the force which had taken the Bastille, brought the king a prisoner to Paris, and captured the Tuileries was not the will of the lawyers and the philosophers. It was the anger and misery and outrage of the poverty-stricken masses of Paris. The way opened to strike at the regime that had ground them down, and they struck. Equality for them was an explosion of wrath, not a social theory.

When the fury slackened and the blood lust turned to shame and apathy, it was the social equality of the lawyers that emerged—the right of the successful to acquire property and to prosper, not the right of every man and woman to share equally in the benefits of society. Yet the revolutionary inter-regnum had been sufficient to suggest to a new generation of more conservative French thinkers—de Maistre, Maine de Biran, de Tocqueville—that if equality in society is pursued by leveling down and uniformity, the end may be attainable only by a degree of governmental intervention that puts political liberty in danger. The natural inequality of talents requires perpetual vigilance on the part of authority if one man is not to profit by his brains or his health or his skill to pull ahead of a less gifted neighbor. If a solution is sought by the abolition of private ownership as such—as the Levelers had begun to suggest a century before—the citizen is placed in a position of total economic dependence upon the community which employs and maintains him. The powers of government vastly increase, and this means, in concrete terms, the powers of some men. The possibility cannot be dismissed that the community itself might become the "private property" of the bureaucrats.

The ideal of fraternity also proved tragically ambiguous. Nothing had so uplifted the hearts of the poets and idealists as the prospect of fraternity, of man linked to his neighbor in brotherhood and building with him the new family of mankind. "In that blessed day," wrote Godwin, the leading revolutionary idealist in England, "there will be neither disease, anguish, melancholy nor resentment. Every man will seek with ineffable ardor the good of all." But in that day, the streets of Paris ran with blood; and it was not only the men and women of the *ancien régime* who were sent to death in the name of fraternity. The most generous spirits, the idealists—Condorcet, Madame Roland, André Chenier—followed the same path to the guillotine while the mob howled for their severed heads to be lifted up for public show. And no sooner were the killings and torturings at an end inside France than the armies of Napoleon marched over Europe, liberating with one hand and slaughtering with the other. The gospel of fraternity, by 1815, had proved a gospel of blood.

II

The Revolution produced a division in the mind of Western man that persists to this day. The split has been given many names—liberal versus conservative, progressive versus reactionary, left versus right. But perhaps the most comprehensive description would be one that divided men between optimists and pessimists, between those who believed that the great tides of change sweeping over Western society were driving it onward to a better fortune and those who believed the torrent was making for destruction.

For the optimists, the essential fact in the French Revolution had been the abdication of the *ancien régime*. If excesses and violence had accompanied its disappearance, the blame lay with the kings and the priests who had clung too long to their obsolete privileges. Similarly, the campaigns of Napoleon, by shaking European despotism to its foundations and spreading the new gospel of national will and popular sovereignty, were essentially progressive. The destruction and bloodshed were only incidental. The long-term effects would all be good.

Under these broad headings of agreement, the optimists varied considerably among themselves. In lands where the frontiers of statehood and language did not yet coincide—in Germany, in Italy, and later in the Austro-Hungarian empire—the first dogma of the optimists was unfettered national sovereignty. The achievement of the nation state was the chief preoccupation of German and Italian liberals. True, the process also entailed sweeping away the remains of the old despotic order—the intimate link between altar and throne, the political framework of principalities in Germany, of dukedoms and papal states in Italy. Thus liberalism and nationalism had the same objectives and tended to work together in pursuit of popular sovereignty and the secular state.

In old-established nation states, in Britain and France, liberalism, not traditionalism, was the dominant force. The idea of progress was absolute. What had been cast out was privilege and superstition. What was to be in the future shone in the light of rationality and freedom. Man's mind, released from ancient fetters, would use the methods of science to control nature, to increase wealth and human wellbeing, and to secure "the greatest good of the greatest number." Education would open the doors of learning to all and with it would come self-knowledge and self-control. Men, masters of themselves, would become, by universal suffrage and parliamentary democracy, masters of their state. Somewhere ahead might be even wider vistas—"the Parliament of Man, the federation of the world." There was a general sense that the long tutelage of man was over and he was on the threshold of taking full and undisputed possession of his kingdom.

With our hindsight, we can perhaps say that the optimism of nineteenth-century progressive thought exposed contemporary thinkers to the risk of a certain naïveté. They were not naïve about the same things. The liberals were naïve about economic power, the socialists about political power. That was and perhaps still is the chief difference between them. But the confident, optimistic mood of their approach was identical. The liberals inherited their overoptimism in economic matters directly from the eighteenth-century concepts of absolute property rights and of the workings of the "hidden hand." Their aim was a system in which each man would be left free from outside interference to pursue his own profit and thus serve the common good.

This liberal attitude was strongly reinforced in the early nineteenth century by the emergence of a new class of active aggressive industrialists who, with Puritan zeal and unflagging energy, turned the mechanical inventions of the eighteenth century—Crompton's mule, the spinning Jenny, the steam engine—into the basis of factory production. At the same time, the application of precise methods of thinking to economic phenomena began to produce a school of economic thought, claiming scientific accuracy and laying down the basic laws of economic activity. These laws—of supply and demand—were a secularized version of the old Deist faith in the "hidden hand." Since, the economists believed, supply and demand tended to fall into equilibrium provided no one inter-

fered with their working—more demand encouraging manufacturers to increase supplies, oversupply causing first prices
and then production to fall—the only healthy and prosperous
economy would be one in which no interference hampered the
working of economic law. The new industrialists eagerly accepted a mode of thought so congenial to their thrusting enterprise. Nor, to a generation still believing that men were poor
through their own lack of thrift and industry, was there anything particularly horrifying in one implication of the supposedly new laws of supply and demand—that wages, the price
of labor, could never rise above the minimum necessary to
keep a laborer alive, for if more money were offered, more
laborers would be born and the oversupply would force wages
down once more.

The workers, however, could not be expected to adopt so
confident an attitude. They might share with their masters the
same belief in education, self-help, parliamentary democracy,
and the certainty of progress, but in the early decades of the
Industrial Revolution it was also certain that their present conditions were unbearable. They could not be naïve about the
virtues of unregulated economies. They were working sixty
and seventy hours a week for starvation wages. They had to
look to some power or institution to better their plight. Their
tendency was to turn to the state as the only available means
of help and to neglect the dangers inherent in the concentration of political power at the center. The General Will could
not be in error. It was the soul of the community. The General
Will, expressed by a majority vote, was the equivalent of the
government in power. Such a government could therefore legitimately do anything the majority wished it to do. For the
workers, increasingly conscious that they were the majority,
the state seemed the natural instrument for the achieving of
progress, for the regulation of economic life, and indeed for
the coming of the millennium.

Early socialism was full of an apocalyptic vision of the "new
heaven and the new earth." Socialists remembered the promise
of the Revolution and forgot the Terror. Fourier had visions of
a society of equals, based on unlimited free love, producing

millions of philosophers like Newton and tens of millions of poets like Homer. For him, nature itself is evil only because man is evil. Reform society and nature will be transformed, the sea turning to lemonade and sea monsters into familiar and agreeable companions. Short of such fantasy, early socialists— Proudhon, Robert Owen, St. Simon—were all sustained by a vision of a totally new society where peace and justice would reign and which would be brought about in the main by the action of the state responding to the general will. Even later, when apocalyptic visions had faded and their place had been taken by the sober plans and practical blueprints of the Fabian Socialists, confidence in state action remained unabated, and the gradual building of a new society under complete government management was, theoretically at least, the goal with which democratic socialism entered the twentieth century.

III

So much for the optimists. On the side of the pessimists, the conservatives saw only the dark implications of the Revolution. Some, of course, were conservative in a pure and irrational sense. Like the Duke of Cambridge, they held that "any change in any direction for whatever purpose is strongly to be deprecated." Like the Bourbons in their restoration or Pope Pius VII on his return to Rome, they attempted to restore as far as was humanly possible the *ancien régime* in its ancient state. They forgot the age-long misery and injustice that had prompted the people to rise. They forgot the long terror exercised by despotic monarchy and were obsessed only with the Terror of the despairing people. As Tom Paine contemptuously remarked: "They pity the plumage and forget the dying bird." They saw the nineteenth century as nothing but a steady drift toward popular anarchy and there was not an effort made to arrest the trend—whether by generals, princes, or plain adventurers—that was too crude or too brutal to enlist their support. Napoleon III, Bismarck, Horthy, Mussolini, Hitler—each was certain of the craven support of the extreme right.

But there were other conservatives—if conservative is the correct term—whose pessimism did not spring from the simple, selfish fear of losing their own privileges. The distrustful estimate of the Revolution made by such men as Burke or Maine de Biran or de Tocqueville sprang from a deep concern for human freedom and from the glimpse they caught in the French Revolution of the Medusa face of a new totalitarian form of government. Their hearts were turned to stone not by the vanishing of the *ancien régime* but by the first indication of what the new regime might be—a Moloch of power, swallowing its children together with its enemies and submitting all to a tyranny more demanding and pervasive than any monarchical despotism ever known.

The weakness even in the more enlightened and perceptive conservatism of the time lay in the extent to which it could react only negatively to the future. To be concerned about the dangers of mass rule was legitimate, but to suppose that the will of the few—which, after all, had been the basis of the *ancien régime*—would remain acceptable was to overlook all the deepest causes of popular revolt behind the Revolution. A more constructive approach would have been to inquire how the many could become more responsible and how popular sovereignty could come to express responsibility and common sense, not the anger and revolt of the dispossessed masses.

Light might have been thrown on the conservative dilemma in Europe by a debate that was being carried on at the same time—the first decades of the nineteenth century—in the United States. The Federalists, led by Alexander Hamilton, shared the fears of European conservatives that popular sovereignty might mean mob rule and dictatorship. Hamilton and his group attempted to impose limits on the democratic character of the United States Constitution, with only partial success. But on the economic life of the new community, the Federalists made a more lasting impression. Hamilton's conscious aim was to create an élite based on wealth and property who would, he believed, be sufficiently responsible to govern the new state without "the risk of anarchy." The government—by instituting a high tariff, by according assistance, privileges, and even monopoly positions to business groups, and by promoting monetary policies weighted in favor of the creditor—would foster such a class and the community would accept its national leadership. Such was the Federalist ethic, one not of *laisser faire* and free enterprise so much as of a conscious erection of an autocracy of wealth.

These policies aroused the keen opposition of the Agrarians. With Jefferson as their leader, but with John Taylor of Carolina as their most systematic exponent, they held a different picture of the new American community. Hamilton's aims would, they believed, introduce into the United States the corruptions, the idleness, and the folly which flowed from the protection of privilege under the European *ancien régime*. Yet the alternative proposed by the Agrarians was in many ways conservative. They met the fear that popular sovereignty would lead to mob rule by the expedient of seeking to insure that the mass of citizens did not become a mob. The cities of Europe were full of desperate and dispossessed proletarians, men without responsibility because they had no stake in the community and nothing to lose save their misery—and their chains. In America, such a development would be prevented by basing society on the widest possible distribution of private property—on the farmer and on the mechanic—and by insuring that the fruits of men's labor were not taken away from them. Real wealth lay in their output of goods. Such property was theirs by their own sweat and belonged to them indisputably by natural right.

The Federalists, so claimed the Agrarians, would transfer this real wealth from the mass to the few by creating monopolies, permitting speculation in stocks and land, paying high interest rates on the national debt, and, since it too had a monopoly effect, by instituting a high tariff. These forms of property were not property in the real sense, for they sprang from privilege, not work. But a society which based itself on the farmer working his own land and the industrialist producing goods in fair competition and sharing the profit with his work people—such a society need not fear anarchy or mob rule for each citizen would have a stake in the community.

Nor would its government need excessive powers in order to intervene in the economy—whether to favor the few or protect the many against the few. It could confine itself to such social tasks as the control of currency and credit, which properly fell within its province. If, on the other hand, the Federalist recipe were accepted, America would fall, John Taylor prophesied, under "a vast pecuniary aristocracy" and "the world, after having contemplated with intense and eager solicitude the experiment of the United States, will be surprised to find that no experiment at all has been made."

The immense natural resources of America, the drive and the ambition of its citizens, and the plain fact that most men accepted speculation and privilege in the hopes of profiting themselves, led to an eventual development of the American economy on Hamiltonian lines. As late as the Civil War, it was still possible to see the United States in terms of the Agrarian philosophy, of men creating their own property by their own work with axe and rifle on the frontier or with experimental machines in their own shops. But the vast opportunities for gain to be made from Civil War contracts, the drive to open up the West with the expansion of railroads, the growth of the whole scale of industry—these forces, allied to the driving ambition and will for power of American business leaders, left little beyond a memory of the Agrarian philosophy by the last decades of the nineteenth century. The wide distribution of private property as an alternative to the concentration of wealth and power had failed. The other corrective—a further concentration of power in government—seemed all the more inevitable as a result.

In Europe, too, there were some efforts to find a middle term. Disraeli and his young conservatives evolved the idea of a "property-owning democracy," but the group was more remarkable for reconciling conservatives to the idea of state intervention not only to assist and aid the business classes but also to protect the interests of the workers. In this lay the germ of the "welfare state" in which, by taxation, part of the income of the well-to-do has been passed on in social services at first to the poorer classes of society and at length to the entire community. It is significant that much of the inspiration behind this early recognition of the state's obligation to the masses was derived from Christian thinking—from the reforming zeal of the Evangelical movement, from the influence of the small group of Christian Socialists, from the activities of a Christian nobleman, Lord Shaftesbury, who fought virtually alone the campaign for the reform of hours and conditions in the factories. These interventions, attacked by honest and serious liberals as the ruin of an economic system—which would run smoothly only if left to itself—did somewhat mitigate the rigors of mid-century industrialism.

In Continental Europe, the liberals' confidence in *laisser faire* and the conservatives' harking back to the *ancien régime* hampered the development of any positive social policy for the people at large. Men who, like the Catholic priest Lammenais, tried to bridge the gap, failed between the liberals' indifference and contempt for religion and the Church's fear of the liberals' anticlerical secularism. Yet such saintly laymen as Ozanam in France or such religious leaders as Bishop Ketteler in Germany did not despair of formulating a Christian social philosophy relevant to the new industrial society. When their efforts and campaigns were crowned by the publication of the papal Encyclical *Rerum Novarum* in 1894, the ghost of John Taylor of Carolina, trained in so different a milieu and tradition, might have been amazed to find the extent to which his Agrarian principles had accorded with the Christian teaching of natural law. The right to private property as the fruit of labor, the attack on speculation, the idea of protection for the worker as co-worker in business enterprise, the recognition of the government's duty to control general financial policy—these points of coincidence balance the many differences which nearly a hundred years of industrial development had made inevitable.

There was, however, another striking resemblance. The philosophy of *Rerum Novarum* made as little immediate impact on society as had the Agrarian principles. The day belonged to liberals and socialists, to progressive thought, to the exponents of unfettered business and unfettered government.

13

A Century of Optimism

THE reservations of the conservatives and their attempts to formulate alternative philosophies are not typical of the nineteenth century: a century must be judged by what it hopes for rather than by what it fears, and in many ways the conservatives felt perpetually that they were fighting a rear-guard action. The hope, the confidence, the optimism lay all on the liberals' side. They could feel that they were being wafted forward "on the wave of the future" and that before them was a prospect of progress whose limits no one could possibly foresee.

With our longer perspective, we may now feel that these nineteenth-century believers in progress were like farmers planting their fields high up on the slopes of a dormant but not extinct volcano. Underneath the assured and hopeful surface of progress and betterment, the irrational and untamed vitalities of human existence—nation and property, the tribe and the market—had gained an enormous accretion of strength unmatched by any increase in the means of control or indeed in the belief that control was necessary.

One of the major consequences of the French Revolution had been to throw the whole weight of popular rule behind the nation state. The passions of the multitudes were now drawn out and concentrated upon the images and symbols of their national life. At the same time, the advent of the Industrial Revolution had unleashed, in industry, a new head of economic power to be thrust into the old institution of private property. From being forces, nationalism and property had become battering rams. Since, moreover, no limits were at the time recognized to either—*laisser faire* prevailing in economies, unfettered national sovereignty in international relations—it was impossible to forecast what these mighty hammers would do to human society. They might batter it into pulp; they might be the instruments of building human civilization to an even higher level. The only clue to the answer lay in the belief in progress—the belief that if things were now left to take their own course, the result would be for the better. Yet that belief was largely irrational. It had been transferred wholesale from the supernatural plane—where in the hidden dealings of God with man it might hold good—to the world of time where the floors were already strewn with the wrecks of earlier civilizations. Seen in this perspective, the optimism of the nineteenth century seems perilously foolhardy.

It is therefore important to remember that in the first decades of the national and industrial revolutions, the darker possibilities were almost completely masked by the extent to which progress did appear to be working automatically. The risk of aggressive nationalism was checked internally by the strength and prestige of parliamentary institutions—not of the ambiguous type of the French revolutionary assembly but of the ancient, tradition-hedged, constitutional democracy of Britain.

Externally, the configuration of world politics seemed naturally favorable to peace. Britain had acquired a vast trading empire during the eighteenth century and now, as the first industrial workshop of the world, needed peace to exchange its goods and services. This peace could be underwritten with a minimum cost and interference by the ubiquitous British navy. Within this worldwide *pax Britannica* and shielded by British ships, the Americas were able to isolate themselves from the old centers of war in Europe and to develop their own communities. The people of the United States enjoyed a century of external tranquillity while they carried their political institutions across a whole continent.

In Europe itself, a balance of power had been established after the French wars. France and Germany were of roughly equal influence, Austria-Hungary dominated Central Europe.

The only anxiety—a recurring one—was the waning of Turkish control in the Balkans and the fear lest Russia should thrust in to take its place. Russia, however, was held in check by the vigilance of the British, who were determined to keep the Russians from Constantinople—a "containment" policy which they maintained for a century with only one relapse into actual fighting—in the Crimea in the 1850's. Moreover, it was a time of vast Russian expansion and consolidation eastward. Like the Americans in the New World, Russian colonists spread quietly and peaceably across a whole continent and, settling the Siberian hinterland, reached the opposite shores of the Pacific. In short, the nineteenth-century world was one of apparent elbow room in which the claims of absolute nationalism did not clash too often because they hardly touched.

The Industrial Revolution meanwhile built up each year an ever more astonishing capacity to produce new wealth. Cloth, tools, machines, gadgets, luxuries began to stream from the new factories. In the United States, the achievement of industrialism was more astonishing than in Britain, where manufacturing had begun as early as the fifteenth century. In America, only a decade might elapse between the clearing of virgin forest and the erection of a steel mill.

How could anyone believe, during this first expansion of industry, that its development would bring anything but good to humanity at large? Each nation by concentrating on what it was most fitted to produce would lower the real cost of commodities and enable the world, by a beneficent division of labor, to multiply its wealth by mutual exchange. Free trade would knit the nations together in a peaceful web of commerce and the expansion of each would benefit the expansion of all. These doctrines of Adam Smith were adopted in Britain by the younger Pitt and became a burning faith to such mid-century leaders as Peel and Cobden and Gladstone. They saw the "hidden hand" at work in international as in internal trade and believed that, provided the states set up no impediments in the shape of tariffs or discrimination, a general and international harmony of interest would prevail. Until the later part of the century at least, many other nations followed suit and abolished or reduced their tariffs.

What the men of those days could not be expected to see was the extent to which the relative harmony they observed depended upon a temporary conjunction of political and economic factors. Britain, the first industrial nation, was relatively small and relatively unprovided with raw materials. It needed wider markets for its capital and its goods and it needed raw materials and foodstuffs to feed the machines and the men tending them. It made possible a free circulation of trade because the chief trading currency—sterling—revolved through the whole system, going out in goods and capital, returning in materials and food.

So long, too, as only a few nations had resorted to industrial production, a natural balance remained between the suppliers of industrial goods—largely in Europe—and the suppliers of raw materials—largely overseas. As the century advanced, these underlying harmonies began to be distorted. More industrial competitors entered the field. Sharp conflicts for markets developed and now, since industrialization had become the basis of everyone's livelihood, markets were no longer —as in the eighteenth century—the concern of a few merchants engaged in the luxury trades. They touched the life of every citizen. Yet merchants had helped to wage wars for trade, limited wars suitable to their limited objectives. Now that the whole industrial life of a nation state was in question, would there be less restraint? Might not the unlimited nature of the economic interest and the unlimited claims of national sovereignty lead inevitably to unlimited conflict? But these were questions that did no more than throw a shadow above the horizon of the nineteenth century.

II

If national and economic optimism sprang in the main from a negative source—ignorance of the scale of the forces unleashed and of their equivocal character—optimism based on confidence in reason and science seemed to be based upon the positive foundation of actual achievement. It was a century during which the mechanical sciences fell almost into the routine of producing new marvels every decade—behind steam, electricity; behind the railway, the internal combustion engine and its extension into flight. Space was vanquished, labor enormously lightened, communications opened from one end of the world to the other in a flash of time.

The unfolding of the behavior of living organisms promised rewards as great as those bestowed by the mechanical sciences. Medicine made its vast and beneficent advance. Leonardo's prophetic words—"Thou, O God, dost sell us all things at the price of labor"—seemed about to be magically, unbelievably fulfilled. No secrets would be withheld from the questing mind. The scientific method, applied to any problem of human existence, would give an answer so unequivocal and so rational that men would accept it as unquestioningly as they now accepted the formulas of the mathematicians. And even short of those final certainties, the application of the scientific temper to such fields as organization and administration promised an increase in rationality and efficiency which seemed little short of liberation to those who had dealt with the bureaucracies of earlier centuries. Such reforms as Cardwell's reorganization of the British army or Florence Nightingale's reforms in military and public health gave the impression of rational light pouring into dark places where nothing but confusion, obscurantism, and grievance had reigned before.

In the two great democracies of the West—in Britain and the United States—the temper of optimism was reinforced, not contradicted, by the general religious temper of the community. Calvinism had given to both countries the first drive toward economic activity, personal thrift, and the accumulation of wealth. Now with the benefits of this process undeniably apparent on every side, a milder Calvinism, rid of its preoccupation with death and damnation and settled in the conviction that success and responsibility were an outward sign of inner grace, gave form and comfort to men's private lives. The nineteenth century was not an irreligious century but it was a time during which men came more and more to accept the belief that religion had no special vocation to guide and influence economic or national life. It was an adornment rather than a foundation of society. Thus churches ran the risk to which the Continental Church had already been exposed: of seeming a support of existing institutions and a mere reflection of the contemporary social order. Underneath the exterior form of religion lay the risk of mass indifference, apostasy, and a turning to new gods.

Yet this hazard, like all the other hazards underlying the brilliant and successful surface of nineteenth-century life, was largely hidden from the men of that day. The tremors caused by the French Revolution had been forgotten. The rumbling as of some distant earthquake caught only the most sensitive ears. The farmers labored cheerfully on, tilling their high fields and planting the seed, while the lava flow of the twentieth century was still held behind the lip of the volcano.

14

Return to Determinism

IF AN observer from another world had added together all the national and economic fatalities present at the beginning of our own day; if he had noted the rigidity of frontiers to which tariffs and quotas were being added, the incompatibility of national interests now pursued with the whole weight of popular democracy, the resentments of past wars and past dominations, the ambitions of growing economic power behind restricted national frontiers; if, in addition, he had remarked upon the narrowing of the world under the impact of industrial and scientific achievements in transport and communications, the speed of travel and information, the accessibility of every nation, the diminishing barriers of space—if, in short, such an observer had added together the steadily increasing pressures in the shrinking space, he would surely have foreseen a world society which while becoming (physically) a single neighborhood was riven with hostilities and clashes of interest more intense and more profoundly felt than at any previous time. Could he in these conditions have foretold the preservation of natural harmony? A peaceful world order evolving "from precedent to precedent" to democratic world government? The lion of nationalism lying down with the lamb of human brotherhood? Or would he rather have foreseen an epoch of permanent crisis in which every one of the economic and national fatalities would work itself out in conflict and aggression and, after each burst of violence, smoulder on in preparation for the next?

As the twentieth century opened, it became clear that the great vitalities of nationalism and economic competition were no longer held in check by the chance harmony of the preceding century. The balance of power had vanished in Europe. The Germans, united by Bismarck, had defeated France and annexed Alsace-Lorraine in 1870. They threatened Russia by beginning to move into the Balkan and Middle Eastern vacuum created by the decline of Turkey. They estranged England by a violent colonial and naval policy. They frightened all Europe by their economic and military expansion. Thus the 1914–1918 war was brought about by a complex of causes—by the ambitions of Germany, the fears of its neighbors, the increasing restrictions on European trade, the pressure for colonies in a shrinking world market, the growing instability of Central and Eastern Europe, and the lack of any wider system—even of a marginal Concert of Europe—to hold national power under some sort of check. These were the causes. Between 1919 and 1939 virtually all of them reappeared. Britain and the United States withdrew from Europe, in spite of pledges to France. Once again, forty million Frenchmen faced sixty million Germans who had twice invaded them. Once again, German national ambition went unchecked as soon as it had, under Hitler, started to show its old evil face. The creation of weak nationalist successor states to Austria-Hungary along the Danube and in the Balkans only perpetuated the power vacuum in the heart of the continent. The collapse of the world economy after the 1929 Depression—in one year world trade fell by two-thirds—led to violent political disturbances in Europe: the rise of Nazism in Germany, Italy's plunge into colonial war in Abyssinia. As a result, the first limited attempt at international order, the League of Nations, foundered. Like somnambulists, the powers marched forward to inevitable conflict—and when it came, repeated with a mocking exactitude most of the alignments and enmities of the earlier struggle. Like cause had produced a like effect.

In the world at large, the *pax Britannica* was undermined by the growth of Asiatic nationalism. Two forces were at work. Western education created a new class of Asiatic intellectual leaders imbued with the spirit of Western nationalism. Such men used the West's own ideas of self-rule in order to weaken

Western control in India and South East Asia. At the same time, this mood of Asiatic self-assertion was encouraged by Japan's *tour de force* in transforming itself in a few decades into an industrialized modernized power on the Western model. Unhappily Japan also copied much of the West's earlier aggressiveness. It fought Russia in Manchuria in 1905, invaded China in 1937, and overran South East Asia in 1942. This turbulence hastened the withdrawal of the old Colonial powers and opened the door to Communist infiltration.

The supposed economic harmonies of the nineteenth century vanished over the same decades. Where the early exponents of inevitable economic equilibrium were at fault was in their fundamental assumption that supply and demand would naturally fall into a self-balancing harmony. The play of the free market would allot fair shares—to capital, the owners, and to labor, the workers. The assumption could only rest on some equality of bargaining power between the two sides. But the early industrial workers who flooded into the cities from the surrounding countryside had no reserves, no security, nothing, in short, but the hands they offered for work in competition with thousands of others. In these conditions, there was a tendency for wages to fall to subsistence level. The owners had the power to wait and hence the power to drive the bargain. They were backed, too, by the century-old prejudice in favor of the absolute rights of property. The first decade of industrialism laid the foundations of the slums and tenements of the new industrial cities and saw the growth of a new race of men born in urban squalor and living out a life of unrelieved labor and penury. Between 1830 and 1860, in spite of the vast growth in Britain's wealth, it is estimated that the share going to the workers remained static. At that time, the mass of the people were unable to secure the purchasing power needed to absorb all the flood of goods which the new machines were capable of producing.

These early years of British industrialism were the formative years for much of the world's later thinking about the relations between capital and labor, the plight of the workers, and the pretensions of property. Engels' *Condition of the*

Working Class in England was published in 1845 and probably did as much as any work to fix the bias of Marxism. It is significant that Marx, in his *Communist Manifesto*, gave the inability of the masses to purchase the new goods poured out by capitalism as one of the inherent contradictions of the capitalist system.

Nor was uncertain demand for consumers' goods the only difficulty. The demand for capital also failed to conform to any natural pre-established harmony. From the very origins of industrialism, the demand for capital goods—for factory construction, for plant equipment, for machinery of all sorts— tended to be irregular. The phenomenon of the trade cycle— the fluctuation of an industrial economy between extremes of boom and depression—could be attributed in part to fluctuating demand for heavy capital equipment. Relatively early in the twentieth century, the degree of capital development already achieved in industrialized countries had grown very greatly. Obvious new openings for investment were tending to decline; the capital already invested had clogged up existing channels. Economists began to speak of "the mature economy"—one in which the demands for capital were largely satisfied. It was Lord Keynes in his *General Theory of Employment, Interest and Money* who first drew attention to the consequences of this apparent state of saturation. He pointed out that the old belief of the classical economists in the natural balance of demand and supply rested on the assumption that all the money earned in the process of producing goods would actually be respent, either on consumer goods or upon new capital equipment. If a part of the money was not respent, the consequent falling off of demand would create surplus capacity on the supply side and introduce disequilibrium into the economy. But in a "mature" economy, with a high degree of existing capital development, the inducements to fresh investment might not be attractive enough to draw back into circulation all the money needed to keep the entire productive machine at work. The level of effective monetary demand might in fact become permanently lower than the sum necessary to absorb all the goods the productive capacity of the economy could make available.

This, in fact, was the situation in large parts of Europe in the stagnant thirties of this century. Even in the far wider and wealthier economy of the United States, something of the same trend could be observed. It is true that by 1939 the economy had roughly recovered the productive levels of 1929, the last year before the slump. But under the stimulus of massive wartime investment, the economy of the United States almost doubled in size between 1939 and 1944; the productive machine proved capable of sufficient immediate expansion to carry a mighty arms program and to raise civilian standards of living at the same time.

Yet these difficulties, in the main domestic and internal difficulties, probably had a less disturbing effect than the obstacles thrown up by growing economic nationalism. The old dream of universal free trade had faded, and whatever might have been the chances of natural economic harmony on a worldwide scale, it was clearly no part of the law of nature that a fixed and arbitrary number of national units, each pursuing its own interests within a series of half-closed economies, should by some extraordinary alchemy produce a harmonious result. Nor did they. Not only were individual nations caught in the contradictions—Britain with its swollen population and lost industrial supremacy, Germany with an economic apparatus built to serve a whole continent—but even the general balance of nineteenth-century world trade was undermined. The emergence of the United States as the world's most powerful economy introduced a new and unforeseen factor into international commerce. Here was a nation with large food supplies and highly competitive manufactures to sell and with little corresponding need to import goods from other nations. The natural tendency in the trade of the United States with other nations has therefore been to bring about a constant surplus of American sales over American purchases. Nor has a steady outflow of capital served to compensate for this lack of balance. Throughout the thirties, the outside world was tending to settle its unfavorable trade balance with the United

States in gold. After the war, the dollar shortage became one of the chief long-term economic problems facing the free world.

The failure of United States overseas investment to expand points to another problem. While the twentieth century has brought an incalculable increase in national self-consciousness in Asia and Africa, it has seen no automatic and self-regulating increase in the amount of wealth flowing to the newly aroused peoples. They inhabit, on the whole, the less economically attractive areas of the earth's surface. Yet undirected investment tends to go where the profits are attractive and if a land is poor it attracts no investment and is in no good position to save for itself. Developed markets, on the other hand, attract each other and to a great extent wealth can circulate among the world's well-to-do—and largely Western—nations in a closed circuit which leaves the poverty-stricken areas largely untouched. In fact, insofar as there is a natural harmony in world economics it seems to take the form of "to him who hath, shall be given"—a maxim perfectly compatible with eighteenth-century concepts of property but an uneasy maxim for a century in which Communism, anticolonialism, and Asian and African nationalism are major forces on the political scene.

II

But perhaps the most drastic and grievous change from nineteenth-century optimism to the confusions of our own day lies not in the sphere of untamed nationalism and unruly economics but in the decline of the moral and spiritual disciplines with which men might hope to bring order to a disordered universe. If one thread more than any other is woven through the stuff of Western thinking it is that man has the power and the responsibility to mold society more closely to his heart's desire. The medieval aspiration to renew all things in Christ, the Puritan belief in work and thrift as the tools of the Kingdom, the Deist and rationalist confidence in social reform and even revolution as a means of remaking society—all these philosophies are derived from the fundamental Christian roots of our society with its belief in man as a free agent, morally responsible for his neighbor and set upon earth to remold human society upon a supernatural plan. Even when, in nineteenth-century liberalism, all apparent theological overtones had vanished, the belief in man—in his freedom, responsibility, and social duty—and in the coming of a better society by his efforts still betrayed the metaphysics that had given it birth.

But in the nineteenth century, a profound change began to occur at the very basis of Western thinking. In essence, it was a return to the determinism which Christian thought had banished from the world. Determinism had, it is true, begun its reinvasion with the eighteenth-century belief in a pre-existent harmony and in the "hidden law" regulating economic life. If man ought, in his economic life, to act solely as his material interests guided him, then inevitably some of the most essential elements in human society were removed from rational and moral control and handed over to the goddess Chance or Necessity, and it was only a matter of guess and faith that she was a beneficent deity and not the "savage necessity" of classical thought. But early in the nineteenth century not only economic life but also man himself were withdrawn from the arena of freedom, rationality, and moral choice and plunged into a world of material conditioning. To Feuerbach, for instance, "Man is what he eats." The physical environment into which he is born and the physical heredity with which he enters life determine his thoughts, ideals, and aspirations quite as absolutely as they do his physical needs and desires.

While this belief in the ultimate dependence of man upon his physical organism was beginning to gain currency, it was very greatly strengthened by Darwin's demonstration that species had developed by long processes of evolution in which responses to environment and the struggle for survival had determined which types of animal would flourish and multiply. Man did not emerge created from the hand of God but was the last in an immeasurably long chain of animal development. This demonstration would not have been, perhaps, so much of a shock to medieval Christianity since the partial animality of man had been the basis of much of its ethical teaching. Even so, the amount of pseudoscience incorporated in Biblical teaching—including, for instance, an exact estimate of the date of Creation a few thousand years before Christ—led easily to an apparent shattering of Christian cosmology by the discoveries of science, a further discrediting of the spiritual view of man, and a steadily widening acceptance of human nature as merely part of a natural material order of reality.

Evolution also reinforced the earlier concept of automatic forces at work in economic life. Since the development of all animal forms, including that of man, had depended upon a successful overcoming of opposition from hostile environments or competitive species, it seemed to follow that "the survival of the fittest," as a law of life, could be safely extended to all forms of economic and social conflict. What the French called *"le struggle-for-life-isme"* acquired a considerable vogue. It was carried to the United States by the writings of Herbert Spencer and seemed to justify all the excesses of the new capitalist class rising to power in the expansion of capitalism after the Civil War. Since competition was now shown to be the law of life, and since to survive—by whatever means— proved that a man was fittest to survive, then the more ruthlessly he struggled, the fitter he must be. The philosophy not unnaturally proved extraordinarily congenial to the thrusting leaders of the new industrialism. What they did not see was that in justifying conflict, apart from all ethical considerations, as the basic law of economics, they left their flank open to anyone who might apply the same doctrine not to the ambitions and aspirations of the few but to the drives and desires of the many. If conflict was to be the order of the day, class conflict offered a much wider field for the mobilization of power and emotion.

While Darwin laid the scientific foundations for the fatality of environment, Freud developed the theme of man's ultimate dependence upon his biological drives and necessities. The new sciences of anthropology and sociology undertook to lay bare the physical pre-conditioning of social life. Conditioned without and within, man might retain the illusion of autonomy and self-determination, but it was an illusion to which science gave no warrant. Moreover, scientific proof, in the sense of laboratory experiment, came to an ever greater extent to be the only form of proof believed to give certainty. The bias in favor of naturalist and materialist explanations began to form at the back of men's minds. The sense that nothing had been explained unless it had been linked with a material and measurable cause gained the force of absolute conviction. True, it was combined in most men's minds with a continuing belief in progress. The dominant mood among liberals and socialists was that a "scientific" ordering of society would create the good life automatically. There was little suspicion that there might be no place for freedom, for responsibility, for truth, or for aspiration in a pre-determined world, and that its only rules might be those of physical survival and brute force.

Yet these ominous possibilities were not hidden from all eyes. And since, in any society, it is often the writers of poetic insight who are granted the painful gift of prophecy and suffer an extra sense with which to distinguish the vital from the trivial in the flux of time, it is not surprising that a malaise began to permeate the minds of poets and seers and to give, even to the most optimistic among them, a dark shadow, a foreboding of what was to come—a malaise of which the confident upholders of the new material civilization felt no trace.

For Dickens (whose greatest power as a writer is not perhaps his power of characterization or caricature but his forceful and grimly poetic evocation of the new industrial environment), the new society was not one of hope and promise in which reason and science would liberate mankind but an unseemly proliferation of urban squalor in which the industrial proletariat lived lives of the darkest misery, ruled by iron economic laws of ferocious inhumanity and sacrificed to the System from which a few might profit but which, for the mass, was a determinist hell. In such a society, between the aggressive economic acquisitiveness of the few and the leaden subordination of the many, the springs of hope, the sense of freedom, the vision of a better future began to fade from the more sensitive hearts. It was doubt, not confidence, that tinged Tennyson's finest poetry—"Oh yet we trust that somehow good Will be the final goal of all." And nowhere perhaps is the sense of waning hope and foreboding for the future more keenly expressed than in Matthew Arnold's great poem, "Dover Beach." For him, the passing of religious faith—which to many of his contemporaries still seemed a liberation from dead superstition—threatened to take with it all the values of human society:

> "The Sea of faith
> Was once, too, at the full, and round earth's shore
> Lay like the folds of a bright girdle furled;
> But now I only hear
> Its melancholy, long, withdrawing roar,
> Retreating to the breath
> Of the night wind down the vast edges drear
> And naked shingles of the world.

> "Ah love, let us be true
> To one another! For the world which seems
> To lie before us like a land of dreams,
> So various, so beautiful, so new,
> Hath really neither joy, nor love, nor light,
> Nor certitude, nor peace, nor help for pain;
> And we are here upon a darkling plain
> Swept with confused alarms of struggle and fight
> Where ignorant armies clash by night."

Perhaps the most startling of all prophetic visions into the darkness lying ahead is to be found in the journals of Baudelaire: "It is not," he writes, "specifically in political matters that the universal ruin or the universal progress—for the name matters little—will be manifested. That will appear in the degradation of the human heart. Need I describe how the last vestiges of statesmanship will struggle painfully in the last clutches of universal bestiality, how the Governors will be forced—in maintaining themselves and erecting a phantom of order—to resort to measures which would make our men of

oday shudder, hardened as they are?" Before this prophetic
vision of modern totalitarianism brought about, as Baudelaire
foresaw, in the name of progress, he could only cry: "The
world is about to end. Its sole reason for continuance is that
it exists. What, under Heaven, has this world henceforth to do?
. . So far will progress have atrophied in us all that is
spiritual, that no dream of the Utopians, however bloody,
sacrilegious or unnatural, will be comparable to the result. I
appeal to every man to show me what remains of Life." As
these lines were being written, the vastest, most systematic
and most visionary dream of all the Utopians was being pieced
together across the channel in London, where Karl Marx
worked laboriously at the sacred book of Communism, *Das
Kapital*.

Marx is the link between the hope of the nineteenth century
and the despair of the twentieth century. He is at once the
last of the liberals and the first of the totalitarians. It is in his
writings that determinism ceases to be a trend and becomes
a fanatical gospel of revolution.

15

Communist Panacea

WHEN one remembers that only forty years ago virtually all there was of Communism in the world was a single leader—Lenin, fretting his life away in neutral Switzerland—and a few cells working in secret inside Russia, the expansion of Communism in this century must appear as extraordinary as the worldwide conquests of Alexander and Genghis Khan or—to use a closer analogy—as revolutionary as the Moslem conquest of half the Christian world in the seventh century of our era. Indeed, the resemblance between the two movements covers far more than the speed and extent of their conquests. It can be argued that both are in some measure great Christian heresies. And like Communism, the Moslem faith in its relations with Europe has tended to follow the pattern of relentless pressure on all weak points and undefended frontiers and to advance its banners wherever there were found to be no defenders at the gate. If Russian armies of occupation are in Austria today, so, too, did the Ottoman forces twice advance to the very gates of Vienna, where they were checked only by the ability of the Habsburg dynasty to unite the peoples of Central Europe in a successful policy of "containment."

Even if the scale of Communist conquest is not unique in history, it is nonetheless the most startling phenomenon of our own day, perhaps all the more startling in view of the apparently abstruse and esoteric nature of its doctrines and its crusade. Can men really be stirred to action by the proposition of the thesis of feudalism passing inevitably by way of the antithesis capitalism into the synthesis communism? Is the law of capitalist accumulation one to stir the heart? Are armies to be set marching at the thought of the inherent contradictions in the organization of mature finance capital? Of all sacred books, *Das Kapital* must be the most unreadable— and the least read. Of all prophets, Marx seems to have been the most isolated and unlikeable. Yet today a quarter of the world's peoples are Communist. How has it come about?

Once again, the analogy of Mohammedanism is instructive. Islam derived its power to attract educated and intellectual groups from the use it made of ideas deeply congenial to the Oriental mind. Its rejection of the Greek and Christian heritage of humanism and incarnation in favor of a purely transcendent deity accorded well with the other worldly tradition of Oriental religious thought. At the same time, the Moslem appeal to the people at large lay in the social evils which it promised to redress. Mohammedanism was in part a harking back to traditional intellectual and religious ideas, in part an outburst of social protest against an unjust and unstable social order. Modern Communism has something of the same character. It has appealed to intellectual groups by offering them a systematic rearrangement of ideas long congenial to the Western mind. It has appealed to the masses as a protest against their lot.

Marx did not originate the idea that the material basis of the universe is the full and sufficient explanation of all that happens in it. Diderot and Holbach, fifty years before him, had come to the conclusion that the laws of matter, observed by the new physical sciences, could be found to cover all apparently immaterial phenomena and that the orderly universe, ticking forward according to the laws of its own mechanism, no longer required the intervention of a great Artificer to set it in motion. Marx inherited this temper but claimed to have rendered it truly scientific by introducing into it the notion of the laws of change. This principle of dynamism, again, he took over from earlier sources—from Hegel, who had applied his dialectic not to matter alone but to matter and mind as different aspects of the single Absolute. Marx, in his own view, dropped the "metaphysical nonsense" and applied the dialectic to matter alone. Yet again he was borrowing, for his dialec-

tic in concrete terms was based on the contradictions of private
property, a notion he took over largely from Christian sources
—from the early Fathers, from the Anabaptists and Cromwell's
Fifth Monarchy men.

If one subtracts these sources and looks for Marx's contradictions actually at work in history, the tidy "scientific" pattern is
quickly seen to be quite as notional as Hegel's Absolute, for no
non-Western society, whatever its physical substratum, has
demonstrated the curve of development followed by the West.
Some civilizations remained completely communal and developed a complicated structure of society in which the
dynamic of private property put in no appearance at all; this
seems to have been the rule in the New World. The "feudal"
relationship of landowner to peasant subsisted in India and
China for thousands of years without giving rise to its supposed antithesis, capitalist industry. The merchant class in
eastern lands showed no inherent inclination to burst the bonds
of agrarian society. In India, the caste system, in part racial,
in part religious in origin, created a further bar to dynamic
economic change. The instances could be multiplied without
end. They do not, it is true, subtract from the value of some
of Marx's insights. Before his time, historians had undoubtedly
underrated the influence upon historical development of the
economic substratum of society and its class and property relationships. In particular, the Marxist technique has proved
a fine instrument for uncovering the points of pretension and
hypocrisy in society where men seek to cover self-interest with
a cloak of morality or patriotism. Men's motives are in general
so mixed that the disentangling of interest and idealism has
undoubtedly led to a more true and convincing analysis of the
historical process. The error arose in the claim to have found
a total explanation of society in economic terms and to have
reduced other social phenomena—whether of art or law or religion or government—to the status of mere reflections of an
underlying economic reality.

That such a theory of society was rigidly determinist Marx
would not have denied; but determinism, too, already had a
strong hold on the mind of Europe. The Calvinists had not

ound belief in predestination a bar to purposeful activity.
And quite apart from this spirit of religious determinism, economic theory in Marx's time—from which he borrowed freely
in developing his theory of value—was also largely deterministic, the laws of supply and demand claiming as complete an
autonomy as Marx's very dialectic itself. The significant difference was that Marx's determinism worked to the advantage
of the many, Manchester determinism only for the few. Nor
was Marx alone in believing human beings to be the product
of their environment and heredity. Such ideas gained wide
popularity during the course of the nineteenth century. In
short, the Marxist diagnosis to a great extent only systematized
a number of scientific and rationalist conceptions current in
his time and brought them together in an apparent unity
which is far from being seen in either nature or society. His
attraction lay in an apparently more scientific presentation of
generally accepted facts.

Yet it is not as science that Marxism acquired the driving
force of a crusade. Communism, both in its origins and in its
claims, is visionary and religious rather than rationalist. Each
of its supposedly cold categories is warmed to life by the
power of imagination and prophecy. This supposedly most
"scientific" of diagnoses has the wild apocalyptic fervor of the
Jewish visionaries of old. It may talk of the inherent contradictions of the capitalist system, the law of increasing misery,
the labor theory of value, or the imperialist phase of advanced
finance capitalism. What it offers and promises is a new heaven
and a new earth.

The moral indignation with which Marx berates the capitalists and exploiters betrays the religious roots of his attitude
toward private property. In a strictly determinist system, what
place could there be for indignation? The capitalists were
obeying historical necessity. They could not be blamed for
fulfilling their part in an inevitable historical process. But
Marx had behind him centuries of Christian and Jewish anger
at the iniquities of those who grind down the faces of the
poor. It is the prophet, not the analyst, who speaks. So, too,
in his denunciation of the miseries of the poor and his cham-

pioning of the messianic mission of the proletariat, he draw
upon a religious tradition which sees in the poor and outcas
the specially loved and chosen of God. The notion that the
poor have a charismatic role to play in world history is un
known outside Western society. In fact, judging by thei
private correspondence, Marx and Engels had no very high
opinion of actual working men and women as opposed to the
idealized class-conscious workers of the Communist myth. But
the power with which the idea was charged was drawn not
from scientifically established fact but from Christian roots of
pity and hope. In short, Marx, who claimed the status of
science for his work and denounced all Utopian tendencies as
"sloppy sentimentality," "metaphysical fanfares," and "soulful
ravings," nevertheless drew on an immensely strong visionary
strain in European thought, a strain of sin and judgment and
retribution, a strain of compassion and outrage, a strain of
apocalyptic hope. This, not rationalism, gave driving force to
the criticism Marx directed at existing institutions. This, not
science, moved the workers to accept the new faith.

Marxism's great strength thus lies not in what it offers but
in what it attacks. So long as Western society continues to
exhibit any major flaws and weaknesses, the Marxists can
claim that their prophecies have been proved and that the
capitalist world is collapsing under the weight of its own contradictions. The weakness in their theory is exposed when they
themselves try to erect a new type of society in place of the
Western model. Then the errors in the Marxist diagnosis cease
to be incidental. They become the major structural faults in
the new foundations.

II

The Communists claim that the Soviet Union transcends all
the contradictions of Western society. In place of competitive
nationalism, it achieves the disappearance of national antagonism and the development in their place of international
brotherhood. Nationality in the harmful aggressive sense is,
they maintain, only a reflection of class antagonism and of

the manipulation of national markets in the interests of the
industrial monopolists. Equally they claim that the social
ownership of the means of production will put an end to the
sham democracy of votes without power, of class differences,
and of privileges based upon unevenly distributed private
ownership. In its place is put the real democracy of economic
security and equality. An economy based upon public ownership will distribute as much purchasing power as it creates.
It will avoid the irregularities of the trade cycle. It will never
reach "maturity" until the necessities of all are satisfied and
"to each according to his need and from each according to his
capacity" has become the rule of economic life. In a society
so ordered, state power (which at present is used exclusively
to buttress the claims of the property owners) will be needed
no longer. In a functionally perfect, frictionless society, man
will live in brotherhood and, as medical science advances, possibly forever as well.

If, as Marx believed, private property is at the root of all
evil, then these Utopian consequences should flow from its
abolition. Suppose, however, the evils and contradictions of
society spring from a far wider and more complex set of
sources—then what guarantee is there that public ownership
will have the beneficial effect? In fact, we may say that the
breakdown of the Communist dream and the failure of Soviet
society to solve the problems either of national sovereignty or
of economic democracy spring above all from Marx's failure to
recognize the depth and complexity of the sources of evil in
human society. Like the Utopian socialists, or the makers of
the French Revolution, or the encyclopedists of the eighteenth
century before him, his chief failure was his naïveté before
the fact of power.

Pitchforked into an unknown world, driven through life
blindly to the certain end of death, dependent for every
breath and every beat of the heart on forces beyond personal
control, man is, it seems, essentially insecure. To this fact of
dependence he may react with simplicity and acceptance. But
the perpetual temptation is to react with violent self-assertion
and pride—with the *hubris* of the Greeks, the *superbia* of the

Romans, with the cry of Lucifer, "I will not serve." In no way apparently, can the sense of the self be so aggrandized and reassured as in the domination of other people and in the act of imposing one's own will on the separate egos of other men. Thus, behind all differentiations of class or nation, there is, in the human psyche, an innate tendency toward domination and exploitation. Marx was not wrong to say that it exists and could be fostered in class relations. He was wrong only in not seeing it active almost everywhere else as well.

Behind all the constitutional checks imposed by medieval theory upon the governors of society lay the perception that unchecked power will be abused. Power is never exercised *in vacuo*. It is exercised by men. Expose them to the possibility of unlimited domination and they seize it; all but a minute fraction of them will deteriorate in the process as the ego grows by what it feeds on. This is the lesson of all history. This is the fundamental reason why human freedom fills so brief a span in the long development of man. Marx, however, was a child of Rousseau and of the French Revolution. He believed that there could be a general will to express the decisions of a whole society and that since the General Will would by definition conform to the interests of the majority, then freedom would consist in putting that will into effect. But how could the General Will be discovered? For Marx, the answer was simple. He knew it already. It lay in the socialization of the means of production and the creation of a classless society. The only need was for the workers to realize that such was the case. If they hesitated or proved insufficiently class-conscious, then it was the duty of the elite to carry out the General Will on their behalf, in the calm confidence that it was what they would want, had they sense enough to see it.

At no point perhaps can one see more clearly the divergence between the Marxist concept of "democracy from above" and the Western notion of political freedom than in this matter of the role of the elite. In Marxist practice, the members of the elite are grouped and disciplined in the Communist party. The Party is the General Will of the community in organized form. Since all social development can be objectively determined beforehand by the proper use of the dialectical method, the General Will can never be wrong and the Party can never be divided. It is thus the symbol of the scientific objectivity of the Soviet state. Yet the Party is in fact a group of men, and behind all the sophistries of the argument about the objective determination of policy, the blunt position in terms of power is that a very small group of men—or even one man— are in a position to do what they will with the mass of the people.

In the Western world, the party system has developed on the exactly opposite principle—that no one group of men can safely be left to govern indefinitely and absolutely in the interests of the community and that their liability to error must be checked by the possibility of exchanging them for other rulers. It is true that this principle of basing party politics upon the desirability of a perpetual alternative is not the exclusive basis of Western party government. The two great parties in the United States have probably approached most nearly to the alternation of "ins" and "outs," and this is a source of strength since it mirrors the extent to which the broad issues of society are being settled not by sudden political action but by deep changes in public opinion which find expression in both parties.

More usually, however, parties represent the pressures and interests of different groups—farmers, workers, professional classes—and government the reconciliation of these pressures. Yet under this system, too, the General Will is allowed to well up from below through the process of free discussion and exchange of convictions in the course of which the great ideas of society gain general acceptance and find their way into all political groups. In this fashion, for instance, the general concept of the contribution government can make to health and welfare has become the accepted principle of virtually all Western parties in the last twenty-five years, even though it would have seemed revolutionary fifty years before.

It is only when a single party claims to incorporate in itself the General Will and to express the total truth about society that the Western political system cannot function. The Fas-

cists and the Nazis, between the wars, were such parties and
their coming to power was a return to despotism. The Communist Party as Marx conceived it was totalitarian from the
start. His first claim for it was that every brand of socialism
save his own was false. In the hundred years that have followed, Communist parties have invariably swallowed up their
rivals—as in Russia and Eastern Europe—or sought to make
parliamentary government impossible—as in France or Italy
today. The practice is inevitable, given the Communist claim
to be alone in knowing the people's will. In a real sense, therefore, one may say that the chief feature that distinguishes
party government in the Western sense from the will of the
Party in the Communist state is that Western practice avoids
hubris. The Communist system does not.

Marx's error in relation to nationalism somewhat resembles
his failure to measure the temptations of personal power. Nationalism is to a nation what personality is to an individual.
It is an enrichment, a principle of variety, a precious endow-
ment. Equally it can be the source of exclusiveness, egomania,
hubris, and domination. Marx assumed that all the aggressive
aspects of nationalism sprang from unequal property relations
and international capitalist competition. As the experience of
Russia has shown, they are anchored not in class but in the
human community itself.

Lenin and Trotsky, internationalists by belief and experience, saw the Russian Revolution as one small facet of a
worldwide experiment. For Stalin, who had barely left Russia,
the Revolution was Russian first and could be international
insofar as such a development suited Russian interests. This
difference may not have been explicitly realized. It simply existed as the natural bias of Stalin's outlook—and of the vast
majority of his people. There had long been a violent and
emotional spirit of nationalism at work in Russia. The nation's
relative lack of development compared with the West had
aroused in some the desire to emulate Western society, in
others a violent compensatory Slav nationalism and a crusad-
ing belief in Russia's destiny to lead the world. Moscow
would be, after the Empire of the Romans and the Empire

of the Byzantines, the center of a new world Empire, a "third Rome."

Now there was nothing unnecessarily incompatible between these old dreams of nationalist glory and Russia's new position as the first territorial base of world revolution. In Humpty Dumpty's words, it would depend which was master—new revolution or old nationalism. It is nationalism that has triumphed, old-fashioned nationalism exhibiting all the traits of aggrandizement and aggression which, according to Marx, were to have faded with the passing of capitalism. Inside Russia, the domination of the Great Russians over all other nationalities has been established and all movements towards political as opposed to cultural autonomy among the minorities have been checked. In 1932, for instance, most of the Ukrainian Cabinet was shot. It seems likely that Beria was shot in 1953 for suggesting some mitigation of Great Russian control.

Outside Russia, the Communists have taken over the old imperial mantle of the czars and extended their domination further than the Russians were able to do even at the time of the partitions of Poland: now all Poland is ruled by a Russian marshal. In the postwar Communist double talk, "international" means anything that protects the national interests of the Soviet Union. "National" in the pejorative sense is a fascist, reactionary, Titoist preference on the part of any nation for its own nationalism and its own national interests as opposed to those of Russia. While inside the Soviet Union, artists and writers have been condemned for "internationalism" —in this sense, preferring Western modes and methods to Russian art and culture—leaders among the Russian satellites, such as Rajk or Slansky or Clementis, have been shot for insufficient internationalism—in other words, for preferring Hungarian or Czech nationalism. The apparent confusions are in reality quite clear. Russian nationalism is good. All other nationalisms are bad. It is as simple as that.

The clearest instance of this distinction occurred in the expulsion of Yugoslavia from the Cominform in 1948. The split had nothing to do with Communism. Marshal Tito was at the time probably the most active Communist in Eastern Europe.

Certainly socialization of industry and the collectivizing of agriculture were being developed more rapidly in Yugoslavia than in any neighboring Communist state. Why then should two fraternal Communist powers fall into a relationship of total and open hostility? Once again, the reason was excessively, naïvely simple. Tito did not want the Russians to run his affairs and direct his economy. The Russians believed it was their right, as the leaders of world revolution and as big Slav brothers, to do so. On a straight issue of irate nationalism, the two countries fell apart. With that division—which, had it not been for Russia's fear of Western military action, would doubtless have led to a Russian occupation of Yugoslavia as swift if not as painless as the Communist seizure of Czechoslovakia—the pretense that Russia had any new principle to offer in international relations was finally exploded. The new Communism was the old imperialism writ large. Nationalism merely appeared with more total pretensions by reason of its vestigial link with the idea of a world crusade.

The Russian claim to have based a new Utopia on state ownership of the means of production proves on examination to be equally dubious. The essence of the claim is that public ownership permits the fullest use of resources, frees the economy from the fluctuations of the trade cycle, puts an end to economic imperialism, and creates a new status for workers and peasants in which co-operation replaces exploitation and brotherhood takes the place of class. It is certainly true that state planning has proved capable of vastly extending the Soviet economy. Its growth may even have been faster than the comparable expansion of the American economy after the Civil War, a process which it closely resembles since both expansions took place inside continental economies, with enormous unexploited reserves of raw materials and with no pressure of population upon the land.

As an economic *tour de force*, the Russian state plan hardly compares to that of Japan, whose economic revolution occurred in a small island virtually without raw materials, desperately overcrowded and entirely dependent upon world trade. Nevertheless, the Russian experiment has proved that, given lavish resources and wide elbow room, state action can be used to force the pace of capital expansion and to build with considerable speed a formidable framework of heavy industry. It has shown, too, that a measure of central control over investment can insure steady expansion and avoid the fluctuations which have been endemic in Western economies. It has also shown that in backward communities, in which a steady economic development comparable to that of the West between the seventeenth and twentieth centuries has not taken place, Communism is one possible means of jumping the centuries and achieving parity with Western standards in the shortest space of time. Rapid expansion implies high capital investment, and in backward countries this means low standards of consumption. A planning dictatorship may be better placed to impose this "austerity" than a government responsive to public opinion.

Nevertheless, in the course of 1953, the Soviet experiment also showed that even elbow room stretching from the Elbe to the Pacific is not sufficient to insure against the opposite risk of overexpansion. Since the articulation of all Eastern Europe into the Soviet economic master plan after 1948, the whole emphasis in Soviet policy has been laid upon further heavy industrial expansion. New basic industries—coal, steel, chemicals, electricity—have been undertaken, and this capital expansion, combined with a large arms program and commitments in arms and equipment to China and Korea, has begun to place a grave strain even on the Soviet Empire's wide resources. At the same time, peasant opposition to collectivization in Eastern Europe and the endemic dissatisfaction of the peasants inside the Soviet Union have led to a dislocation in food supplies. In countries such as Rumania and Hungary—traditionally food exporters—conditions of grave shortage have arisen, and inside the Soviet Union agriculture still fails to expand in the same measure as industry.

There are signs, too, that the Soviet citizen is beginning to demand a larger share of the wealth he has created—more consumer goods in place of yet another hydroelectric station, monster steel plant, or record-breaking canal. During 1953, under these various pressures, part at least of the more ambitious plans in both Russia and its satellites had to be postponed or abandoned, steel furnaces left half built or new factories arrested at the foundation stage. New inducements were offered to the peasant to stay on the land and to produce more food—from his private plot as well as from the collective farm. Promises of more and better consumer goods became the staple of political speeches and the most influential economic planner in the Soviet sphere, Mikoyan, urged the Ministries and officials concerned with consumer goods to learn from Western methods of advertising and sales technique in an attempt to find out what the consumer really wants. The whole crisis shows that the fluctuations of the trade cycle are not the only dislocations to which an economy may be exposed. Overambitious planning can lead to so great a lack of balance between sections of the economy that the machine breaks down for lack of such essentials as enough food or a sufficient flow of raw materials. In Western terms, such a crisis would be called one of inflation or overextension; its effects are as economically disturbing and socially dangerous as the crises of deflation in past Western experience.

Mikoyan's hint on salesmanship has more than a passing interest. It suggests in fact that one of the most searching tests of the Soviet economy lies ahead. As every Western power has discovered in developing a war effort, it is possible to keep a whole economy fully at work, provided capital goods are being planned on a wide enough scale—and provided the economy commands sufficient resources. In the early stages of any economy, the building of basic industry is likely to be the chief economic task; and this stage, in which consumer choice is least important, lends itself well to mass planning, as does a war effort. (Whether a government could ever have invented the industrial system *de novo* will now be forever unprovable. Industrialism was in fact evolved by the creativeness of independent entrepreneurs in Britain and America. Every subsequent state system has only copied their pioneering venture.) The challenge to stability and sustained expansion begins to develop when the large capital needs of the economy are satisfied and the variable and unpredictable play of consumer choice begins to exercise a more decisive influence. This phase has barely begun in Russia. So far, therefore, the Soviet experiment in state planning undoubtedly proves that government control of capital expansion can prevent fluctuations in the economy. It tells us little or nothing about the compatibility of total state planning with a prosperous and varied peacetime economy based on consumer choice.

III

It is when one turns to the political and social consequences of Soviet state capitalism that the Marxist claim to have created a new type of society begins to appear most dubious. In the international field, state ownership of the means of production has proved no obstacle to imperialism, supposedly a by-product of private capitalism but possibly an inevitable consequence of power and aggressive nationalism. Two essential features of imperialism—the subordination of colonial markets to the interests of the metropolitan power and direct investment in colonial resources to insure control of materials and profits—have both reappeared in Russia's relationships with Eastern Europe. First by means of reparations (East German reparations came to an end only in 1953) and later by direct control of satellite plans through the Committee for Economic Co-operation—Comecon—the dominant role in East European trade has been taken by Russia. This in itself need imply no discrimination and could offer the satellites the prospects of growing markets in the U.S.S.R. But one of the reasons why Tito broke with Russia was that Soviet goods were overpriced and Yugoslav goods underpriced in their trade agreements. The Russians have also—like the Nazis between 1935 and 1939—bought Balkan products cheaply and re-exported them for "hard" currency. These tricks of trade have been reinforced by direct Soviet investment in Eastern Europe. Soviet companies own and manage a number of large firms in Germany. All uranium mining is a Soviet preserve. Austrian oil is Russian-owned, Rumanian oil is exploited by a

Soviet-Rumanian oil trust. Similar joint companies control river traffic on the Danube, Hungarian bauxite, and Eastern European airlines. All this amounts to a pattern of imperialism which is rendered more onerous by the fact that the Soviet living standard is still lower than that in most of Eastern Europe and the movement to siphon off wealth from the satellites is correspondingly greater.

Against the disadvantages may be set the industrial development fostered by Russia in Eastern Europe. Yet, as was shown in the crisis of 1953, this development depends upon the maintenance of adequate supplies of goods and raw materials. If Russia itself is not fully supplied, the satellites are likely to be even more sharply pinched. In short, it is as yet far from clear that the whole pattern of forced heavy investment has been sound. New Zealand or the Scandinavian lands, countries with balanced industrial and agricultural development, might have provided a happier and more prosperous model.

Soviet claims to have laid the foundations of a workers' and peasants' paradise are even more unreal; and again, if one must fix the blame on one factor more than on any other, it lies in the Marxist naïveté about power. State ownership of the means of production entails inevitably the concentration of political and economic power in the hands of the same men. These men are not abstractions. They are living human beings with all the urges and insecurities of the normal human temperament. Moreover, they will tend to be the most aggressive and practical and most obviously qualified for success and promotion. Paradoxical as it may seem, this new race of bureaucrats, party organizers, and managers, also appears to have been exposed to a competitive atmosphere in which there is neither scruple nor compassion, and which to a great extent resembles the conditions under which nineteenth-century industry was built up in the West. Within the Five Year Plan, the success of separate industries and indeed of individual factories depends upon fulfilling and overfulfilling the "norm" of output set for the particular branch. But in an economy in which the flow of raw materials tends to be erratic and is often inadequate, and in which skilled labor is still in short supply, fulfilling the norm in one factory often depends upon successful piratical raids on neighboring factories and industries or on compelling ministries to disgorge vital supplies and materials —if necessary at the expense of other sectors. In this highly competitive atmosphere—in which political as well as economic success and security depend upon achievement—the new tribe of managers seem to have acquired the vigor, self-reliance, self-help, contempt for weakness and failure, and indifference to the human factor which Marx and Engels found and condemned among the owners and managers of the Manchester School.

In Russia, however, the struggle for survival of the new managerial classes is rendered more envenomed by the concentration of economic and political power. A man's flank is open to his rival's accusation not only of economic incompetence but of political unreliability as well. Behind the risk of the unfulfilled norm lies the possibility of being accused not only of incompetence but also of sabotage. And behind sabotage lies the shadow of the secret police.

The managers, in spite of this insecurity, at least possess the fruits of office and, given the very low standards still endured by Russian laborers, the gap between highest-salaried manager and lowest-paid worker is far greater than in the United States. Moreover, the standard of living is still different in quality as well as quantity. In industrial America, many workers have the same type of material living conditions as their employer, but they have less. In Russia, the gap between manager and worker is often still the difference between Western and Oriental living standards.

Nor is the worker much compensated by what Marx thought would be an inevitable increase in status and dignity. In fact, the boss is more remote in a nationalized industry run from Moscow than in the average Western firm. Trade unions are part of the national and Party apparatus to insure productivity, to fix wages and norms according to state policy, to be alert for signs of unrest, and to uphold factory discipline. In Russia, at least, this type of unionism is now almost as old as the Revolution, although complaints in the newspapers suggest much underground resentment at injustice and political favoritism in the plants. But in Eastern Europe, Soviet-style trade unionism was imposed on workers who, especially in Germany and Czechoslovakia, had experienced trade-union autonomy of the Western type. The revolt of the East German workers in June 1953 was an entirely spontaneous outburst of despair and protest against a state-run economy which set ever higher norms and lower rewards for work and used the unions as a party police.

Nor was loss of status the only grievance. The first action in many East German towns was to march to the prisons and release political prisoners. Behind the discipline of the factory and the perpetual vigilance of Party-controlled unions lies the risk of deportation to correction camps, of disappearance to the labor colonies of the Arctic, to mines and penal settlements. The extent to which slave labor has become an integral part of the Soviet economy is hotly disputed. What cannot be disputed is that the concentration camp is a recognized part of the Soviet penal system. Thus the "new" society reverts to the patterns of slavery of archaic man.

Nor have the Soviets so far fared better in agriculture. Collectivization has been in force for nearly twenty years and the peasants, as the concessions of 1953 have shown, are as wedded as ever to the memory of private property. The ultimate Soviet aim of turning agriculture into an industrial process and the peasants into wage earners living in urbanized surroundings—"agro towns"—has not been abandoned. But the obstinate determination of the peasant to grow more and work harder on his own private plot stands—as always—in the way. Nor are Soviet doctrinaires for a moment shaken by the fact that small landowning farmers, working co-operatively in Northern Europe, have a productivity three times as high as that of Soviet agriculture. The Soviet aim is not only economic. It is political. A landowning farmer class would enjoy a potential economic independence which might endanger monolithic Communist control.

IV

After the French Revolution, thoughtful men were profoundly impressed and disturbed by its brief showing forth of total dictatorship. They came to believe that any attempt on the part of the community to concentrate all power—moral, political, and economic—in the hands of the state and to use that power to bring about an earthly Utopia could result only in unmitigated despotism and the defacement of humanity. They appealed to the older tradition of Europe—incorporated in the political systems of Britain and America—to the separation of powers, to the supremacy of law over government and governed, to the idea of a religious loyalty which transcends the state, and to a modesty in political aims which could recognize that paradise cannot be built and ordinary men deified by violent acts of state.

The first thirty years of the Soviet experiment have undoubtedly borne out these fears. Probably no state in history has violated more systematically and purposefully the rights and safeguards of individual citizens and of subordinate communities, or justified its activities with a more righteous faith in the infallibility of its policy. Men are sent to labor camps in the name of freedom, minorities are wiped out in the name of liberation, at least a million peasants are starved in the name of more efficient agriculture. Yet even those who foresaw, as did Baudelaire, the necessary connection between the establishment of a state Utopia and the use of inhuman violence against all those judged not to fit into its Procrustean bed—even they probably had little suspicion of how far the oppression and the distortion of reason would go. They were barely aware of the extent to which industrial and scientific developments were bound to strengthen the hands of despots and weaken the natural resistance of citizens. Modern transport alone makes possible such acts of state as the deportation of two-thirds of the inhabitants of the Baltic countries to the Soviet interior. Modern radio and telegraphy penetrate the remotest corners of a country, where ignorance and indifference might once have preserved people from the contagion of uniformity. Modern propaganda is inconceivable without the radio industry or without such vast business enterprises as the Soviet publishing houses which flood Russia and the Russian empire with Communist literature.

Above all, it is doubtful whether some Communist refinements either in diplomacy or in the penal system would have been conceivable without modern discoveries in the physiology of the mind. Torture has been used in previous political systems. Its aim—hideous enough in all conscience—was to produce verbal conformity by the fear of pain. It left the will intact; it only asked for a lie. Fortified by new knowledge, the Communists use a type of psychophysical torture—in which sleeplessness and endless questioning are a central technique —in order to change the will itself and to produce men who come to believe the lie laid on their lips by their executioners. The white-faced automata in the Soviet courtroom using the very language of their accusers are men from whom not only liberty but humanity itself has been subtracted. The technique is odious enough when it wrings from purged Soviet leaders the confession that they have been "in the pay of the imperialists" from the first day of the Revolution. But at least these are men of the Party reacting according to the Party's own inner laws. The sense that humanity itself is outlawed arises when Catholic cardinals confess to Communist crimes or United States airmen sign statements that they have used bacteriological warfare against Koreans and Chinese.

It is at this point that the Western mind begins to understand fully what Marxists mean when they say, as Lenin said: "We repudiate all morality derived from nonhuman and nonclass concepts. . . . We say that our morality is entirely subordinated to the interests of the class struggle of the proletariat . . . we do not believe in an eternal morality." Silone, the great Italian anti-Fascist leader, abandoned Communism on precisely this point. At a meeting of the Comintern in Moscow, an English trade-union delegate complained that his new instructions did not square with the policy he had recently been instructed to pursue. He was told to carry out the new while appearing to carry on with the old. "But," he protested, "that would be a lie." The laughter which shook the Soviet leaders at the naïveté of this reply was the force which drove Silone from the Party.

There are those, nevertheless, who believe that the present phase of total despotism in Russia is essentially ephemeral, that it represents only a temporary dictatorship of the proletariat entrusted with the task of consolidating the revolution and creating an ample, stable economy. Now that the Soviet system has made in thirty years the transition from the wooden plow to the atomic pile, they think, a freely flowing and wealthy economic system will soon make possible the relaxation of political control and genuine political democracy will evolve from the substructure of socialist ownership. The brief liberalization of penal policy under Beria after the death of Stalin has been taken as a pointer to show that the Soviet people's desire for greater freedom has, as a result of economic maturity, become an active factor in Soviet politics. True, Beria was quickly purged, presumably by those who are not interested in liberalization. But a rift had appeared in the dark and leaden sky of totalitarian control. Was it the first light of a new dawn?

The world may devoutly hope so, but when an attempt is made to envisage the direction of a genuine slackening of control, the result is not reassuring. Would Great Russian nationalism be so far relaxed as to permit the revival of national autonomy not only in Eastern Europe but in such areas as the Ukraine, in which centrifugal tendencies have regularly had to be controlled by force? Would—indeed, could—trade unions be detached from the state and Party apparatus? Would more than one party be permitted to organize the political life of the people? Could there be a departure from compulsory Marxism as the religion of state and the forced content of all education? One reaches the inevitable conclusion that it is only to the degree to which Soviet society ceases to be formally Marxist that it can achieve a measure of freedom. How tragic, then, must seem the suffering and agonies, the deportations and decimations, the slavery and privation imposed and endured in the name of the Marxist myth. Baudelaire's "dream of the Utopians . . . bloody, sacrilegious [and] unnatural," must be counted one of the most devastating of the collective aberrations of mankind.

FOUR

POLICY

Economics of Welfare

Yet the aberrations of humanity need not, any more than the errors of individual lives, entail pure loss. The warnings are there to be heeded. The lessons can be learned. The challenge is to learn them in such a way that the typical swing of the pendulum of error—from one extreme to its opposite—is avoided; and this, as the whole post-Communist history of the West makes clear, is anything but an easy operation.

The National Socialist Counter-Revolution in Germany is the extreme example of the false reaction to Communism. The root of the evil lay, in the first place, in the extent to which Nazism was a blind reaction of fear. If Hitler had not been able to exploit Communism as a threat to everything the wealthy, the professional people, or the shaken middle classes hoped to preserve—their status, their respectability, their property—he could never have used methods of violence, deceit, and total illegality to defeat the equally violent, deceitful, and unconstitutional Communist Party organization. Nazi propaganda painted Communist aims and methods in a bestial light to cover its own bestiality. Only fear could have blinded decent, conservative people to the violence that was being committed in the name of anti-Communism. And blind, irrational fear appears to have this psychological consequence: that it lays panic-stricken men and women open to precisely those terrors they fear the most. Thus Hitler was able to destroy law on the pretext of saving it, undermine free government on the ground that he was its only safeguard, bring all property under state control with the explanation that he was the champion of private enterprise, and finally open the gates of Europe to Russian Communism on the excuse that he and he alone knew how to fight it.

So much for the negative reaction. The positive basis of the Nazi Counter-Revolution was no less destructive. In order to fight Communism, Hitler drew on the arrogance, the unlimited pretensions, the unbridled assertiveness of Western nationalism. This force, which had already unleashed one appalling war in the world, in Germany had the additional bitterness of remembered defeat. In Hitler's hands, it became an instrument of paranoiac unreason. He attempted to base a world system on the alleged innate superiority of a single racial group. He carried the exclusiveness of nationalism to the pitch of scientifically murdering practically the entire community of European Jewry. He reduced the Slavs in his brief empire to the status of slaves and helots. He worked out in extreme institutional form and with the total logic of the lunatic the unlimited pretensions of Western nationalism. In other nations, some modesty, some respect for law, some lingering sense of a wider worldwide community had put a certain restraint on the arrogance of national sovereignty. In Nazism, each Western people had to see its own worst instincts with the mask down and all restraints thrown off. This was what revolutionary nationalism could look like *in extremis*. This was the monster of pure violence and pure irrationality that had been growing up in Europe for the last four hundred years and now stood revealed, a mystery of nihilism and pure destruction.

This frightful experience revealed once and for all the destructive forces concealed within the drives of national arrogance and irrational fear. As in the release of atomic power itself, their conjunction let loose more or less incalculable and unpredictable violence. Nor is there any reason to suppose that the experience, once made, could not be repeated. It is for this reason that many people in Europe, who have lived through the Nazi revolution at close quarters, observe with what some Americans think is exaggerated alarm the phenomenon known as "McCarthyism" in the United States. It is not that they deny the risks of Communism or question for one moment the dangers of the Soviet government's worldwide conspiracy. It is not that they equate the deeply rooted American democracy with the flimsy façade of the Weimar Republic. Yet they recoil from methods which recall ominously those of the Nazi dictator. The exploitation of unreasoning fear and the creation of general distrust on the one hand, the emphasis on nationalist separatism on the other, have in them the seeds at least of a type of anti-Communism which, in Europe only two decades ago, destroyed law, destroyed government, destroyed all forms of freedom, destroyed free enterprise and free trade unions, and opened the way to unlimited war. Communism must be countered; but if it is countered by the wrong methods, the results are ultimately undistinguishable from Communism itself.

Communism, in short, will not be defeated if the Western world tries to counter it by falling back on the uncontrolled vitalities of our age. Unlimited defense of absolute property or unrestrained reliance upon nationalism offer no answer to the Communist challenge—for they are, in fact, the destructive forces which helped to bring Communism into being and would, even without Communism, tear the world apart with social strife and international conflict. Nor will Communism be defeated by anything as blind and unconstructive as fear. The Western world needs above all, in the light of Communist criticism, to reconsider its own basic institutions and, in the face of the false philosophy of Communism, to re-examine its own fundamental beliefs. There are no surface solutions in this struggle. Communism is at once the cumulative effect of Western errors and the inexorable criticism of them. It can be countered only by defense in depth.

II

There is usually a time lag in people's thinking about society. Some thinker crystallizes a view of man and of his social relationships—as Marx did a century ago—and the ideas acquire an independent life of their own and continue to influence policy and break governments and create revolutions whether or not they bear any resemblance to fact. Rousseau's noble primitive man uncorrupted by government was one such pregnant myth. A large part of the mythology of our modern world can still be traced to Marx, for no writer since him has produced a view of society so charged with myth-making power. The Marxist criticism of the free world is not only the daily fare of at least a third of the human race; it also lies embedded in the instinctive thinking of millions of workers even though they are, in fact, prepared to fight strenuously to rid their unions of Communists. It is the submerged gospel of the European Left. Above all, it is the pattern of thought upon which men in all countries will tend to fall back, if crises and instabilities reappear in the West, simply because it is the most systematic and the most familiar critique available. When disturbances as shattering as the 1929 depression strike society, the forces and issues involved are too vast to be unraveled by everyday processes of thought. Men have to revert to generalizations and myths in order to think about them at all. Hence the attractiveness of Marxism, with its apparent power to put every phenomenon into its proper place in a total explanation of man, society, history, human destiny, and ultimate salvation.

In the Marxist picture of Western society, certain fundamental causes of instability receive special emphasis. They each relate to those lawless forces of absolute nationalism and absolute property which, even without a Marx to underline their destructiveness, would have shaken the Western world to its foundations. The Marxists point in the first place to economic nationalism which, they maintain, is the ultimate cause of war between the nations and the driving force behind imperialism. Their next target is private capitalism, which, in their theory, deprives the worker at home and in the colonies not only of sufficient purchasing power but of status and dignity as well. And the evils they believe to be inherent in both economic nationalism and private enterprise they trace back to the same source—the institution of private property. It is private monopolists who use national and imperial frontiers to restrict and manipulate markets. It is private owners who exploit the worker and keep from him an adequate share of the community's wealth. The abolition of private property and the introduction of state ownership are thus the solution to all the innate contradictions of the Western world.

In order to counter this Marxist critique, it is not enough to point to the failure of the theory in Russia. The challenge is the extent to which the weaknesses attacked by Marx still persist in Western society.

In one field at least, Marx's criticism has proved sufficiently wide of the mark. In his contemptuous estimate, Western political democracy was a sham and the government no more than "the managing committee of the bourgeoisie"—in other words, a direct instrument of class rule. He underestimated the transforming effect of a steady widening of the franchise in the West and the pressure of a large popular vote upon the functions of government. In place of narrow class interests there grew up the idea that the proper aim of the state was to secure the common good and the general welfare. This transformation cannot be attributed to any one group or philosophy. Disraeli, a Tory statesman, first used tax money for public sanitation and workers' dwellings. Bismarck, an ultra-conservative, was a pioneer in the field of contemporary social insurance. A Liberal, Lloyd George, introduced it into Britain on the advice of another Liberal, William Beveridge. The Fabian group among the Socialists popularized the notion of state action to promote general welfare. Neither Gladstone, who reintroduced Pitt's income tax, nor Sir William Harcourt, who proposed death duties, could be called wild revolutionaries. In fact Christian conscience, not radical Utopianism, was the mainspring of their policy. All these converging influences helped to create the climate of the "welfare state," that of a popularly elected government using money raised by taxing wealthier members of society in order to forward the purposes of the whole community.

This concept of welfare and insurance has gone far to falsify one of the most fundamental of Marx's predictions of disaster —that the workers under capitalism must grow ever poorer and thus never provide a market sufficient to absorb industrialism's growing supplies of goods. The extent of "built-in" purchasing power in a modern Western community is difficult to estimate, but it is undoubtedly great enough to falsify predictions based, say, on the depression of 1929. At that time, particularly in the United States (where, in general terms, welfare services have been a product of the post-1929 New Deal), the unemployed worker had little or no cushion of aid and insurance. When he dropped out of work, he virtually dropped out of the market. In the Atlantic world today, certainly, he no longer does so.

Yet it cannot be claimed that the new welfare policies of the West are a complete answer to Marx's criticism. There is much in the Marxist attack they do not even touch. State welfare does not of itself abate national pretensions. It has as yet been extended only very marginally to colonial or backward areas. The British government's Colonial Development and Welfare Fund is based on principles similar to those underlying the idea of domestic welfare. The wealthier community passes on, by means of taxation, some of its resources to the poorer areas. Point Four programs have the same intent. But, so far, it can hardly be said that it is settled policy to base Western relations with Africa and Asia on the welfare principle.

Even within the national community, welfare policies have their limitations. They represent a method of dividing wealth. They are not necessarily a means of expanding it. If the taxation from which welfare is derived discourages enterprise and hampers expansion and invention, it could conceivably become a policy of reducing real wealth.

Perhaps the greatest limiting factor in any policy of state welfare is that, valuable though it is, it has no decisive effect on the question of man's status in free society. The transfer of wealth by the impersonal agency of the state does not essentially lessen the sense of division between "we" and "they"; "we," the workers, the underprivileged, the people at the receiving end; and "they," the privileged, the wealthy, the classes that must be "soaked" to support us. Passive citizenship —the passivity of the man who, sometimes resentfully, pays his taxes and the passivity of the man who, often indifferently, accepts the benefits—effects no fundamental transformation of the barriers in society, no deepening of social responsibility, no growth of brotherhood. The welfare state is, socially, a great advance on the old "divine right of property holders." In a sense, it represents a return to Europe's older tradition, that property is a trust as well as a right. But it is not the full recipe against all Western forms of instability nor the final answer to the gospel of Marx.

For this reason, the Marxist idea of state ownership has until recently exercised considerable fascination on Europe's socialist parties. The left wing is still committed to it. In Asia, it is accepted doctrine. The argument runs that the potential inhibition to expansion entailed in high welfare taxes would vanish in a state-owned system since, today, it springs in the main from the dissatisfaction of private industrialists. Under common ownership, too, the worker would acquire full status. The General Will of the community would control everything. The citizen, a mystical fraction of that General Will, would control everything as well. The factory would be "my" factory, the management "my" management. Estrangement would vanish. Passivity would disappear.

Yet recent experience in Britain points away from state ownership as the community's panacea. The fact is significant for there has been time in Britain for a limited experiment in nationalization and also for some second thoughts upon the experience. The result of this process is that a section of the Labour Party and most of the major trade unions have come to regard nationalization as a secondary issue. It is virtually omitted from the new Party program. The reasons for this change of position are complex but they all have this in common—that the practical results of nationalizing an industry bear almost no relation to the "myth" from which the policy of nationalization was first derived.

The worker's status in a large public corporation is identical with his position in a large private corporation. The tendency is for him to feel, perhaps, rather more remote from management and from the levers of power. The experience of nationalization has, moreover, entailed the learning of some practical lessons on the nature and function of profits. The idea dies hard among the workers that profits are the fruits of exploitation. They still carry with them the aura of illicit earnings, dubious speculation, and class greed. Yet it has become obvious that a public corporation, where presumably all these turpitudes are absent, must aim at making a profit. In fact, it has to make precisely the same kind of calculations as does a private firm. The margin over and above costs of production—which in Marx's simplified economics is the surplus sweated from the workers—has in fact to cover managerial salaries, expansion, replacement and obsolescence costs, risks of competition from new inventions and substitutes, and also simple uncertainty—the hazards of major disturbances in the economy.

Nationalization does not even affect the question of the payment of interest on borrowed capital. To the worker, dividends seem essentially a part of the profits which are being drained out of the enterprise to provide incomes for idle rentiers. In fact, such payments are in large measure part of the costs of production. They are the means of coaxing savings into an enterprise and of insuring that they do not go elsewhere. Businesses which provide services needed by the community can earn the profits which in turn permit them to attract more capital. Businesses which are not satisfying demand, cannot. Obviously, the process can be disturbed by speculation or by monopoly. Yet the division of the community's savings between various competing economic purposes remains an essential decision in any economy, collective or private, and profit making is a means of determining the optimum division of capital, particularly in an advanced economy with a very wide range of consumer choice.

But perhaps the factor which, more than any other, has introduced new directions into socialist thinking in Britain has been the realization of the scale and size of operations that are involved in a wholly public economy. This has brought with it the fear lest the dwarfing of man apparent everywhere in modern mass environment may not be aggravated to an intolerable degree by the transfer of ever more power to the state. The public corporations themselves will tend to be monsters in which the industrial worker is lost. They in turn will be instruments of a state in which all economic and political power is concentrated. The fate of workers and farmers and professional people in Czechoslovakia since 1948 offers daily evidence of the agony imposed on an advanced Western society by the new Communist Leviathan.

Democratic socialism does not, it is true, envisage dictatorial government, but there is a limit to the extent of control and vigilance which any parliament can exercise. The British Parliament is already so overburdened that a large amount of legislation is drafted by the civil service, passed by an enabling act, and imposed on the citizen without even the most cursory Parliamentary examination. If Parliament were made ultimately responsible for every enterprise in the country, its powers of effective control would become correspondingly negligible. Government would be conducted by a bureaucracy—benevolent, one might hope, but exposed to all the temptations of absolute power. In a mixed economy, on the other hand, the pretensions of management are checked by the unions, by other competitors, by public opinion, by political pressure and parliamentary authority. The principle of the division of power is still effective. It is such considerations as these—in short, a concern for freedom—which, more than any other factor, have produced new thinking in the European Left.

This attitude does not entail any abandonment of the belief that the state has a positive role to play in the economy. No agency save the government has the range of authority, of information, and of general oversight necessary to insure policies of high and stable employment and steady expansion in the economy at large. The only limitation on the state's responsibility in this essential task of regulating the economy's general climate lies in the fact that, in virtually every country today, the factors making for equilibrium or instability are international and national governments have neither the scope nor the resources needed for dealing with them.

17

Worker or Partner?

EVEN if public ownership of the means of production does not provide an automatic solution of the instabilities and contradictions of industrial society, this is not to say that the problems themselves no longer exist. Class divisions remain a fact. The gulf between the mass of the workers owning little or no property and the much smaller managerial, professional, and property-owning groups has not been bridged, even if in America, Britain, and Scandinavia it is no longer the source of bitterness which it is still, say, in France, where the actual share of national wealth going to the workers is lower than before the Second World War. These contradictions are the fault lines in Western society at which the Communists work away, trying to gouge them wider and slip in the explosive charge. Then, when a major crisis of economic instability shakes the community, the fault lines widen of themselves. The worker who is unemployed feels in a bitter and intensified form the inferiority of his status. Before, the community ordered him about. Now it has not even any use for him. The colonial plantation worker finds his income quartered, yet the base of his security in the old tribal society has been shattered beyond repair. Bewildered and angry, both are ready to listen to the first agitator who will show them that their condition is the result of the System and can be remedied when the system is totally overthrown. Thus it is not enough to say that public ownership is no solution, for the continuance of the present system is no solution either. The problem is to seek a prosperous, stable, and human order by means which do not risk its humanity in the process. There are at least signs that in the last ten or fifteen years some new processes of thought have been at work in this field.

The first characteristic of the new approach is that it is tentative and experimental. Yet it is perhaps this absence of total solutions and total claims that is its most encouraging feature. Marx, who never managed or administered anything in all his life, infested Western thinking for a century with sweeping generalizations and massive myths: men could hardly be thought of as individual human beings living local, concrete lives, for their whole existence was translated into terms of classes and trends and iron laws and historical necessities—all intoxicating to the poet, the philosopher, and the intellectual, but not necessarily close to the reality of industrial life. Nor were Marx's opponents immune from the temptation to make myths. The notions of complete and unfettered free enterprise, or of absolute private property, make up in their way a set of generalizations equally broad and equally remote from the daily problems of production and management.

The second point is the extent to which the new trends have developed most widely and successfully in the United States. Nothing illustrates more starkly the force of myths than the way in which men of the Left in Europe have ignored the transformation that has come about in American industrial society. Wedded as they are to their belief that the United States is an advanced case of monopoly capitalism, they have, it seems, taken few opportunities to study, scientifically and objectively, the concrete facts of the American economic system. The transformation of labor-management relations, the growth of bonus, productivity, and profit-sharing schemes, the experiments in industrial self-government and even private collective ownership—all these are virtually unknown outside America. Yet added together, they amount to something very close to a revolution.

The starting point of recent thinking in the United States tends to be the actual place of men's work—the factory, the enterprise—and the solutions it strives for are grounded not so much in general laws or philosophical principles as in the concrete daily experience of factory life. It is, after all, in this actual environment that men experience their problems, their difficulties, and their frustrations. Moreover, the enterprise, the business corporation, is the primal unit of the industrial order, the master institution whose needs and rhythms tend more and more to determine the life of the community. The essence of the business enterprise is that it is a co-operative venture, each group, whatever its functions, depending upon the work of others. Workers are powerless without managers, managers are handicapped without technical experts and research staff, the enterprise may need external sources of capital and hence shareholders. Yet these various groups are also to some extent in conflict over the division of the income earned by the enterprise. It has one first economic duty—to pay its way; if it does not, everyone suffers. But this overriding aim can be achieved under very various conditions of internal distribution of income and there is tension among the various groups to increase their share of the enterprise's earnings. The essence of modern thinking is the effort to discover and stress the elements not of conflict but those of co-operation in the enterprise. One step is to dispel ignorance and to attempt to set before the workers' leaders the facts of the profit-and-loss account. Joint committees of labor and management are established to keep open communication between the various partners in the industrial process and to insure that the prospects, possibilities, and difficulties of the enterprise are fairly grasped. This step, however, does little to associate the worker directly with his firm's successful functioning. Many businesses go further and seek ways and means of associating the employees with the earning of profits. Workers are encouraged to become owners of shares themselves, either by the issuing of employee shares below the market price or by the distribution of bonus shares. In some enterprises, a proportion of the shares are placed permanently in a trust fund and the income from the shares is spent in the interests of the workers in the enterprise by a committee elected from among the workers themselves. Other firms have taken the working force into partnership, allotting, for example, fifty-one per cent of the shares to the employees. The patterns vary, but the aim is the same—to give the worker a stake in the enterprise over and above his wages which enter into basic costs of production, and in this way to relate the worker directly and imaginatively to the success of the business.

The granting of a share in profits from a possibly remote management to workers who are expected to be grateful does not, however, meet the workers' concern with status. It may smack too much of paternalism, of a labor policy which reconciles the worker to his chains by making them golden. The desire for status is unavoidable and unquenchable in Western society, in which the leaven of equality has been so long at work. It is not enough to meet it in society at large by greater opportunities for education, wider avenues of professional recruitment, and a taxation policy which works against the accumulation and inheritance of extremes of wealth. All these policies help to set the tone of society, but, if they do not penetrate into the factory itself, they will only make more obvious the contrast between the democratic assumptions of society in general and the dictatorial structure of industry.

In Germany, the trade unions are eager to assert status, equality, and responsibility by appointing trade-union representatives to the managing boards of major industries—the so-called *Mitbestimmungsrecht*. In Britain, trade unionists are appointed as a matter of course to the boards of public corporations. But this solution presents real difficulties. It must be repeated that the first task of management is to insure that the enterprise is prosperous. If the business cannot pay its way, there is an end to all efforts to improve its structure or ameliorate working conditions. Making an enterprise pay is a highly technical and complicated process and if workers are to be associated with management the step can be justified only if they bring the right kind of competence to the task. Above all, they cannot act purely as workers' representatives. The bargain to be struck with the workers is part of the picture management has to bear in mind, but it is not the primary question. That question remains the profitability of the concern as a whole. In a word, management has a task which is determined not simply by conditions inside the factory but also by hard objective facts such as the state of the market, the availability of raw materials, and the competition for skilled labor. To assess them is a highly skilled technical performance which can no more be determined "democratically" than the stresses of a bridge can be decided by a majority vote.

Is there then no place for responsibility and status among the workers of the enterprise? If a factory were no more than a place where goods are manufactured at competitive prices, such might be the case. But it is also a human society of work, a place where numbers of men and women spend a large part of their working life, where their happiness or unhappiness is made and where the actual quality of their life is largely determined. Inevitably, much that goes on in the factory is only indirectly concerned with purely economic processes, and the more the functions which do not require an exclusively managerial decision are delegated to the working body and to its elected representatives, the more the factory in free society can come to adopt the pattern of responsibility prevailing in the community outside.

A number of firms in the United States have experimented in setting up factory committees, elected by the workers, which have exclusive responsibility in such fields as sport, amenities, and the canteen, and almost exclusive responsibility for health and safety in the factory. Where the firm itself is running its own pension, security, or bonus plans, or has set up a fund for profit sharing, these, too, should very largely be determined by the factory committee, management intervening only to set the scale of the firm's contribution or to check abuses. A further wide variety of issues which concern both labor and management—such as apprenticeship, training plans, the hiring and firing of labor, absenteeism, and all forms of factory discipline—are usually agreed between management and the unions. Such issues could be transferred to the factory's organ of self-government. Above all, the factory committee would be the channel through which the basic economic factors governing the industry and the firm could be communicated to the working staff and through which, in return, the work force as a whole could be enlisted intelligently in the problems of productivity.

Some critics may argue that the development of responsible self-government in industry must weaken the powers of the unions and therefore will never be acceptable to the mass of the workers as an alternative to the old—though discredited—ideal of nationalization. But in fact, the position of trade unions would be far more uncertain in a wholly nationalized industrial system than in an economy still based upon separate autonomous units under a variety of management. In Russia and Eastern Europe, the unions are mere branches of management: the trade-union movement is one large company union linked to the single management of the state. The establishment of factory self-government, on the contrary, would need to be rooted in a strong trade-union movement.

II

To give the worker both stake and status in his own enterprise would go part of the way toward closing the rifts in our modern industrial order. But there is some irrationality to be abated on the side of management. It is the essence of Western thinking about power that it should never be dissociated from responsibility. In the particular case of property, the deepest tradition in the West has been that the justification of private property lies in the fact that the man who personally owns property is most likely to administer it responsibly. Ownership implies control and control, to be efficient, must be personal. The teaching of the Schoolmen starts from this premise—that property held in common is likely to be maladministered and thus that in the interest of society property may be privately held. Later, both John Locke and Adam Smith saw the justification of private property in the fact that a man had used his own labor to work his possessions up from the state of nature. These doctrines were perverted into the doctrine of absolute property rights, divorced either from responsibility or from personal effort, and they in their turn have given rise to the opposite perversion, that private property is itself illegitimate—a doctrine which works out in practice to the by no means self-evident proposition that no one but a state official can be entrusted with the administration of property. Yet this second perversion seems likely to prevail—and has prevailed over a third of the human race—unless Western thinking about property can be restored to a rational foundation in responsibility and effort.

The typical institution of modern industrialism—the business corporation—is owned nominally by its shareholders. It is widely recognized that this ownership is, for the mass of shareholders, largely a myth. They have not the faintest notion of how the business is conducted nor any interest in finding out, provided it continues to pay its dividends. They have abdicated the control which traditionally goes with ownership to the managerial group which may or may not be shareholders. Since control should rest on effort and responsibility, their abdication is natural and inevitable. But the system is left saddled with the myth of ownership. And it is a harmful myth for it leaves the mass of the workers obscurely aware that they are working for an anonymous crowd of investors who, in the workers' view, do nothing for the enterprise except pocket the profits. (When the invested money is inherited, the workers are not far from the mark.)

The simplest and most direct method of ending this universal state of absentee landlordism could lie in formally completing the divorce which already exists between management and ownership. The ownership of shares should no longer confer rights of control. Ownership in the strict sense of implying complete responsibility and authority could be limited to trustee shares which would be permanently vested in the board of directors. "Shares" would still be bought and sold and earn dividends, for a business needs to continue to compete for capital in the capital market, but they would earn no more than their owners want them to earn and that is an economic reward. In a sense, business corporations based upon trustee shares would then resemble corporations under public law—hospitals, universities—and would come to enjoy the same unquestioned acceptance. The proposal is not revolutionary. Some large enterprises—the Tata group in India for instance, the large Burroughs-Wellcome pharmaceutical concern—are

lready "owned" altogether or in part by trusts in which the
tock is vested. Nor need the new pattern cover firms below
certain working force or family firms of the first generation.

The ultimate test of management lies, however, in the mar-
et itself. Since 1945 there have been signs of a renewed reali-
ation in Britain and Europe that one reason for the flexibility,
nventiveness, and power of the United States economy has
een its higher degree of competitiveness. The cartel in Ger-
nany, the price ring in Britain, the multitude of closed cor-
orations in France, have all helped in creating an arthritic
ondition in the European body economic which, in France at
east, has sometimes a look of *rigor mortis*. For this reason such
noves as the pooling of the coal and steel industry in Western
Europe and the consequent removal of internal protection are
mong the most hopeful developments in building a new,
vealthier, and more efficient economy on the east of the
Atlantic.

If these reforms and modifications of business structure are
rought together, they can be seen to add up to a philosophy
f work and society in keeping with the deepest traditions and
nsights of the West. By leaving all but the major acts of economic policy in the hands of separate corporations, the com-
nunity preserves in its economic life that decentralization of
lecision and division of power which are the essence of free-
lom. At the same time, the new concept of the corporation
goes some way toward reviving the notion of property as a
ocial trust. The creation of organs of self-government in the
actory makes it possible for the worker to carry over into in-
lustrial life the self-reliance and responsibility which he is sup-
osed to demonstrate as a free citizen in his community.
Co-operation on a basis of partnership between labor and management within the factory gives institutional force to the un-
lerlying economic fact that modern industry is essentially a
ocial and collective operation. And the extension of profit
haring under any of its various forms is a method by which
he corporation itself can help to strengthen the mass market
nd to lessen the disparities of wealth and opportunity. Taxa-
ion and wider openings for education will no doubt remain

the chief instruments of equality, but better status in the factory and a direct sense of sharing in its profits are powerful contributions industry can make to the Western ideal of an open society.

There is little point in discussing whether such an approach to the problems of property and of industrial life is based on conservative or progressive principles. To preserve freedom in the twentieth century is in one sense conservative, for certainly we have enjoyed it in the past and under modern totalitarianism would enjoy it no longer. On the other hand, many of the steps needed to preserve freedom—such as the modification of national sovereignty or the abandonment of absolute property rights—appear to be revolutionary for they work against the tendencies of the last four hundred years.

Yet in this matter of property, the reformers can at least plead that their principles are rooted in some of the oldest trends in European thought. It is in Christian teaching that the social duties of property have been most constantly underlined. The organization of medieval economic life tended toward the co-operative form of guild and corporation. After the interregnum of absolute individualism and absolute property rights, the industrial process itself has reimposed a co-operative form on modern business. There is at least a chance that industrial society, instead of evolving towards more and more massive institutions until finally the state absorbs all, may be stabilized in a co-operative, decentralized system, divided in power, co-operative in spirit, and allowing free play for the energies of man. The obstacles in the way spring from labor's continuing resentment at its status and from the unexploded myth of absolute property. These are the poisons which are still at work, producing the rash of discontent or the total infection of Communism. Purge them, and the West has the means of building an industrial order which is both social and free.

18

Beyond the Nation State

STATUS and partnership are not all that men and women ask from the economic system in which they work. Security and stability concern them no less. In fact, in modern society, fear of unemployment remains the darkest of the shadows thrown by the past. In an industrial order, a man out of work is almost a man out of life. His kind of work requires the co-operation of hundreds of other workers and of the great machines. When they stop turning, his capacity to work stops with them. Waiting for re-employment, he must become, after a certain time, resentful and neurotic. The day of the agitator opens with the alienation of the masses from free society. Nor is the collapse of confidence confined to the workers. In the thirties, many men of education and background on both sides of the Atlantic turned to Communism in sick disgust at the waste and misery they saw around them. This mood, rather than positive loyalty to Moscow, accounts for the Leftward trend of younger intellectuals before the war. It was the selfishness and heartlessness in their own society that repelled them. By the same token, they ceased to support Communism once they became aware of the even stonier and infinitely more systematic heartlessness of the Soviet system.

Economic stability is thus at the core of any policy for strengthening the foundations of free society. But, at once, the obstinate fact has to be faced that in our modern interdependent world any policies for full employment or for expanding the economy can be effective only if they are based upon international co-operation and agreement. In other words, exclusive economic nationalism is now, if anything, a greater obsta-

cle to economic stability than faulty attitudes toward property
and responsibility within the domestic community. The Marxist challenge covers more than the status of the worker and
the expanding of his purchasing power. In condemning unrestrained economic nationalism and its extension into imperialism, Marxism attacks forces, attitudes, and institutions which
are still built into the very foundations of the Western world.

For nearly a century, belief in the absolute nature of property has been undergoing modification. The significant fact in
relation to nationalism, on the contrary, is that it has succeeded
so far in overcoming every movement to lessen its exclusive
claims. It has done so even when those movements had behind
them the explosive energy of revolution. The United States began not as a nationalist undertaking but as a new political experiment. Some of its founders—Jefferson, for instance—believed that its principles of federation and free government
would ultimately spread to all mankind. Every race contributed to the further growth of the experiment. Yet "American-
ism" as an exclusive sense of national separateness has played
a considerable part in United States politics and is still a lively
force. The French Revolution began as a new dawn for humanity and ended in Napoleon's version of French imperialism. In our own day, Great Russian nationalism has muffled
the international aspirations of Communism. China, the lat-
est revolutionary, marked its victory by invading Tibet and
threatening the independence of South East Asia, both areas
of former Chinese imperial ambition. A force which can thus
master all the supposedly supernational movements of the age
reveals itself as the first energy, the deepest vitality, the most
instinctive conviction of the modern world.

Are we, then, to suppose that no counter-action is possible
against the all-conquering force of modern nationalism? There
is, at least, the language of fact. No rational man can deny
the basic physical changes which have occurred in our universe in the last hundred years. It now takes less time to girdle
the earth than it took during the eighteenth century to travel
from Boston to Philadelphia or from Edinburgh to London.
Even if still only a small fraction of mankind uses the new

means of transport, the physical interconnectedness of those who stay at home is equally a fact. The Malayan peasant's decision whether or not to hand food through the stockade to a Communist guerrilla may be determined by the opening or closing of an artificial-rubber factory in the United States. The chocolate eaters in London and New York help to fix the income of cocoa farmers in the Ashanti. A United States tariff controls the livelihood of Swiss watchmakers, a shot fired in Korea raises the price of the Australian wool clip. However violent the effort made at various times—for instance in the thirties—to insulate national economies from the forces of change or development or collapse at work in world trade, the web of commerce has grown so strongly that today the nations appear to have only two choices: either to make the intricate system function or else to strangle in its tangled skein.

But it is above all in the sphere of warfare that the implications of our interconnectedness are most inescapable. The hydrogen bomb has reached a stage of destructiveness at which one bomb is sufficient to wipe out the largest city. Yet no part of the world is out of the range of a potential aggressor. No continent is removed by more than a few minutes' firing time from the site of one or another projector of guided missiles. Such is the vulnerable and crowded world in which we live. There is a possible analogy to our condition in an earlier phase of Western history: in the hill town of San Gimignano in Tuscany, the visitor today may smile at the fantasy of its myriad high towers, each attached to a family mansion and each used, it appears, as one more base for attack upon the rival across the street whenever political rivalries and vendettas split the little town into an anarchy of warring factions. But our world today is not much wider than the city boundaries of San Gimignano. We, too, are building the equivalent of towers to our own houses from which to hurl atomic weapons at rivals across the frontiers which are little wider in time than a village street. We cannot escape from this foreshortening of our world, for every month, our test pilots with all the resources of science behind them are achieving fresh velocities beyond the speed of sound and the designers of armament are plotting the

parabolas along which rockets with atomic war heads may one
day pass at the speed of light. This is our world, as confined
and vulnerable as an Italian hill city, its sovereignties almost
as laughable as the old family feuds, its killings as fratricidal,
its warfare as likely to destroy in one holocaust family and
neighbor and town.

Few people deny these facts. On the contrary, they have
passed into the realm of truisms before they have had time to
impress themselves on peoples' minds and hearts as being actually true. "We need some form of world government" is a
statement which receives the same kind of assent as, say, "honesty is the best policy." People do not dispute it but they feel
that, as a principle, it is unlikely to stand up to the pressure
of interest and ambition which are the stuff of real life. Similarly, the ideal of world government cannot offset what is still
the accepted habitual mode of international relations, in other
words, unchecked and unregulated national sovereignty. This
peculiar dichotomy is obvious in the two efforts made so far
in international society to set up an organized framework of
world government. First the League of Nations and now the
United Nations have been based upon the recognition that the
world society of nation states needs some common institutions
and some legal restraints to convert it from perpetual anarchy
into something more resembling an orderly human community. At the same time, the first principle of anarchy, the unchecked sovereignty of the nation state, is enshrined at the
center of the Charter, in the absolute veto of the great powers.
This veto was not the work of the Communists—although, being in a minority, they have used it most frequently since 1945.
It was solemnly written into the Charter on the insistence of
all the great powers, who thus betrayed their inability to conceive of a system in which final authority could be anywhere
but in a nation state. In the same way, the families of San
Gimignano, although they elected a mayor and a council and
made a show of hiring municipal officers to keep the peace,
could not, when it came to their deepest interest, see further
than building towers and pouring lead on their neighbors. In

he shrunken world of atomic power, our own aberrations may
e more tragic but are they any less absurd?

Yet even if the physical and scientific realities of our world
demand some form of effective international government, it is
qually a political reality that the subjection of a quarter of
he globe to Communist dictatorship makes a single function-
ng world authority inconceivable for the time being. The dif-
iculty does not simply lie in the doctrinal division. Any world
ociety would include an immense diversity of philosophies
nd economic principles and even varying degrees of freedom.
The United States is perhaps the best analogy we have for a
lural international society: the differences in outlook and
tructure between, say, the states of Mississippi and Massa-
husetts do not preclude their partnership in a common union.
The union, too, by expressing the general direction of Ameri-
an society toward freedom and opportunity, influences slowly
ut steadily the outlook and practice of its member states. A
vorld society would doubtless include a very wide diversity of
olitical and social forms, but its general aim and pressure
vould be toward freedom and the rule of law. So long, how-
ver, as Soviet society is based upon the opposite principle—
nd indeed upon the extension of the opposite principle—world
rder of an organic type remains out of reach. The fact which
nore than any other precipitated the American Civil War was
he belief that slavery, far from growing obsolete within the
riginal slave states, was beginning aggressively to claim the
ight to spread to the rest of the Union. The great obstacle to
ny form of functioning international order today is that there
s no fixed frontier between slave and free and no apparent
nd to the pretensions of the Communist slave states to spread
heir "peculiar institution" to the rest of the world.

The specter of "permanent revolution" still haunts the international stage. The Soviet strategists have not yet abandoned
he apocalyptic approach of Marx—that their doctrine must
either conquer or destroy the world. Wherever dams and obstacles to their advance are established, the pressure is maintained, the flood sweeps on, seeking out the weak sections of
the dyke, the rotting wood, the crumbling soil. And wherever

such a point of weakness is exposed, there the Communists will be found at work. Newly fledged trade unionists in Africa, landless Chinese in Malaya, unemployed intellectuals in India, British electrical workers disgruntled over wage rates, Italian sharecroppers looking for land—the raw material the Communists seek to manipulate is ubiquitous and the Communist activities have one invariable aim, that of making all save the Communist form of society intolerable.

Nor is it simply a question of undermining the West's weak points. Where the use of direct force promises relatively painless results, force is used. This calculation—a false one as it proved—launched the attack on South Korea. The Chinese Communists, on this principle, have reinforced the Vietminh forces in the Indo-Chinese war. Nor is the threat confined to Indo-China. The Communists apparently intend to use Indo-China as a base for the disintegration of Burma and Siam and the creation of a greater Thai state under Communist control. The impression is that of an endless chain reaction of calculated violence in which each frontier gained provides the stepping stone for the attack upon the next. In these circumstances, there is no foundation stable enough to make possible the building of any structure of world government.

The Western policy which has come to be known as "containment" is simply the Western reaction to this orthodox Communist strategy. Its aim is to insure that at no time will the non-Communist powers appear weak enough or divided enough to invite Soviet miscalculations and adventures. It is not aggressive. On the contrary, its chief aim is to check opportunist aggressiveness on the other side. Soviet policy has, on more than one occasion, shown a tendency to what Stalin once called "dizziness from success." Containment is a sober policy designed to prevent such dizziness. Above all, it is an essential step in establishing some sort of reliable frontier which can be taken as a starting point in international relations on a worldwide scale. A frontier may not be the ideal in our narrow atomic universe, but it is infinitely better than the perpetual insecurity of no frontiers at all.

The difficulty inherent in practicing containment is not that is a policy of the minimum, a sort of *faute de mieux* for genuine world order. For the democracies of the West, it is very nearly a maximum, straining their resources of imagination and statesmanship to the utmost and showing almost no sign of becoming a settled principle in their dealings with the Communists. In theory, it is the obvious course of wisdom to remain strong and to remain united. In practice, all the instinctive pressures work the other way. Free nations, whose governments depend upon the verdict of an electorate, have a natural tendency toward appeasement. The man in the street dislikes arms, he objects to conscription, somewhere in his subconscious he still believes that armaments cause wars and that an "armament race" ends in disaster. If other powers build up great armies and threaten aggression, he tends to place a touching faith in conciliation and negotiation. In the thirties, the men of the Right appeased Hitler. In the fifties, the men of the Left appease Moscow. But the mood is the same, an essential Micawberism, a hope that something will turn up, that tension will slacken of itself, that expenditures on arms can be diverted to social services or to world development or to private spending, to anything rather than the first foundation of national life, which is security.

The pursuit of unity is no less hazardous. It is an undeniable fact of Western history that alliances based purely upon defense and aimed only against some form of external pressure have no inner cohesion, no élan, no powers of development, no ultimate tendency towards a "more perfect union." They are normally at their maximum efficiency on the day that they are signed. Thereafter, like the innumerable solemn leagues, holy alliances, and eternal covenants in Europe's checkered past, they fall apart on the reefs of unsolved national interest and mutual distrust.

The North Atlantic alliance, the central institution in the West's policy of containment, is, like every previous alliance, at the mercy of these two forces—democracy's tendency to reject the cost of military preparedness and the natural centrifugal tendencies present among separate national and sovereign states. By an unlucky chance, there is some evidence to suggest that the two tendencies are reinforcing each other and thus hastening the processes of disintegration. The desire to keep defense expenditure to a minimum and to spare the greatest possible number of young citizens from the burden of carrying arms has led to at least two decisions among the Atlantic part ners that have later been shown to have incalculable political effects. Neither Britain nor the United States has been anxious to increase the size of its armies. The discrepancy between the number of divisions the two powers and their allies could put into the field and the huge armies maintained by the Communist dictatorships can be partly bridged by technical superiority and by the fact that the aggressor needs bigger battalions than the defender. But a gap remains and the proposal to fill it with German soldiers, made only four years after the defeat of the Nazis, has proved to be almost too much for the frightened French. It has also provided the excuse for the anti American policies pursued by the Bevanite wing of the Labour Party in Britain.

The second decision may well prove to have had even more disturbing political consequences. Again, both Britain and the United States have decided to reduce expenditure on arms. In America, in order to insure that this cut did not entail any lessening of security, the policy has been described as one that concentrates on atomic weapons through which greater destructive power can be achieved at less cost. It is easy for Communist propaganda to paint this as a decision on the part of the United States to withdraw its land forces from Europe and the Far East and to defend its allies—if defense becomes necessary—by "liberating" them after an atomic holocaust. The propagandist's task has been made easier by the United States hydrogen bomb tests conducted early in 1954 and by the confusion of mind created by the official announcement that America's answer to aggression would be "massive atomic retaliation at a place and time of its own choosing." Here, according to the Communists, was the United States pledging itself to make every war a hydrogen war and to launch the ultimate destruction of human society.

Neutralism—the desire to keep out of the struggle at all costs

—is an inevitable by-product of war. But it is an almost irresistible reaction to atomic war. The very theory of collective security itself, upon which the North Atlantic alliance and the Anzus Pact in the Pacific are based, appears to break down when atomic war is in question. Only two or three powers possess atomic bombs. The addition to either side of other nations lacking the decisive weapons does not seem to be likely to make much difference. Above all, the destructiveness of the weapons is such that neither side can win any victory save that of universal ruin. Why join in such senseless slaughter? Why take sides at all? The hydrogen bomb has created arguments for neutralism so new and powerful that they strike at the very heart of the Atlantic alliance—or indeed at any other enterprise of Western collective defense in Asia, in the Pacific, or in the Middle East.

There can be little doubt that the essential enterprise of containment, of maintaining unity and strength in the face of worldwide Communist pressure, will slacken and fall apart unless the Western powers are ready to devote new thought and new energies to the maintenance of their alliance. The first need is to reconsider defense policy in the light of the conditions created by weapons of almost total destruction. The possession by both sides of the hydrogen bomb may well prove a strong deterrent to general war. The Russians would not risk an all-out struggle over the Berlin airlift. Nor would the Western allies take the risk over Korea. Yet limited wars are possible, are happening, and appear to be the Communists' chief means of fretting away the frontiers of the free world. Paradoxically, therefore, the more the Atlantic alliance relies upon atomic weapons, the less it may be able to cope with the kind of wars that are likely to be fought.

In such wars, armed manpower and "conventional" weapons are decisive. This fact suggests that the Atlantic powers, while maintaining their apparatus of hydrogen bombs as a deterrent to universal war, have primarily to deal with the challenge of the Russian and Chinese mass armies and with the Communists' readiness to use these reserves in frontier wars which, beginning as civil wars, become wars of limited intervention. It may well be that this challenge can be met, in the short run, only by maintaining more men under arms in the West, highly armed and highly mobile, to insure that such Communist ventures as the Korean aggression or the possible Vietminh attempt to disintegrate Burma and Siam are stopped short at the first hint of trouble.

Western forces of this type would bear some resemblance to an embryo world police force. They would need, as an international force, to be recruited with some regard to differences in population. A proportional contribution would put an end to the present situation in which France, a nation of some forty millions, is supposed to maintain the bulk of the land armies in an alliance which includes one hundred and sixty million Americans and fifty million British—with a backing of another thirty million in the English-speaking Commonwealth nations. In short, the maintenance of the Atlantic alliance seems to demand a greater military commitment from Britain and the United States, whatever their deeply rooted prejudices against large military establishments. It is no part of the law of nature that either country should be secure with precisely that degree of mobilization that it finds acceptable and comfortable. It is a disturbing thought that Rome finally fell because citizens would not man the frontier and the legions had to be recruited from barbarians instead.

But in the longer run, there is only one method of dealing effectively with the mass armies of the totalitarians and that is to press, argue, and persuade these nations into disarming. Disarmament is the West's first interest and should be the perpetual aim of its activity and diplomacy. The reduction of all armies by an agreed ratio, based presumably on some proportion of population together with length and vulnerability of frontiers, should be the theme, day in, day out, of Western statesmanship and propaganda. The control of atomic weapons—which the Communists have succeeded in making the central point of disarmament—is almost certainly less crucial, for these weapons are now so terrifying that they are to a very great extent their own deterrent. It is the land armies that begin all minor wars. It is with land armies that aggressors

ill still run the risk of hostilities. In fact, only when land
mies are reduced and an international police force estab-
hed does it seem safe to set about the international regula-
on of atomic weapons. Otherwise the greatest deterrent to
tal war, the hydrogen bomb, will have been removed before
e chief instigators of war, land armies, have been brought
der control.

II

If disarmament became the central theme of Western diplo-
acy, this fact alone would go some way to arrest the present
rift toward resentments and misunderstandings among the
tlantic Powers. It would be some check to neutralism. It
ould provide some other context than that of fear. Even so,
a alliance based purely upon the negative task of containing
ommunism remains a very limited and unreliable instrument
f co-operation. Of itself it does little to meet the wider prob-
m of achieving the measure of Western economic stability
eeded to carry simultaneously a defense effort and an ex-
anding civilian economy. It does nothing to meet such urgent
roblems as the development of less advanced areas and the
eation of conditions in Asia or Africa or Latin America in
hich Communism can no longer use local poverty and
espair as the incitements to limited war. The framers of the
orth Atlantic Treaty recognized the limitations of the purely
ilitary approach when, in Article 2 of the Treaty, they pro-
osed wider social and economic tasks for the Organization
nd appointed a secretariat with responsibilities beyond the
mited sphere of defense. This aspect of the alliance has, how-
ver, gone almost entirely by default. The Western allies are
o nearer common economic and social policies than they were
ve years ago. In fact, they are further away, for the effect
f the passage of time, unless positive countermeasures are
ken, is to whittle away hopes and efforts.

This failure to follow up the first promise of Atlantic associa-
on is all the more unfortunate in that, over the last four years,
considerable unanimity of opinion has grown up on the

steps to be taken to give the Western alliance—and hence t[h]
security of the free world—a solid economic underpinning. T[h]
Gray Report, the Bell Report, the Rockefeller Report, t[h]
Douglas and the Randall Reports—all these various reports [b]
American experts, not to mention as many more by other of[fi]
cial agencies, have recommended some or most of the maj[or]
lines of policy needed to insure economic stability and expa[n]
sion in the West. The difficulty lies in the unrepentant n[a]
tionalism of the Western partners and in the hold on the
minds exercised by exclusive doctrines of national self-intere[st]
Yet there is not a modification in economic policy that mig[ht]
be made as part of an agreed plan for an expanding wor[ld]
economy which is not an infinitesimal scratch compared wi[th]
the hatchet blows of unregulated economic crisis or of t[he]
enormous defense programs which will be necessary if Allie[d]
disunity now give the Communists the opportunity to ta[ke]
over a further segment of the free world.

Let us suppose, therefore, that statesmanship and the lon[g]
vision are sufficient in the West to counter the temptations [of]
national short-sightedness and immediate drift. The task woul[d]
then be seen to be to give economic substance to a gener[al]
strengthening of the Atlantic community. A possible agend[a]
has to a great extent been laid down in the various Report[s]
The achievement of convertible currencies and eventually [of]
a single currency, the underpinning of this currency by t[he]
maintenance of balanced and expanding trade, the develo[p]
ment of new sources of food and raw materials to sustain e[x]
panding activity, the finding of capital for investment for th[e]
development and for maintaining high employment—these a[re]
some of the headings which appear in one or other of th[e]
Reports and which would be the first responsibility of th[e]
Atlantic community.

The machinery for acting on such a program should not b[e]
too difficult to devise. One could envisage the setting up, un[
der the authority of the existing Atlantic Council, of a numbe[r]
of special committees or commissions to deal with specifi[c]
points of the program—a Commission for Currency and Trad[e]
for instance, and a Commission for Development. The tim[e]

ble to be followed by such bodies would be dictated by the
rgency of the problems they had to meet. The two greatest
obstacles to the free flow of trade are inconvertible currencies
nd direct obstructions in the shape of tariffs, quotas, and
ther discriminatory restrictions. At present, many nations fear
o relax their controls over dollar purchases because their hold-
gs of gold and dollars are so low in relation to their volume
f trade that even a slight turn in the dollar market might
peedily exhaust their reserves. Britain's reserves, for instance,
re in the neighborhood of $3 billion. Yet sterling covers nearly
o per cent of the world's trade and exchanges worth $40
illion. Similarly the reserves in gold and dollars at the dis-
osal of the International Monetary Fund are only about $3
illion. Yet world trade involves commercial exchanges to the
alue—in all currencies—of more than $70 billion. The cover
s thus inadequate to a turnover on such a scale since the
ominant position of the United States makes the dollar the
nost sought-after of currencies.

A first step toward a fuller and freer flow of trade might
herefore lie in the establishment of a new Monetary Fund—
r an expansion of the old—on a scale sufficient to cover the
ormal fluctuations of worldwide trade. The gold and dollar
ontent of the reserve fund might then be in the neighbor-
ood of $10 billion. The procedure used to build up the re-
erves of the first International Monetary Fund could be em-
loyed again—each nation contributing a share of its national
ncome—but it would probably be necessary to add to each
ation's contribution some additional sum proportionate to the
xisting level of its reserves. This measure would insure that
he new fund had ample supplies of the currency—dollars—
vhich would, in the first years at least, come under particular
train.

Given the backing of this reserve fund, the nations might
nove to convertibility at once, while still retaining as a safety
neasure some restrictions on trade. The next five or ten years
ould be designated as the period during which restraints
vould be removed, first the discriminatory restraints and then,
y reciprocal agreement, the barriers thrown up by tariffs.

During this experimental period, it would be the task of the Commission for Currency and Trade to study all points of stress and devise remedies. For instance, it might be found that France had developed a permanent debtor status or was rapidly exhausting the dollar reserves of the fund. Equally, it might be found that the United States remained a steady creditor. The Commission would be required to study the disequilibrium as exhaustively and dispassionately as the Marshall Plan agencies used to study the condition of the various European economies and then to put forward the remedies needed to restore balance. The permanent creditor might be required to proceed more speedily with tariff cuts or to increase its immigration quota or to make more capital available. The debtor member might be required to rationalize parts of its economy—agriculture in France is an obvious example—to reduce its internal price level, to devalue (since currencies would still no doubt be separate), and as a last resort to consider whether new patterns of investment and a new policy for migration might not be necessary.

In a sense, recommendations of this type involve no new departure. The High Authority of the European Coal and Steel Pool already has powers to impose levies on trade and to use the funds for the redevelopment of areas in which competition has closed pits or furnaces and is creating unemployment. Such readjustments are much less drastic than the risks entailed in taking no co-operative action. They have the added virtue of being sought calmly and rationally in the normal processes of economic co-operation and not in blind panic under the inexorable pressure of economic collapse. Moreover, extreme modifications of policy would probably remain exceptional. The existing patterns of trade already spring in large measure from natural foundations in geography, transport, the location of raw materials, and accessibility to markets. Provided the Western powers give themselves the reserves, the time, and the elbow room within which to act, they can develop, without undue dislocation, the expedients which they need.

In fact, they have already proved that they can do so. After

he First World War, the entire Western world embarked upon
carnival of boom and bust. A vast postwar inflation was
ollowed by the collapse of 1921. Another inflated bubble of
rosperity exploded in 1929. After the Second World War, on
he contrary, the processes of recovery, guided since 1947 by
lose international consultation, have been incomparably more
rderly and have included such stupendous feats as the re-
overy of Western Germany and the maintenance in the
Jnited States of an economy double the prewar scale.

After a ten-year experimental phase—or possibly a longer
eriod, for what is ten years in the trade of all mankind?—it is
ossible to hope that the main points of stress will be apparent
nd the appropriate methods to deal with them will be agreed.
ome barriers will no doubt remain. For instance, a measure
f tariff protection may be needed to maintain standards of
iving in countries where labor is highly paid against the com-
etition of extremely low-cost producers. Other tariffs may be
ecessary to preserve strategic industries in uncompetitive
reas. A free world economy can undoubtedly carry some
ariations and modifications, just as the United States economy
as carried differential freight rates and other obstacles to com-
lete mobility. The point is to reduce restrictions upon trade
o the lowest practicable level and not to use them as the first
ine of defense in national policy.

Nevertheless, there are certain conditions under which any
xperimental advance toward more freely moving trade will
nfallibly fail. No trading system yet devised can stand more
han a certain degree of deflation and unemployment among
ts partners. No conceivable trading system can withstand the
trains imposed by a general collapse of domestic production.
Nor is there any use glossing over the fact that every other
conomy in the free world would adopt such policies quite
ruitlessly if the most powerful free economy—that of the
United States—were not prepared to maintain its own levels of
rosperity. Thus the first duty that the United States must
ulfill, if it is to develop the leadership which belongs to it by
virtue of its scale and influence, is simply to maintain the
phenomenal standards of its economy. There can surely have
been few less onerous costs of leadership in the history of man.

19

A Prosperous World Order

WE RETURN, then, to the question of maintaining high and stable standards of domestic production. Most economists are now agreed, with whatever difference of emphasis, that the fundamental aim of a policy of full employment is to maintain a balance between the supply of goods an economy is able to produce and the demand which is generated by the various stages of the productive process. If consumption, government expenditure, and private investment add up to roughly the entire potential output of the economy, demand will be maintained and stability unimpaired. It is therefore the government's duty in its annual estimates of the economy (which, in sharp distinction to the estimates of thirty years ago, are now reasonably accurate) to judge when there will be a shortfall in consumption, in investment, or in its own expenditures.

If such a shortfall is likely, the government can adopt a variety of expedients. It can remit the lower levels of taxation to encourage mass spending. It can foster more investment by increasing its own orders to industry or by remitting taxation on fresh capital expenditure. It can directly increase its own outlay in public works or social security or aid to schools and hospitals. If it feels that higher taxation on large incomes—which are less likely to be spent—is not a judicious method of raising revenue for its own extended program, then it can, in slack times, carry an unbalanced budget and use its deficit as an instrument of inflation. Alternatively, the course of wisdom might seem to be in putting aside funds for the depression by higher taxation at the peak of the boom. In other words, the state appears to need a ten-year capital budget

lesigned to act as a regulator to the economy in addition to
ts annual estimate of current revenue and expenses. The es-
ence of all these measures is, however, the same: that de-
nand and supply be held in balance. In a backward economy,
he balance would no doubt be maintained by greater empha-
is on fresh investment. In a mature economy, the maintenance
f consumption would be the first objective.

The United States, alone among the world's economies, can
pproach the issue of full employment without a perpetual
ackward glance at a potential crisis in its international bal-
nce of payments. There are no materials necessary for the
naintenance of production which the dollar will not buy.
There is no dollar sent out into the world to purchase goods
vhich will not sooner or later be gratefully respent in the
Jnited States market. The problem in America, where not more
han about six or seven per cent of the national economy is
nvolved in foreign trade, lies essentially in the maintenance of
lomestic demand. Much of it today is probably self-sustaining.
Social insurance, pension, and welfare schemes have grown
enormously. Speculation is less, the self-financing of industry
greater. The government is likely for years to come to make
sizeable expenditures on arms. Yet there are strong reasons for
avoiding overoptimism in this field. Nothing would give
greater encouragement and scope to the Communists than the
onslaught of a Western depression. Nothing is more certain
han that free economies have undergone violent depressions
in the past. Moreover, though policies applied in time can be
marginal, applied too late they have to be vast.

It would seem, therefore, to be the path of wisdom for any
democratic government to have ready prepared its methods
of expanding demand in times of threatened recession and its
timetable for carrying out such a policy. The aim should be
to stimulate demand over the widest possible area and to insure that the capital-goods industries receive their share of the
renewed activity. The proven effectiveness of an arms effort is
just this immense stimulus it gives to heavy industry and the
extraordinary variety of demand which it creates. The nearest
approximation to an ideal policy would thus be one which

combined an arms program's wide powers of reactivating the economy with a rather more useful and less lethal end product.

Is such a program conceivable? Among various possibilities there is one which has had some success in the past and which seems particularly appropriate to the youthful marriages and high birth rate of the United States. Its essence might be a federally financed increase in the already massive provision of new homes. If such a program were extended to include the rebuilding of slum areas, there would seem to be almost no limit to the demand it could satisfy. One might even imagine, more ambitiously, a fifty-year plan to renovate the substandard towns of the whole continent, for certainly there is no greater single source of misery than filthy, vermin-infested homes, overcrowded, crumbling to decay, and housing the future delinquents of society. Housing and slum clearance programs probably did more than any other single policy to lift Britain from the bottom of the depression after 1932. Expanded federally financed housing may well have helped to end the downturn of the American economy in 1949. And if one could for a moment subtract from the French economy its insoluble problems of foreign trade, it can be said that nothing would so restore French morale and weaken the influence of Communism as a systematic program of house building. The thousands who live in perpetual squalor and, in winter, on the borderline of death by exposure are those who swell the Communist vote and watch indifferently the political maneuvering of a system which leaves them to the hopeless degradation of slum life.

II

A domestic program of housing and urban redevelopment is not, of course, an exclusive policy for full production. Another obvious possibility lies in a rehabilitation and expansion of the United States highway system. But a housing program would go some of the way toward maintaining demand in the event of a future decline in arms production or a normal down-urn in the economy. By the same token it would help to maintain international trade by insuring against a catastrophic fall in United States imports. Yet today, in spite of high employment and a vast arms budget, the United States trade deficit with the world is in the neighborhood of $3 billion. At present, the disparity is met partly by restrictions imposed on American sales abroad, partly by American military and paramilitary aid. It is, therefore, impossible to avoid the question whether, given this ominous unbalance in external trade, an American program for full production should not include more than purely domestic policies.

The reaction against all forms of further foreign aid is natural and widespread in the United States. Over $30 billion have been given away since 1945. Yet the world is still in turmoil. May not any attempt to continue the policy simply entail throwing good money after bad? There is, moreover, a deep instinctive distaste for the idea of governments giving or lending capital. It appears to be part of that conspiracy to extend governmental powers against which many Americans feel it their duty to battle. The case for including assistance to other nations in any United States program for high and stable production must, therefore, be closely argued and must include overwhelmingly cogent reasons before it is likely to modify America's understandable mood of disillusion and distrust.

A useful starting point is, therefore, the argument of direct national self-interest. As the Paley Report has shown, if the United States economy is to expand on the scale needed even to maintain present standards for a soaring population, it must be able to satisfy a steadily mounting demand for raw materials many of which are only to be found outside its boundaries and most of which require years of intensive development before they are ready for industrial use. In advanced communities, the expansion of raw-material supplies does not present private enterprise with insuperable difficulties. But some of the richest reserves of special ores lie in territories where the foundations of a modern economy have barely been laid. A hundred years ago, private enterprise was willing to provide basic services. British firms laid out the public utilities of Latin America and undertook municipal contracts from Athens to Singapore. Today, this type of investment is no longer profitable. Moreover, it shares, together with many other forms of private investment, the disadvantage of exciting local nationalist prejudice. Under these conditions, it is possible and indeed likely that the expansion of primary production needed to sustain the growth of the American economy may not occur.

It would, on the other hand, be perfectly feasible to devise programs whereby the preliminaries to large development schemes overseas were provided by intergovernmental lending while private enterprise undertook the expansion of raw materials and trade in which it was particularly interested. The largest capital scheme under discussion in Africa, the Volta River Project, follows this pattern. The British and Gold Coast governments may provide the capital for building the port, the railways, and the power required in the scheme. A Canadian company—Aluminium, Ltd.—might lease the bauxite deposits, set up the aluminum factory and smelter, and produce the aluminum. The division of capital between the public and private participants in the scheme would be roughly equal. It is not impossible to conceive of an extension of this principle according to which public funds might be used to provide underdeveloped areas in Africa, Asia, and Latin America with basic services—roads, railways, ports, public utilities and town sites—while local and foreign private enterprise were given inducements to co-operate in developing local materials and fashioning the web of trade. Conceived on a sufficient scale, a series of such "continental plans" would offer the triple benefit of expanding world supplies of raw materials, of creating wider demand for manufactured goods and, by means of the American contribution, of helping to fill the gap in the world's trade balance with the United States.

Nor is the interest in such plans confined to the economic advantage. At present, there is comparatively little disposition in the United States to question aid given to other nations to defend them against Communist attack. Subsidies and shipments of arms to military allies have a sufficiently long history in the relations between nation states to arouse little prejudice and less comment. The fact remains, however, that the likelihood of a frontal attack by Communists on neighboring territory has very much diminished since the United States taught them the lesson in Korea that painless aggression is a thing of the past. The chief technique of attack practiced by the Communists in Asia and Africa is that of internal infiltration, making use of every opening given by poverty and starvation and hopeless misery. These they compare with the high standards of the West and declare that the West has gained its wealth by exploiting the toiling millions in less favored areas. Communism, on the contrary, comes among them as a gospel of salvation which will give them not only wealth and stability but also equality with the West. It offers them freedom from want and "freedom from contempt" as well. Against such techniques, the shipment of arms is all but useless.

Is it therefore not legitimate to regard economic aid given to underdeveloped areas as a straightforward means of national security? To give only one instance, if the Indian Union were to sink, by reason of its poverty, into a welter of separate states in which Communism steadily gained ground, the insecurity of the Western world would be so vastly increased that even greater outlay on arms would be needed than is spent today. Yet if, in the period of India's Five Year Plan, only a billion dollars were invested in Indian basic expansion—in other words, about one-ninetieth of the free world's annual arms bill —the consequence might well be to insure the success of the Plan and the confounding of Communist hopes and schemes. It is blindly conventional nationalist thinking to accept the pursuit of security as legitimate only when it takes the form of sending an ally tanks and armored cars. If the object is the same—to check Communism—and if the aim can be better achieved by the dispatch of bulldozers and tractors, what is the precise metaphysical difference which makes a tank legitimate and a tractor the object of attack and suspicion? The one is as much concerned with national security as the other. The only distinction is that, given Communist techniques of infiltration and disruption, a far higher dividend is likely to follow from economic aid in Asia, Africa, and the Middle East than from the simple shipment of arms.

There is thus a definite economic and strategic advantage to be gained in including foreign aid in long-term plans for Western economic stability. Needless to say, such a policy could not be confined to the United States, although as the center of the free world economy and its greatest creditor, its participation would have the most beneficial effect in terms of balancing international trade. But all the nations of the West have a comparable interest in world stability and security and it is not difficult to devise a scheme whereby every country with a national income per head of over a certain figure—for instance, $500 a year—should contribute one or two per cent of its total national income to an Atlantic Development Fund, administered by the Commission for Investment and charged with the responsibility of using its capital to give the maximum degree of security coupled with the most rational development of resources. A one-per-cent levy on the dozen countries who would qualify for participation would place about $5 billion at the Commission's disposal each year—certainly not an excessive sum in view of a United Nations estimate that the minimum annual requirement of capital to insure some expansion in the underdeveloped areas is in the neighborhood of $19 billion. Yet even $5 billion a year of certain income would enable the West to formulate sustained plans for assistance and development. Even $5 billion would be enough to set the tide of propaganda working against the Communists. Even $5 billion would begin to turn the promise of the Western way of life from words to deeds. And no one can estimate what such a reversal would mean in terms of battles won because they had never to be fought and of lives and assets saved from destruction.

III

Yet there must be some who wonder whether the full promise of Western society can be contained within such a profit-and-loss account. Is this the only motive, the only aspiration

behind a policy of aid to less-developed areas? Is there to be
no more to it than an exact calculation of national interest and
a careful decision that it will in the long run cost the good
Samaritan more to leave the wounded man in the ditch than
to bind up his wounds and carry him to the inn? We are
confronted here with one of the most obstinate prejudices in
our Western mind—the deep feeling that there are no moral
obligations which stretch beyond our own frontiers. The prejudice cannot yet be argued away, for with most people it has
not reached a point where it even needs to be defended. It is
still self-evident, a fact of life, a part of the structure of the
universe. It may be true that the members of the white race
in the last four hundred years have occupied and developed
all the best, most pleasant, and most fertile areas of the world,
that they have an average standard of living anything up to
eight times as high as that of the peoples of India or South East
Asia, that their average expectation of life is above sixty years,
that of India about thirty, that only one in thirty of their children dies in infancy while in Burma the proportion is one in
five—all this may be true and yet seems to possess no more
particular significance than that the Himalayas are high or
that the tropics are hot. Such facts are still seen as normal
features of the pattern and structure of the universe. Certainly
they do not yet bind the conscience, trouble the spirit, and
affect the will of Western man.

Yet it may be that, in this field of the needs and miseries of
the human race, we are about to witness a revolution as startling as that which overtook men's thoughts about the absolute rights of property in the course of the nineteenth century
and one which is, to a curious degree, comparable to the earlier
change. The fundamental character of that change lay in the
acceptance of the idea that property did not confer an absolute right, that no man, in the complex and interconnected
world of modern industry, could claim that his wealth was his
own entirely by his own exertions and that he had complete
and final say in its disposal. In place of the old absolute
concept of property, there grew the realization that all wealth
is in some measure a trust, that all material wellbeing owes so

much to the community which protects it and to the fellow workers who help to create it that every man owes a proportion of his wealth to society and to his neighbor, above all to those of his neighbors who, through no fault of their own, have inherited the darker side of life. The great revolution expressed in progressive taxation and in social welfare—which more than anything else has turned Communism into a spent force in so many Western nations—is fundamentally an acceptance of solidarity, of responsibility, and of common humanity—but all, so far, inside the frontiers of the nation state.

Yet today the conditions which made absolute property rights obsolete within domestic society are beginning to prevail in international society as well. The wealth at the disposal of the Western nations is theirs today by inheritance and fortune. Each Western citizen is born, like a child of the Victorian upper class, into a world of privilege and ease. He will not drag out an existence under relentless suns or in the perpetual damp heat of the tropics. He will not live under the shadow of starvation, malarial, tuberculosis-ridden, carrying in his frail body disgusting parasites bred in filthy water. His health, his cleanliness, his good food, his clean water—these are the unearned increments which are his by the accident of birth north of Cancer and south of Capricorn. At the same time, some of his wealth today is preserved by preventing the poorer peoples of the world from moving to land under his control, although—as in the case of Canada, Australia, and even the United States—resources are not yet fully developed. Part of the wealth of the West has also been created by the labor of men and women who live in the world's tropical slums or, like the African slaves, were removed from there to work in the white continents. The peoples of Africa and Asia did not choose to be drawn into the Western web of wealth; white men created a unified world economy and pressed them into its service. Some benefits flow back to them, no doubt, just as the factory worker of Victorian England gained marginal rewards from the success of the new industrial system. Yet they are rewards that express chance, not solidarity. Thus the relationship today between the privileged nations of the West and the underdeveloped areas of the world offers a startling analogy with the conditions which prevailed within early industrial society when Marx and Engels wrote their indictments and predicted the ruin that lay ahead.

It is therefore possible—indeed more than possible; it is likely—that unless some modification can be introduced into our Western concept of national self-interest comparable to the modification of the old absolute concept of property, the prophecies which Marx made in vain of the disintegration of domestic society in the West may yet be turned in judgment against the West's relations with the world's backward areas. Lenin may be proved to have seen further than his master when he prophesied that colonial territories would be the Achilles heel of the West. Equally, however, the prophecies can once more be proved false and empty if the Western powers modify their national policies—as they did their notions of property—in the direction of solidarity, responsibility, and brotherhood. Today, we have no more than inklings of the needed change. Our present insights are perhaps comparable to the efforts of private reformers and private charities in Victorian England to effect the revolution in men's thinking on the responsibilities of private property a hundred years ago. Point Four programs, the Colombo Plan, Colonial Welfare and Development Funds, Technical Assistance from the United Nations—all these separate ventures illustrate the first attempts of Western man to establish a new relationship between the wealthy nations of the world and their straitened brethren. What is lacking, however, is any deep-rooted conviction that some transfer of wealth from the Atlantic world—where it is mainly concentrated—to the underprivileged areas represents, not choice and charity, but the obligations of justice and brotherly love.

IV

Inspired by a wider vision, underpinned by long-term economic agreements, served by functioning joint commissions, an Atlantic Community might come to represent the first full experiment in free international co-operation. Its development would give the lie to the Marxists. Neither economic contradictions nor national hostilities would tear the free world apart. History itself would be compelled to revise its judgments, for here would be the first example of a great society drawing back from the ruinous pursuit of unlimited national sovereignty and unchecked economic interest, taming those ferocious forces and achieving instead a worldwide order in which the vitalities of race and of possession acknowledged control.

Yet it may still be asked whether the creation of an Atlantic Community, however open and co-operative, may not have the effect of limiting and hampering other possibilities of international co-operation, some of them perhaps on a wider scale. For instance, while it is possible to conceive of the Asian nations remaining in the British Commonwealth and of new African nations taking their place beside them, could India or Pakistan or Nigeria or the Gold Coast be expected to seek integrated membership in a union which would be predominantly white and, in its early stages at least, unavoidably hostile to the Soviet world bloc? The answer, however, should not lie in failing to create an Atlantic Community. It could be sought by means of recognized degrees of membership. Some associates, by their own choice, would not enter the military community; Sweden and Switzerland in Europe would fall into this category, and India is an obvious example in Asia. Their policy need not entail any lack of readiness to defend themselves and the Atlantic Powers would go to their assistance if they were attacked simply because aggression must be checked wherever it occurs. But they could remain outside the fusing of military forces and command undertaken by the full members of the Atlantic Community.

On the other hand, it is at least likely that most Asian and African nations would wish to be associated fully with the West in an economic community, since their urgent need for development and investment and trade makes some form of international co-operation essential. One can, in short, envisage a core of Atlantic nations linked fully by the whole range of communities set up under treaty and around them a penumbra of associated states, attached to the inner ring for specific purposes. In this way, too, the special and traditional links of Commonwealth countries with Britain or of the Latin American republics with the United States could be preserved and even grow stronger, for it is clear that the greatest disruptive forces in the world today are military weakness and economic instability. A strong and prosperous Atlantic "core" might have very greatly enhanced powers of attraction for the states lying on its fringe.

Nor is an Atlantic Union any obstacle to the steady development of the United Nations. The United Nations would continue to exercise all its functions as the only meeting ground of the whole world community of nations, whatever their political allegiances. The Atlantic States could use their resources to support the United Nations programs of economic and social advancement, and, in their dealings with unaffiliated Asian or Middle Eastern States, their most useful instrument of policy might often be a United Nations agency rather than one of their own commissions. Indonesia today, for instance, is in desperate need of assistance to build up an administrative structure and to restore internal order. It is unlikely that it would ask help directly from the Western powers. But a United Nations mission, reinforced with Atlantic financial and technical backing, might well be admitted to assist in essential reforms.

Above all, the United Nations would continue to be the neutral meeting ground with the Communist states. So long as this channel of communication is kept open, the world retains a symbol and hope of the unity it must seek in the atomic age. The division into blocs of final and uncompromising hostility is not made absolute. A little rift remains for reason, negotiation, and compromise, and on one occasion at least—the ending of the Berlin siege—it has proved wide enough to open the way for a settlement.

Yet to some people the main objection to an Atlantic Community lies precisely in this risk—that it will divide the world finally into two blocs of uncompromising hostility. They believe that there are forces in Russia, particularly since the death of Stalin, that are making for the relaxation of tension and that, provided the Western powers do nothing to check or shrivel these growing points of a more liberal order, the next decades may see a transformation of Soviet society and the emergence of a free community from the totalitarian chrysalis. This argument, however, assumes the complete abandonment by Soviet Russia of the aim of ultimately controlling the world. It is conceivable that after long years of coexistence with a strong, stable, Western order, the aim might be tacitly allowed to go by default. But it is most unlikely that the central point of the Marxist gospel would be abandoned so long as it seemed to have a reasonable chance of succeeding. The best hopes of success lie, as the Marxists repeat day in, day out, in the national divisions and economic incoherences of the Western world. Continue them, and automatically the Communist ambition to exploit them is kept alive and eager. End them, and the Communists may sooner or later accept coexistence as a fact.

There remains one last obstinate—though opposite—objection. It is that an Atlantic Community is unsatisfactory not because it does and risks too much, but because, on the contrary, it falls so far short of world government. The logic of the world demands a single center of authority. What is the use of work for such partial solutions? Will it not deflect energy from the real crusade? Will it not confuse people's minds and lead them back into the byways of old divisions and hostilities and away from the wide horizon of the world state? Perhaps the most simple answer to these doubts is that men must begin where they can. At present there is only one pretender to world order, the Soviet Union. The Western world is divided into an anarchy of conflicting nationalities of which the only likely outcome is to give the Communists their chance to unite the world under their authority. If a world order is to be anything but totalitarian, then the Western nations must at least create a nucleus of free co-operation, and if they cannot begin in an Atlantic Community, then certainly there is no other starting place available to them. An Atlantic Union may fall short of that unity which technically, scientifically, and economically the modern world requires. It falls short of the international hopes nourished in the West's liberal tradition. It falls far short of that brotherhood of all humanity which the great religions have planted as a dream in the human heart. But at least it is a beginning, and if men can learn, within a Western community based on common political and social ideals, to tame their arrogant nationalism and to abate their economic pretensions, they will at least have undergone the best possible preparation for a world society, against the day when it is possible to build one and to build it free.

FIVE

FAITH

20

Faith and Freedom

HOWEVER rational, however compelling, however logical the arguments for Western unity may be, however obvious the benefits of economic co-operation, however hopeful the promise of amity between the nations, one may still question whether reason or logic, of themselves, are enough to change the direction of Western development. The vitalities that must be mastered are the fiercest in the world. They appeal to the ultimate instincts in mankind—the protection of the tribe and the struggle for physical survival. Reason may be outmatched in its struggle with such giants. Has Western man other forces to summon to his aid?

There is, of course, the fact of fear. It is not to be despised. Many things have been accomplished in recent years—including the groundwork of the Atlantic alliance—which would never have been achieved without Soviet pressure. Moreover, even if the Soviets were outwardly unaggressive, they could still—like their totalitarian brethren the Nazis—inspire in the West a salutary fear by demonstrating, in its ultimate stages, the rake's progress in which all Western civilization is to some extent involved. Both these systems of absolute dictatorship have sprung from the Western world. Both have carried to an extreme degree principles and policies which have already made their appearance in the West. The nationalism which Hitler turned to a horror of blood and butchery presides in a sedate form over all Western democracies. The confidence in state action, the glorification of technology, the unlimited faith in science, the centralization of decision, and the subordination of law to so-called mass interests—all these, which in an extreme form have gone to set an inhuman stamp upon Soviet society, have helped in the West to create communities in which the individual citizen feels overwhelmed, isolated, and helpless before the anonymities of public and private bureaucracy. We are right to fear these vast distortions of tendencies already at work in our own society. Both the Soviet and the Nazi systems must stand as dread reminders that in the twentieth century, the line of least resistance in politics tends toward the full apparatus of totalitarian rule. It is not wrong to fear such warnings. It is the beginning of wisdom.

But fear alone is a poor counsellor because it is essentially negative. The Western world cannot combat Communism on such a basis. A people guided only by fear leaves all the initiative and all the advantage with the other side and is reduced to a blind defensive maneuvering in order to counter the other's positive actions, to inferiority, to loss of control, and in all probability to ultimate defeat. Throughout history, the men with a positive goal and a persistent aim have had their way. Like artists at work on the raw material of stone or wood or canvas, they have imposed their vision and drawn the rough vitalities of human existence together into new patterns of society. True, the materials have often proved recalcitrant and the vision has been distorted. Yet such ideals as the Greek *polis*, the "chosen people" of Jewry, the unity of Christendom, the American Republic—or indeed the Dictatorship of the Proletariat—have proved instruments in the hands of men by virtue of which the forces of hunger and power and fear, which are the inchoate stuff of existence, have been molded into something nearer the visionaries' desire. If, in the second half of the twentieth century, the Western peoples have lost all their visions and dreamed all their dreams, then the world is open to the powerful myths of the totalitarians. The society which they picture may be in many respects a nightmare, but nightmares are potent in a world without good dreams.

The West will prove more vulnerable than any other society if it abandons the pursuit of visions and ideals for, more than any other community, it is the product not of geographical and racial forces but of the molding power of the human spirit.

Geographically, Europe is no more than the small Western promontory of the land mass of Asia. It is "Europe" solely because its frontiers mark the frontiers of Christendom. Racially, the United States is a melting pot of every nation under the sun. Only by force of an idea—the "proposition" that men are created equal and possess inalienable rights—has it risen to be the most powerful community in the history of man. Both European society and its extension into the New World have been sustained by a unique faith in man—in his freedom, in his responsibility, in the laws which should safeguard him, in the rights that are his and in the duties by which he earns those rights. So accustomed are we to this view of man that we do not realize the audacity which was needed to bring it into being. At a time when humanity was subject to every physical calamity, when perpetual labor was needed to wring a livelihood from the soil, when the fatalities of tempest and sickness and the general recalcitrance of matter lay heavily upon man's spirit, and when the world, unpenetrated by rational discovery, was a vast unknown—in such a time, the Greek and Jewish forebears of our own civilization made their tremendous acts of faith in man and in his destiny. They declared him to be the crown of the universe. They saw nature as a field open to his reason and his dominion. The Greeks affirmed his power to build a rational order, the Jews proclaimed him a co-worker in the coming reign of righteousness.

It was because this picture of man was so high and so untrammeled and its ambition so vast that it led to the discovery of material instruments of mastery, to science and industry and all the material means of our own day. Man is not master of the universe because he can split the atom. He has split the atom because he first believed in his own unique mastery. Faith led to the material achievement, not the achievement to the faith. In fact, now that the means of mastering the environment, of building—physically—a better world, are more complete than ever before, it is a paradox that the faith is slackening. The men of the West believed in man's high destiny and in his power to remold society in a divine pattern more entirely when their physical means were inadequate and their control marginal than they do today when science and industry offer unlimited opportunities of creation. The reason is that the old audacious view of man and of his destiny was sustained only by faith. Reduce man to a creature of his environment, projected from the fatality of birth by anonymous forces on to the fatality of death—then he is ready to surrender his freedom, his rights, his greatness. He is ready for dictatorship and the slave state.

The human heart has both appetites and despairs which rational codes alone are unable to control. Man is lonely. He is not self-sufficient. He rebels against meaninglessness in life. He is haunted by death. He is afraid. He needs to feel himself part of a wider whole and he has unassuageable powers of dedication and devotion which must find expression in worship and service. If, therefore, there is no other outlet for these powers, then the community in which he lives, the tribe, the state, Caesar, the dictator, become the natural and inevitable objects of his religious zeal. Religion is not abolished by the "abolition" of God; the religion of Caesar takes its place. And since, for a few men, the need to worship is satisfied in *hubris*, in the worship of the self, the multitudes who look for a god can nearly always be certain of finding a willing candidate. In times of crisis, when insecurity, anxiety, loneliness, and the meaninglessness of life become well-nigh insupportable—how can a man tolerate years without work in modern industrial society?—the hunger for godlike leadership, for religious reassurance, for a merging of the self in the security of the whole becomes irresistible. Even when faith in God survives, the desire wells up for strong government. Where religious faith has vanished, all the energies of the soul are poured into the one channel of political faith. In our own day, Communism and National Socialism have proved to be powerful religions and have brought back into the world the identification of state and church, city and temple, king and god which made up the monolithic unity of archaic society and the universal servitude of archaic man.

Few deny the historical role of Christianity in creating a double order of reality and a division of power out of which the possibility of freedom has grown. Even the most doubtful must confront the fact that totalitarian government in its extremest form has returned when the waning of religion left the altars of the soul empty and turned men back to the oldest gods of all—the idols of the tribe. Nor is it easy to conceive of any means other than religious faith for preserving a genuine division of power in society; for if man is no more than the creature of his environment, and a product of his social order, on what foundations can he base claims and loyalties which go beyond the social order? From what source can he draw the strength to resist the claims of society? To what justice can he appeal beyond the dictates of the state? The state is by nature so powerful and compelling and voracious an institution that the citizen, standing alone against it, is all but powerless. He needs counter-institutions, above all the counter-institution of the Church, which of all organized bodies alone can look Caesar in the face and claim a higher loyalty.

It is, however, one thing to argue that a recovery of faith in God is necessary as a safeguard of Western freedom. It is quite another to put forward sociological and political and historical facts as the basis for a revival of faith. Such a procedure runs the risk of resembling the hypocrisy of eighteenth-century cynics who argued that religion was good for the poor because it kept them contented. Faith is not a matter of convenience nor even—save indirectly—a matter of sociology. It is a question of conviction and dedication and both spring from one source only—from the belief in God as a fact, as the supreme Fact of existence. Faith will not be restored in the West because people believe it to be useful. It will return only when they find that it is true.

II

But can modern man accept such a possibility? The whole trend of four hundred years of rationalism and science has taken him in the opposite direction—toward acceptance of a single material universe which is the sum of all there is and has no place for gods, for supernature, for First Causes or Creators claiming the worship and obedience of man. After so much conditioning in the idea of a single natural system, can man find in his contemporary universe any trace of a supernatural order of reality, any hint that the faith which once sustained his civilization is not a helpful myth but still the essential map of human destiny?

Perhaps the surest starting point for such an inquiry—and it is idle to speak of a recovery of faith unless such an inquiry is undertaken—lies with the fact of the existence of a physical universe. One of the problems that has puzzled mankind ever since man began to reflect upon experience is that of "being" itself. All our knowledge of physical reality, from its minutest atoms and impulses up to its most awesome manifestations in mountain ranges or volcanic eruptions, suggests that each physical phenomenon has a physical cause behind it and that it is not in itself a sufficient explanation of what and why it is. Yet if the whole physical universe is made up of dependent substances, each requiring an explanation, then the sum of reality is still only a sum of dependent things and it does not seem that all dependent substances added together can somehow add the quality of independence to themselves merely, as it were, by huddling together. Logically, they seem to demand a self-explanatory self-subsistent ground to account for their existence. Some scientists, believing the whole of the universe to display evidence of declining energy, hold that a physical act of creation once took place to launch the whole complex phenomenon of physical reality—a theory which seems to imply a Creator behind the act of creation. A more recent theory suggests that the total universe is maintained by a constant pouring into the system of interstellar gas out of which are condensed the galaxies, which in their turn breed stars whose explosions precipitate the planets, on one of which —our own—we know life exists. But this theory, while solving the problem of the appearance of the solar system, leaves us with the problem of the interstellar gas. How does it appear? Has it a cause? Or alone of all the physical phenomena of which we are aware, has it no cause? Its supposed continuous creation at least suggests something behind it which does the creating.

But even if the mind can grasp and be satisfied with the idea of interstellar gas as the uncaused, self-subsistent ground of physical reality, this prop breaks down when we turn from matter to mind, from physical reality to the field of rationality and reason. One of the great progenitors of our civilization, the Greeks, believed that rationality is evidence of the divine in nature. If it can be shown that the very notion of rationality can have no place in a single material order of nature, then the presumption must be that there is more than a material universe and that any account of reality must include other than purely material factors. In ordinary daily common sense living we do, of course, make constant distinctions between purely material facts and sensations and something else that seems to be beyond and apart from them. We do not confuse mind with matter. We believe we understand what we say when we distinguish between rational and irrational behavior. We think we can see the difference between a valid and an invalid inference or conclusion. To put the distinction in concrete terms, a man undergoing a nightmare has vivid mental images which may cause him to call out, to wave his arms about, to get up, and even to threaten violence. Similarly, a man overcome by a fit of rage or under the influence of drugs may commit crimes of which he would normally be believed incapable. In none of these cases do we consider the man's mind—his rational nature—to have been at work: he has been overcome by irrational forces, by the store of uncontrolled sensory images and desires in his subconscious, by a flood of sensation, by the physical effect of some narcotic substance. These material powers have invaded his mind and taken over control.

So strong is this belief that rationality is something apart from material and emotional causation that the followers of Marx have mobilized it into a most potent weapon against Western society. It is their contemptuous charge that Western freedom, Western law, and Western idealism are all cloaks for the greed and rapacity of Western economic exploitation. They attack the validity of Western ideas on the grounds that they are only projections of self-interest and class feeling. In another field, Freud has helped to confuse conventional morality by reducing much of it to the rationalization of unconscious drives and impulses.

But here is the puzzle. If the whole of reality is made up of a single material process, it follows that mind can be only the by-product of the physical brain and that every thought is materially conditioned by the sensations and impulses which have previously been registered in the physical organism. This, briefly, is the view of mind held by those who believe only in a single material order of reality. In fact, it is the view they must hold, for if mind were something else, their theory would be wrong: there would be one point in nature to which material conditioning did not provide the full explanation; mind would be the entry point of another order of reality, the chink, however tiny, through which might stream another radiance, the light of the Logos itself, the fount of truth.

Is mind then the projection of the physical organism? If it is, all our thoughts have at some point physical origins. They are all rooted in what, in our everyday language, we call irrational facts, facts of temperament, physique, heredity, or environment. Each of these facts, used to explain a single happening, would, as we have seen, destroy the credibility of the explanation. Add all the single happenings together to make up the whole universe and is there any more room for reason? By choosing a single material order of reality, we seem to exclude rationality altogether. And this possibility has very serious consequences for thought.

A passion for truth is generally held to be among mankind's noblest aspirations. All the world religions have affirmed that God, in some mysterious fashion, is Truth. At this stage of the argument, we can at least maintain the negative point that in a universe without supernature, without some order of reality apart from material happenings, there can be no such thing as truth. Valid argument, rational deduction, proof itself are alike impossibilities. When Marx says that law and custom and idealism and religion and theories and ideas are all byproducts of the material process of production, he clearly means us to believe the statement. But on his own showing, his statement, like that of any other idea, must be the product of a certain stage of economic development. It is no more "rational" than the theories of capitalism it is used to demolish.

Similarly with every other argument, if statements are no more than certain rearrangements of impulses in the speaker's brain; if, as Dr. Thomas Huxley once said to the British Association, "the thoughts to which I am now giving utterance and your thoughts regarding them are expressions of the molecular changes in the matter of life," then they can be observed and noted but they cannot be said to "prove" something any more than an attack of measles can be looked on as an argument. They simply occur.

Some materialists would attempt to get around this difficulty by saying that thoughts have been rising in human minds for thousands and thousands of years. Some thoughts give their thinkers greater chances of survival than others. Over the millennia ideas have been weeded out by process of elimination—the thinkers of inefficient thoughts succumbing, the thinkers of self-preserving thoughts surviving—until today, the thoughts we call true are really those which have helped the human organism to exist and develop. But this whole argument, to be convincing, depends upon the validity of a chain of argument. It depends upon a number of inferences about the past, it depends upon judgments on the efficacy of heredity and upon deductions based upon the supposed survival of the fittest. But if all these mental processes of judgment, inference, and deduction are simply the mental reflections of material cerebral patterns, of the dance of atoms in the cortex, in what sense can they be said to be true? And if the inferences and the deductions are unprovable, the theory is in the same state.

Some thinkers, faced with these difficulties, have solved them by giving up the idea of truth. They no longer claim that the mind can give a true account of external reality. But it can know that certain things work out according to predetermined physical tests. Some of these help human wellbeing and it is enough to concentrate on them and leave abstruse problems of truth to the philosophers. Yet even the claim that truth cannot be known is, presumably, a statement of fact, a statement about the limitations of the mind, and as such it puts in its claim to be true. If, however, the mind is a physical substance, causally determined by other physical substances, it cannot tell us, one way or the other, which view of its powers is correct. As Professor J. S. Haldane once wrote: "If my mental processes are determined wholly by the motions of atoms in my brain, I have no reason to suppose that my beliefs are true . . . and hence I have no reason for supposing my brain to be composed of atoms." Even if we can in theory dispense with truth—and it is difficult to believe that anyone should seriously consider abandoning one of mankind's deepest and most disinterested pursuits—the claim to truth or the desire for truth seems to re-enter by the very door through which it has been expelled.

Rationality and the pursuit of truth—the great inheritance from the Greek world—can occupy a place in a purely material order of reality only, as it were, by stealth. Strictly, they have no right to be there. Nor does the other deepest element in the Western tradition—the intense Jewish concern with moral righteousness and the sense of God as the supreme Good—find any easier entry point into a closed material world. If there is no more in the universe than material facts and causations, goodness or the Good can be only a by-product of material processes. Great efforts have been made in the last century to trace the meaning of goodness back to its supposedly material source—in individual or collective interest, in emotion, in the desire for self or group preservation. Indeed, such theories are inevitable, if there is no more than a material universe. If goodness cannot be reduced to material interests and emotions, the universe cannot be seen as a single natural process: another loophole opens in nature, another order of reality may obtrude reflecting a transcendent and absolute Perfection.

Yet to believe that goodness is ultimately reduceable to material components is a much more troublesome process than it may seem at first. To go back to our everyday thinking, we distinguish very easily between the good and the self-interested; in fact, it seems part of the essence of goodness to be disinterested. If material causes can be found for supposedly "good" conduct, its goodness begins to fade. For instance, if we say "Miss Smith has given up everything to look after her troublesome and ailing old uncle," we are inclined to applaud her spirit of self-sacrifice. If, however, the rider is added, "She also expects to inherit his large fortune," the goodness of her behavior is open to doubt. Yet if material causes prevent us in individual instances from calling actions or personalities good, where is there place for goodness in a universe which contains nothing but material causes?

An answer can be attempted by moving from the individual to the collective level. It is the wisdom of the race or the tribe bent on self-preservation that has given rise in individual minds to judgments of value. Courage or self-sacrifice are "good" because both are necessary to the survival of the community. The essence of the idea of Good is that it compels obedience. We feel we ought to acquire characteristics or undertake action which we believe to be good. But this reaction is due to the fact that millennia of collective conditioning and disciplining have induced in us this conditioned reflex of obedience. The belief that the good has a claim on us, the whole concept of conscience, duty, and obligation which is inextricably tied up with the idea of the good, can be traced back ultimately to such purely material causes as physical survival and tribal taboo.

But, if this is the case, how has the distinction come about between the good on the one hand and the merely useful or expedient on the other? It is a fact that if we are told that the root of our morals is only expediency, or social use, then the hold of morality on our conscience instantly begins to slacken. We can accept a morality based upon social utility only if we believe the wellbeing of the greater number to be more valuable—to contain a higher good—than our own individual wellbeing. This is itself a moral judgment. But if it is only a reflection of long collective conditioning, it ceases to be binding on our conscience.

The puzzle is to account for "goodness" at all as a powerful factor in our mind if it disappears on being reduced to material interest. If there is no such thing in reality as goodness, how did it ever come to be invented or invoked? When the supposed conditioning of mankind began, why was the appeal made, beyond fear and discipline, to the idea of goodness constraining the conscience? The possibility that "I ought" is more than a Pavlovian reflex is suggested by the fact that the moment I am told it is just a reflex, I cease to feel that I ought to take any notice of it. And yet the notion of goodness and duty exists. How did it arise?

III

By formal rational argument, it is thus possible to come to a point at which the mind acknowledges the fact that some Ground or Foundation of reality, of being, underlies the multifarious physical universe, and that this same Ground is, in some sense, the source and sustainer of reason, truth, and goodness, all of them inexplicable in purely material terms. In fact, in the highest reach of unaided human speculation, the Greeks did succeed in bringing humanity as far as this point. When St. Paul spoke to the men of Athens, he found among their altars one dedicated to "the unknown God." But can we go any further than a concept of the Godhead which is indeed removed only by a hairbreadth from the unknown? Supernatural Reason as the source of rationality may be a logical necessity but a logical necessity can appear very remote from the strivings and sufferings of humanity. How can we advance beyond this point and learn not only to recognize the existence of an independent, self-subsistent Reality, but furthermore to see It no longer as an "unknown God"?

The problem here is essentially no different from that in any other field of inquiry. In our present epoch, with its enormous accumulation of specialized information, no one can hope to enter fully into any sphere of knowledge without devoting to it much time and energy. If someone wants to deepen his understanding of science, he applies first of all to the acknowledged men of science who have devoted their lives to science. For art he goes to the greatest artists. Moreover, to secure any degree of mastery in a subject, he realizes that he must to some extent practice it experimentally. Music, for instance, does not reveal its highest delights except to those who can master a score or play some form of instrument. In many fields, the average inquirer is entirely dependent upon the knowledge and information of others. Since, then, we have to accept the fact that most of our knowledge is derivative and depends for its certainty upon the confidence we can place in the honesty and veracity of other people's witness, there is nothing contrary to reason in accepting facts on the basis of other men's evidence. We do so all the time.

Let us suppose, therefore, that a group of men come to us singly with tales of an unknown country which they have visited. They describe its landscape and they tell us of the route they took to get there. First of all, we notice that each witness tends to tell the same story and to describe the same road. Then we notice that they are drawn from almost every class of society and from every nation under the sun. Then with increasing surprise we discover that they are not the only group of witnesses. In every age, men similarly drawn from different peoples and different vocations have left behind them evidence of a similar journey and a similar discovery of the distant land. What would be a rational response to this weight of evidence and this "cloud of witnesses"? Should we not, in normal life, believe in the existence of their discovered country, accept their account of its landscape, and also accept as a fact their advice that if we could but set out on the same journey with the same map and the same kit, we too should find the land and find it to be as they had promised?

This is an exact description of the human witness to the fact and nature of the final self-subsistent Reality. The country which has been mapped is the divine landscape of God. The route that has been followed is the road followed by the mystics and the saints. If we wish to know more of the nature of the Godhead, these are the men and women to whom we must turn. Yet as soon as the terms are changed from a natural to a supernatural landscape and from a physical to a religious route, the old doubts and skepticisms creep back. Is this witness really reliable? Are we not in fact back in a private world of imagination without external reference, among dreams and hallucinations and even the symptoms of hysteria? The procedure of seeking knowledge by going to those with the best claim to have it may work well enough among the concrete realities of daily life and scientific experiment. But this land of religious and mystical experience is essentially relative, varying from tradition to tradition and land to land and essentially private, expressing no more than a personal state of mind. How can it claim authority or induce belief?

The first point to be clarified is that the knowledge of the Godhead proclaimed by the religious leaders of mankind is only in part relative. There is admittedly a great difference in their attitude toward creation and toward material things. It is an important difference which has vitally affected the development of human history. But in describing the essential nature of the divine Ground of being, the ultimate Reason from which all rationality is derived, all ages and all traditions give testimony to the same facts. They are also unanimous in their description of man's relation to this divine Reality and of the means he must take to unite himself to it in such a way that his whole life falls into place, finds its true north, experiences the peace of mind and soul which is sought restlessly and vainly among material things, and finds "the glorious liberty of the sons of God."

According to this universal testimony, God is the Source, Reason, and Ground of all things, the Being which alone makes the idea of existence itself conceivable. This Ground can also be known under the form of the various absolutes—Goodness, Truth, Beauty—which are inexplicable in terms of ordinary material experience. The fullness, the plenitude of the good, the true, and the beautiful are in God. Moreover, this order of Reality which is supreme and transcendent and the Ground of everything else is also immanent. "The Kingdom of

Heaven is within you." In the depths of our being, at the point of our soul, we are united with the source of Reality. In the words of Hindu philosophy, "That art thou." In the words of the Christian mystic Eckhart, writing in the high Middle Ages, "To gauge the soul we must gauge it with God, for the Ground of God and the Ground of the soul are one and the same."

But how are we to know God? Once again, the evidence is unanimous. God is known by means of love. Love in this sense has nothing to do with emotion or sentiment. To love is to desire the Good. The completely disinterested act, undertaken because the mind wills to do good, unites the soul with God, for to love Him is to do His will. Similarly, in our relations with other human beings and indeed with all created things, our desire must be to procure their good and to respect their nature. In the words of William Law, the great eighteenth-century mystic: "By love I do not mean any natural tenderness, which is more or less in people according to their constitution; but I mean a larger principle of soul, founded in reason and piety which makes us tender, kind and gentle to all our fellow creatures as creatures of God and for His sake." Here, if anywhere, is the fundamental root of Western freedom—in this metaphysical sense of the infinite value of each human soul before God and the infinite respect each man owes to his neighbor's liberty and wellbeing.

A steady, selfless wish for the good of others is, however, intensely difficult to achieve if we are entangled deeply in our own immediate aims and satisfactions. Hence the universal teaching of the need for detachment, for self-naughting, for serving men and controlling things always with an idea of procuring their harmony, order, and peace and not with the intention of bending them this way and that to satisfy the nagging desire of the separate self for possession or power. The great poet and mystic of the Moslem Sufis, Rabi'a, speaks thus of disinterestedness: "God, if I worship Thee in fear of hell, burn me in hell. And if I worship Thee in hope of Paradise, exclude me from Paradise; but if I worship Thee for Thine Own sake, withhold not Thine Everlasting Beauty." Or we may take the more homely words of the gentle saint,

François de Sales: "I have hardly any desires but if I were born again I should have none at all. We should ask nothing and refuse nothing, but leave ourselves in the arms of divine Providence without wasting time in any desire, except to will what God wills of us."

This need of detachment is the deepest ground of the moral law, for the commandments of truth and honesty, of chastity and sobriety, of mercy and forgiveness are all but different aspects of this deep respect for all creatures and this fundamental desire to do them good. The sense of St. Augustine's "Love God and do what you like" becomes more evident. If your will is so trained as to wish only good to your neighbors and your desire is directed wholly toward the supreme Good of God, then your free actions will flow from this innate spiritual health of mind and spirit. Equally, the soul bent only on the passions and hungers of the self will flout his neighbor, disturb his peace and freedom, and build institutions and societies mirroring and perpetuating aggression and greed.

It is the testimony of all these witnesses that the man who wholeheartedly pursues the Good, loving the Supreme Good that is God and loving his neighbor and all creaturely things, will find his way to a direct knowledge of the Ground of his own and of all being. As his own selfish aims diminish, there is ever more room in his being for the desire for the Good which is the love and life of God. This turning from self-centeredness to God-centeredness brings with it a peace and radiance of living which makes the saint a light to men. And as love of God increases, and love of self drains away, a man may achieve a direct union of loving knowledge even with God Himself. On this point, too, the witness of the mystics who have actually crossed the threshold of the uncharted land is unanimous. Consciousness goes out beyond all sensible experience of ear or eye or touch to know the unknowable and to experience a joy so extreme that no language is adequate to describe the ravishment of the soul as it meets, in its own depths, the Ground of its own life and of all reality.

The insights achieved by men of pre-eminent goodness, by saints and mystics, are rendered more remarkable by the testimony of two other kinds of witness. Saints display the genius of goodness. By devotion, contemplation, and the most unrelenting study and detachment, they reach mankind's deepest vision into the nature of the good. In another field, the artist must achieve a comparable dedication. He devotes his life to the pursuit and study of reality under its aspect both of beauty and truth, and he brings to his labors the concentrated effort and total dedication without which few discoveries or fresh insights are ever achieved in life. And again, in another sphere —that of the study of reality under its physical aspects—the scientist works with comparable devotion and detachment. The saint, the poet, and the scientist are the seers, the visionaries, the explorers of the world. The remarkable fact about their testimony is that each in his own field reaches recognizably similar intuitions into the ultimate nature of reality.

In our own day, the importance attached to the poet's role is perhaps less than it has been in the past. The degree to which the poets feel this loss of authority perhaps explains why so many poets today write for a private audience in language and images often incomprehensible to ordinary men and women. Yet this present withdrawal does not alter the fact that in the finest poetry of the world, we are compelled to admit the activity of a greater power of penetration into the nature of things than is found in us ordinary citizens who are caught up in the round of daily duties without much time for reflection or "to stand and stare." The greatest poetry gives us a sense of light thrown onto dark places and of horizons widening as we read. It can show us our own nature as we have not recognized it and point to significances in the sensible world beyond those which an uninstructed eye or ear can catch. The deepest poetry seems essentially to have this quality of recognition. For a moment, it brings a feeling of comfort and stills the restlessness of heart and mind.

The point at which great poetry reinforces great holiness is here in these moments of recognition, for the almost universal evidence of the poets is that behind the flux of nature there is a universal ground, a Oneness which, if we could leave the eyes of flesh for the eye of purified imagination, would be apparent to us. In the words of Blake: "If the doors of perception were cleansed, everything would appear to man as it is, infinite." Wordsworth is the poet who strove most persistently to convey the sense of a greater reality lying behind nature and filling it with "intimations of immortality":

> "Even such a shell the universe itself
> Is to the ear of Faith, and there are times,
> I doubt not, when to you it doth impart
> Authentic tidings of invisible things;
> Of ebb and flow and ever-driving power;
> And central peace, subsisting at the heart
> Of endless agitation."

Perhaps the most moving of all intuitions of the One behind the many is in the *Adonais* of Shelley:

> "The One remains, the many change and pass;
> Heaven's light for ever shines, Earth's shadows fly;
> Life, like a dome of many-coloured glass
> Stains the white radiance of eternity."

And almost the same image is to be found in the Christian poet Henry Vaughn, who wrote a century before:

> "I saw Eternity the other night
> Like a great Ring of pure and endless light
> All calm, as it was bright
> And round beneath it, Time in hours, days, years,
> Driv'n by the spheres
> Like a vast shadow mov'd . . ."

The poets, too, have divined the mystics' knowledge of infinity and reality lying at the base of each human spirit, at the point of the soul, at the core of individual existence. In Wordsworth again we read:

> ". . . Whether we be young or old
> Our destiny, our being's heart and home
> Is with infinitude and only there."

Even where the sense of oneness is not explicit, poetry is

constantly seeking by its use of images to bring together into a sort of order and relationship the multiplicity of sensations, impulses, and reactions which crowd disorderly in the human mind. Harmony is one of the deepest powers in poetry and harmony is an instinctive knowledge that there is pattern in the flux, order behind multiplicity, a oneness in manifold events. The most poetic images are those which echo through our minds, touching chord after chord of memory and bringing all the disparate sounds together into some felt unity. It is as though the essence of great poetry is to wean us back from the incorrigible multiplicity of our ordinary seeing to the single vision, the single eye which, in the words of the Gospel, makes the whole body lightsome.

If the authority of the poets is not what it once was, that of the scientists at least is unimpaired. They are the wise men, the Magi of our day, and from one end of the world to the other they are accepted as seers and diviners of reality. Their witness, too, is especially significant since for centuries the divorce between the religious and scientific outlook has seemed so wide that any light science may throw on the insights of religion has a special validity, like the grudging praise of a lifelong adversary. In one respect at least, religion and science are in complete agreement. If the central intuition of religion is the One behind the many, so is it the central working hypothesis of all science. The aim of all pure scientific thought is to bring more and more of the observable universe under the governance of single laws. Science does not prove the unity and uniformity of nature. Its proofs rely on the intuition of such a unity. You cannot, for instance, prove probability by the number of recurrences of any given event that you have already observed. Those recurrences are minute compared with all the possible occurrences between now and the end of time. You argue that the recurrence hitherto observed will extend into the future because the probability that uniformity and unity hold good in nature is a direct intuition of the mind into the nature of reality. The few cases observed would prove nothing, unless probability were already assumed. Thus at the core of science lies an intuition or a working hypothesis which is hardly distinguishable from the central intuition of religion, that nature is intelligible and that there is a discoverable One behind the manifold of existence.

The firmest proofs of religion are rooted in the nature of reality—in the necessities of reason, in the underivative character of such concepts as truth and goodness. Since, however, the Western mind has in the last century become more and more accustomed to think of proof in the pragmatic terms of modern science—a thing being "true" if it can be shown to work—it is perhaps worth remembering that even here in the sphere of pragmatic proof faith and science conform to a similar pattern and claim a comparable validity. The world which science lays bare, in its capacity as weigher and measurer, is one of soundless, colorless impulses of energy which under given conditions appear to behave in certain ways. This clearly is not reality as such for, at the very least, reality must be allowed to be colored, scented, and noisy—qualities which do not appear in the scientific picture. Yet science can predict up to a point how, under given conditions, this queer universe of energy will behave. Proceed in a given way to set up your experiment and the experiment will work; and, on the theory of probability, repeat the same conditions and the experiment will work again. Thus, even if science cannot say what reality is, still less say whether its abstracted picture is "true," it can say that certain methods of handling reality work.

What is perhaps not very generally realized is that if this is the full extent of science's claim to lay bare reality, religion can proceed with much the same degree of certitude. The saint can say: "This universe I tell you of, in which God's being and energy and love fill all reality and in which the base of your own soul is anchored in the Source of Being, may seem to you very far removed from the colorful material reality which you meet every day. But is it stranger than the colorless, soundless energies of science? Stranger than the notion that you are sitting this moment upon an intersection of physical impulses? Than that reality is a dance of electrons? The energy of God and the energy of nuclear power are equally remote from daily experience."

But, some will say, we can prove the existence of nuclear power by setting up immensely complicated experiments, processing matter through them, and at the other end receiving a predictable explosion. "Then," the saint continues, "I say that the experiments of the religious life work in exactly the same way. We, the scientists of goodness, tell you that if you will take the raw materials of your all too human mind and body and process them through the laboratory of detachment, humility, prayer, and neighborly love, the result will be the explosion into your life of the overwhelming love and knowledge of God. Do not think you can know God except by hearsay unless you submit yourself to this experimental process, any more than you can produce nuclear fission without an Oak Ridge or a Harwell. But we promise that if the experiment is carried out under clinically pure conditions—as it has been in the life of the best and purest of mankind—then the result is scientifically certain. The pure of heart shall see God. That statement of fact is as experimentally certain as that H_2O is the constitution of water, and it is proved by the same experimental means."

If science is known by results—and this is in fact where its certitude rests—so, too, are the truths of religion. The experimental tests of religion are more delicate and unstable than those of science, for the raw material—the heart of man—has not that implicit obedience to the law of its own nature which is observable in metals or minerals or even living tissues. Inconveniently but gloriously, it has a free and unconditioned element. Again and again, in the laboratory itself, the experiment is botched. Yet where it is triumphantly concluded—in a Buddha, in a Lao-tse, in a St. Francis of Assisi, in a St. Peter Claver or a John Woolman—the experimental proof of religion shines forth with a light no less clear than that of science.

We are back once more with the earlier analogy of the travelers who come to report the existence of a far country. We shall have little inkling of its nature unless we set out on the route for it, following the map of the saints and mystics who have taken the road before us. There is no other road but the way of humility and love and detachment from personal longings and ambitions. It is frankly a way which most of us do not care to follow beyond the first mile or two. But for those who persevere to the end, the "spiritual city" is no mirage. There awaits, in experimental fact, the infinitude for which we are made, the peace that surpasses all understanding, the love and union of God Himself.

IV

To these central facts—a God who is Source and Sustainer of all reality and individual souls capable of union with the Godhead—the witness of the great world religions is virtually one. The sense of timeless Unity underlying the multiplicity of creation is to be found in every great tradition. So, too, is the concept of man, the amphibian, belonging both to the world of eternity and to the world of time. But after this point, there comes a cleavage between the approach of Eastern and of Western religion. In the main religious traditions of the East, the world of time is a world of illusion, a snare of troubles or delusions from which the goal of each separate soul is release into the peace of union with the divine Ground of being and loss of all trace of separate selfhood.

For Christianity, on the contrary, time is God's creation as well as timelessness, and the tremendous vocation of man is to remake not only his own destiny but that of the material universe as well. Admittedly, this ambition of "renewing all things" is a dangerous one. If religion's aim is to transform the whole of society, it exposes itself to formidable risks. It is condemned to come to grips with the vitalities of life which, although neutral in themselves, can all too easily become instruments of destruction. Without authority there can be no social order in an imperfect world, but men who exercise authority are exposed to the special temptations of power. Institutions entail a similar ambiguity. Effective social action demands a measure of organization. The more successful the action, the larger the organization will tend to grow. Yet in the growing complexity and impersonality of a large administration lie temptations to pride, power, and ambition which smaller groups do not present.

The more vital the interests which institutions protect, the more imperious the temptations they involve. Primitive tribal groups fight to maintain control of grazing grounds and hunting reserves. Their most recent successors—the nation states— fight worldwide wars for survival. When primitive economic life develops to the point of needing some division of labor, the share of wealth received by each partner in the economy becomes a new center of conflict, classes organizing to defend their own or to override others' interests. Even the smallest and most fundamental human institution—the family—has become at certain times and in certain societies a center of violent social strife, of vendetta and blood feud, with family leagued against family in the same city and liquidating each other with the ruthlessness now reserved for national or civil war. Yet each form of organization—family, vocational group, city, state—is legitimate, rational, and indeed essential, for no work of civilization is possible without the co-operation of more than one human group. It is simply a tragic fact of human experience that any organization, merely by existing, can become a potential center of ambition, fear, greed, or the lust for power. Like all other material things, organizations are ambiguous, being vessels equally of creation and destruction.

Within the range of human institutions, religious organization contains temptations more searching and subtle than any included in purely secular life. All too often men feel that their loyalty to their religious society absolves them from the restraints they would impose on their private actions. Men who would not be ambitious for themselves are "ambitious for God." The phenomenon is described by William Law as "turning to God without turning from self." All the lusts and prejudices of the heart are retained but identified with some supposedly religious cause. "Pride, self-exaltation, hatred and persecution, under a cloak of religious zeal," Law continues, "will sanctify actions which nature, left to itself, would be ashamed to own." This difficulty is not confined to religion. Nationalism, patriotism, family affection, liberty itself have been the excuses for high-minded crime. But the scandal is especially keen and demoralizing when those who claim to preach the love of God and man are ready to burn and torture in the name of love.

For this reason, Eastern philosophers have argued—and still argue today—that the betrayal of Christianity lies with those who have made of it a historical religion, active in time and committed to the renewal of "all things." These critics claim that only a purely otherworldly religion of Eastern stamp can mend the ills of humanity and lead man back to his true center. If this world is seen as an "insubstantial pageant," as illusion, as the *maya* of the Hindus, then peace, tolerance, and fellowship become possible in human society. If no material thing is of any importance and nothing of value is to be achieved among the dreams and illusions of material existence, the believer will seek neither earthly kingdom nor earthly church. Nor will he use material means—violence, for instance, or the authority of institutions—to bring people to the true day-spring of existence. Hindu and Buddhist religion has been, they point out, profoundly tolerant and peaceable. Its missionaries carried Hindu and Buddhist faith throughout Asia without a single crusade or holy war. The ascetic, the enlightened man, the fakir, the guru led men gently by wisdom and supereminent example and preached "sorrow and the ending of sorrow" solely by nonviolent means. This peacefulness springs essentially from a world outlook in which matter is an evil dream, for if matter is evil, who will seek to use it as an instrument? Only when men raise their eyes from time to timelessness, when their whole aim is to pass from the frets and desires of separate existence to the peace of annihilation, of losing all separateness in the Whole—only then will peace and tolerance reign in earthly society which knows itself to be what it is—illusion.

In a sense, this doctrine is an extreme form of the ideal of detachment preached by all great world religions. But its extremeness creates the dilemma: It is rational to believe that the aim of human existence lies beyond material things; but is it rational to conceive that aim to lie in extinction? Why, if the separateness of the self is pure evil and if absorption without residue in the Whole is the only aim of being, should anything separate ever have come into existence in the first place? How from the impersonal abstract Unity could personal concrete beings have come into existence? If they are errors, who bred them? The Unity? In which case, the Unity includes errors in its own nature. Something else? In which case, the Unity is not the whole.

Moreover, in the packed and complex life of time, the practical consequences of a timeless religion may not be as universally desirable as the critics of historical religion claim. If the whole of matter is an illusion, why trouble about it? The philosopher turns his back on the transient world but the world goes on just the same—only without what might have been his saving intervention. A religion which seeks nothing is too abstract for the many. Therefore the common religion of India still bears the stamp of the ancient fertility religions. Until the other day, the cult of blood lived on in the worship of Kali—it was Europeans, not Indians, who put an end to the Thugs who worshiped the goddess with a bowstring around the throat of their victims.

The social consequences, too, were not always happy. Hinduism and Buddhism were spared the shame and horror of having wars waged in their names. Equally they did little to stop warfare. Wars between tribes and states were no less frequent in the Oriental world than in the West. There is, it is true, an exception to the warlike character of Indian history. Asoka, the great Mauryan king, proved that Buddhism applied to politics could produce a cult of official tolerance. His reign shines like a beacon in the antique world. Yet it was a single beacon, for his reign was unique.

Perhaps the greatest difficulty the exponents of timelessness have to face is the fact that India's timeless religion rested upon a social structure which, for irrational and perpetuated injustice, has almost no parallel in the West. The Aryan invaders from the North used their religious system as one more means of compelling the black Dravidian stock of the South to confine themselves to the menial work of society. The caste system, backed with all the authority of the priests, brought into being in India some seven thousand years ago the type of society which Dr. Malan seeks to introduce into Africa today. But no sustained attack upon the system came from the timeless philosophy of the Hindus. Shankara might write: "Caste, creed, family and lineage do not exist in Brahman [the All]. Brahman has neither name nor form, transcends merit and demerit, is beyond time, space and the objects of sense and experience. Such is Brahman and 'Thou art That.'" But if caste did not exist, there was no need to do anything about it. No one can doubt the splendor and purity of the summits of Indian thought nor question the value of its spirit of tolerance and detachment. But the problems of time are not automatically solved by the sheer pursuit of timelessness. They can be ignored and grow more rank and more encrusted, as in each generation the weight of human passion and human self-interest piles up against them.

Yet perhaps the greatest difficulty to be faced in the Eastern view of material reality as illusion and evil lies in the fundamental question why, if it is delusion, it came into existence, and for what purpose a divine Creator called into being a universe of total meaninglessness. Christianity may bear upon itself the marks and wounds of time. It may need to learn more fully the Eastern passion of pure detachment and to eschew forever the pursuit of spiritual ends by violent means. But at least it has confronted the mystery of physical reality and found in it, not illusion, but the sublimest drama ever revealed to the mind of man.

The physical universe, in its stupendous richness and variety, is without doubt a profound mystery. The questions which the Almighty leveled at Job to illustrate the gap between the Mind that made the world and human intelligence still hold good for modern man:

"Where wast thou when I laid the foundations of the world? Who hath laid the measure thereof, if thou knowest? Or hath stretched the line upon it? Upon what are its bases grounded? Or who laid the cornerstone thereof?

"Shalt thou be able to join together the shining stars the Pleiades or canst thou stop the turning about of Arcturus?

"Canst thou bring forth the day star in its time and make the evening star to rise upon the children of earth?"

Yet if this bewildering panorama is studied, as natural science has made it possible for us to study it in the last hundred years, some hint of pattern seems nonetheless to emerge. Even if the possibility of purposive creation is dismissed and the processes of blind determinism are accepted, the direction of those processes is at least significant. A type of life on earth has evolved over the millennia which, with all the false starts, tragedies, holocausts, and blind alleys, has moved from the conditioned and limited to the increasingly free and undetermined. Indeed, one of the preconditions of advance appears to have been the avoidance of perfect adaptation to environment. When life becomes fixed in too complete and rigid a physical form, the least unbalance condemns it to destruction. The evolution is from matter to powers which are increasingly difficult to express in terms of matter. Choice, curiosity, questioning, inquiry, deduction, the powers of the questing mind—in a word, a certain freedom—appear to crown the present stage of evolutionary advance; and even those who do not accept the idea of a spiritual order would not deny that if advance is to continue, it is unlikely to take the direction of purely material mutations. Reason, however evolved, holds the key to the future.

To a Christian, this sense of a shadowy pattern underlying the immensities of nature is in no way remarkable. Although no human mind could have invented such a plot to the history of humanity, the plot, once unveiled, is consistent with what a man might gropingly know of his Creator. The highest good of which reason has any experience is disinterested love. Faced with the vast conundrum of why a self-subsistent, perfect, timeless First Cause should will anything to exist beyond Itself, our human reason can dimly grasp that the aim might be the creation of beings capable of conceiving disinterested love and giving it freely back to the primal Giver. The kind of universe in which such beings could be drawn from nothing—from the dust of the Scriptures, from the microscopic cells floating in warm shallow primeval seas of evolutionary theory—is as inconceivable to us as it was to Job. No one faintly knows what kind of a universe he or she would find credible. But some of the aspects of this particular universe which are as puzzling to us as to Job himself seem to divulge a part of their meaning if the purpose of creation is indeed the exchange of disinterested love.

A condition of such love is that it should not be balanced against some system of exact rewards or punishments. Love which knows that every demonstration will open the cupboard door would quickly degenerate into self-interest. The fact that the wicked flourish like the green bay tree has always been a scandal to the would-be just. No poet has expressed the agony more keenly than Gerard Manley Hopkins:

> "Wert thou my enemy, O thou my friend,
> How wouldst thou worse, I wonder, than thou dost
> Defeat, thwart me? Oh the sots and thralls of lust
> Do in spare hours more thrive than I that spend
> Sir, life upon thy cause."

Yet consider the opposite—a universe in which every virtuous act were followed by earthly success and every aspiration toward the good—which is the essence of the love of God—were instantly rewarded with mental ease and physical comfort. Under such conditions how soon would a selfish calculus of advantage stifle that pure disinterested search for the good which is the crown of every moral being, that spendthrift love which repays neglect and indifference with devotion and fills up with its own full measure the inadequacy of another's response, the love, one should remark, most prized by the world's greatest creator, Shakespeare, the love of Imogen, the love of Cordelia, the love of the dying Desdemona? It seems as though the very disharmonies and injustices of the universe are a condition of producing its supremest good. As the great nineteenth-century liberal Walter Bagehot wrote: "We could not be what we ought to be, if we lived in the sort of universe we should

xpect . . . a latent Providence, a confused life, an odd ma-
erial world, our existence broken short in the midst are not
eal difficulties but real helps . . . they, or something like
hem, are essential conditions of a moral life in a subordinate
eing."

This "confused life" and "odd material world" seem essential
o man's full stature in another sense. An energy of the mind
kin to love is that of creation. Man cannot create from noth-
ng. Equally in a completed, regulated universe he would have
othing to create. But in this earthly arena of growth and
hange in which in fact he finds himself, he possesses within
nd without the raw materials for his creativity. Both in his
wn physical organism and in the social organism to which he
elongs, the physical vitalities of growth, survival, and repro-
uction are the given materials out of which, by the higher
owers of reason and moral choice, he labors to produce the
hole personality and the balanced social order. The vitalities
hemselves are almost neutral. They can be used to build or
o destroy. Like an artist, man has to learn both to work along
he grain of his material and to subordinate it to the ideal
orm at which he aims. In a perfect universe, man the creator
vould have no place.

And this, perhaps, is another way of saying that the basis of
oth disinterested love and of creativity is freedom. Constraint
estroys both the lover and the artist. Yet if a man is to be left
. measure of unconditioned living, he is left with the power of
hoosing well or ill. His power to create is inevitably balanced
y his power to destroy. It is almost as though, at the un-
maginable origins of life, the Creator had faced the choice
vhich all forms of authority must face—parents, guardians,
chool teachers, governments: Is the system to be a benev-
lent despotism in which the power of choice is reduced to a
ninimum and with it the power to disrupt? Or shall the risk
f freedom be run? Shall it be love or the rod? It seems that
n our universe the risk, in spite of all its appalling conse-
uences, has been run. The love is not to be compelled; the
ood is to be chosen, not imposed. Freedom is to be a reality.
t will not be limited by preserving men from the power of

choosing wrong. They are to be left the full range of self
determination.

Equally, the consequence of wrong choice, setting in mo
tion, as it must, a causal chain of disaster, must be endured
That "the wages of sin is death" is probably as inherent in
the nature of reality as that to fall down a sixty-foot cliff break
the body. For the Christian, the Creator's answer to the risk
inherent in freedom is not to abolish them but to share them
Himself. The gap opened by false choice between man and
his true nature, the barriers thrown up by the recurrence and
perpetuation of wrong choosing, will be overcome by God
Himself taking on the full burden of humanity and working
out in His own flesh the consequences of man's freedom to
choose both good and ill. When He meets the disciples on the
way to Emmaus, He asks the mysterious question, "*Ought no*
Christ to have suffered these things and so to enter into hi
glory?" A God who had taken the risk of freedom and then
left the world unaided and unpitied to its consequences would
seem, surely, an intolerable divinity. Only a God who had
shared to the last limit of suffering in the evils that flow from
human freedom can be manifest as a God not only of justice
but also of mercy and compassion.

Other world religions have hints and glimpses of the opera
tion of the divine pity. The Hindu avatar, the Buddhist bo
dhisattva represent the concept of the timeless one appearing
in time to release man from the bondage of the world. In
Christianity the Incarnation contains far more than the con
cept of simple deliverance. Deliverance as an end in itself im
plies the worthlessness and meaninglessness of created things
Christianity rejects this contempt for the work of God's hands
God takes on human nature not only to repair the ravages of
false choice, but to restore humanity to its true dignity as the
vehicle of supernatural life, the "temple of the Holy Spirit."
Christ, the second Adam, is the firstborn of a new race of men
who, as the spiritual kingdom is spread on earth, will achieve
a unity of nature and supernature comparable to our present
union of mind and animal nature but transcending it as ra
tional life transcends the sentient life below it.

These "new men," these saints and mystics, may be as obscure and apparently powerless as the first human beings must have seemed, in the dawn of rational life, to the larger mammals among which they lived. Indeed, each stage of evolution would have been completely mysterious had we not been reading the story backward. There is no reason to suppose its next phase will be more obvious or sudden than the last. But we can at least observe some faint analogy between the emergence among scattered human beings of rational power and the appearance, in the saints and mystics of the world, of more than ordinary vision and capacity. Surveying the human scene, we can at least doubt whether men of any other type—the conquerors, for instance, or the despots or the economic empire builders—seem to carry in them the smallest seed of a more than rational life.

It is thus the unique character of Christianity, among all the world religions, to have grasped not only the infinitude of the Creator but also the dynamism of His creation. For all its evil and suffering and sin, the world is rescued from the last horror —the horror of meaninglessness. History may be difficult to decipher but it is not a mindless record of violence and pride, of conquest and defeat. The effort of man to remake himself in the image of his Maker and to remake the world in the pattern of a divine order gives greatness and significance even to his failures. Since he is finite and free, he must sometimes fail. Since he has God-given reason and grace, his story is nonetheless one of slow ascent. In every other tradition, the height of vision seems to have reached no further than a static perfection or else the ultimate gulf of infinity. It is only in Christianity that Creator and creation are understood together in a dynamic relationship of freedom and love.

v

Yet to say that in Christianity man can find the profoundest insights into his own nature and into the meaning of history leaves him confronted with the tragic fact that, at present, these insights carry with them the differences and even animosities of a divided Christianity.

Few can doubt the extent to which the hostilities, the mutual martyrings, the displays of hatred and scorn between Christians have brought Christianity itself into contempt and caused men to turn to irreligion or to the timeless religions of the East in order to be rid of the all too worldly disputes within the Christian family. Yet it may be that the time of these scandals is drawing to a close. Some of their virulence sprang from the use made of religious differences by politicians anxious to advance their own national interests. It was in the era of state religion, of the union of altar and throne, that the Christian communions prepared for themselves a later loss of spiritual power. Today, not only is the divorce between Church and government complete in most parts of the world, but, in place of the old union, there has broken out a persecution of the Church by the state—a condition, as the early Christians discovered, not incompatible with spiritual vitality. If the Christian communions have drawn from their three hundred years' entanglement with the civil power the realization that the independence of the two authorities is the best guarantee for both, one great cause of strife will have been removed.

It may lessen, too, another obstacle to understanding, the past readiness of most Christian communions to use force where persuasion failed. This tendency was strengthened by the state which, having fixed the religion of its citizens, saw in heresy the risk of treason. But the thumbscrew and the stake did not restore orthodoxy to religion; they all but drove religion itself away. Today, however, Christians no longer use violence. It is used against them. Throughout Eastern Europe, throughout China, they are returning to the condition of the primitive Church in which they suffer all things in their witness against the worship of the modern Caesar.

With these vast obstacles to good will removed, we may hope that the reunion of Christendom may begin at the point at which the greatest harm has been done—at the point where mutual charity has been lost. We do not know what form such

a return to Christian unity may take. We do not know what
diversity of rite or discipline will be compatible with the essential oneness of Christian truth. But it seems clear at least
that argument and reasoning will not produce unity if the desire for unity is lacking. And how can such a desire be born
among men who still cannot distinguish between rejection of
an error and profound dislike for the one who errs? It is charity
that is the bond of perfection, it is by love that the Christian
is to be known. Those who pray for the restoration of Christian
unity have to pray first of all for the restoration of mutual
love.

If the future of a reunited Christendom is obscure to us,
how much more uncertain is the prospect of religious unity in
the world at large. The strength of the outward thrust of the
West in the last four hundred years has driven many non-
Western peoples to defend their identity not only by imitating
Western nationalism but by clinging with a new fanaticism to
their old religious traditions. In the Moslem world, the asceticism and orthodoxy of the Wahabites was as much a reaction
to the West as was the modernizing temper of Kemal Ataturk.
British influence in India provided one impulse toward the
nineteenth-century revival of Hindu religion and philosophy.
In Japan, Shintoism has been fostered by the government to
prevent the adoption of Western technology from extinguish-
ing the separateness of Japanese culture. The decision of the
Far Eastern rulers in the seventeenth century to exclude the
Christian missionaries of the West would have been repeated
in the nineteenth, if the local governments had still enjoyed
the power to do so. The preaching of Christianity has seemed
to them the Trojan horse of Western control. Today in China,
the Communists persecute Christians on the ground that they
are the fifth column of "Western American imperialism."

Yet this fact of Communist persecution is a reminder that
one era of Western relationships with the East has come to an
end and that a new phase is at least conceivable in the con-
tacts between the great religions of the world. It may be that,
to generate the physical and intellectual energy necessary for
the great task of unifying the world, the peoples of the West

needed the intolerance, the pride in their own achievement, the deep sense of superiority which, between the sixteenth and the nineteenth century, made them irresistible—and largely intolerable—to the other nations of the world. Now that, physically, the task is done and mankind must learn to consider itself a single family inhabiting its one small home in infinite space, the Western peoples have lost their unquestioned predominance. But they are likely, as a result, to lose their power of arousing intense resentment.

On their own side, there is infinitely more understanding and respect for other traditions and cultures than was the case even a hundred years ago when "the heathen Chinee" was a figure of fun and the religions of the East were dismissed as darkest superstition. There is now, with greater learning and greater humility, a new readiness to follow the wisdom of those Jesuit missionaries who held that the essence of Christianity could be given to Indians and Chinese only if Christianity were restated in terms of their own religious tradition and philosophy. We in the West, who are convinced that time has meaning and that God works in history, cannot believe that the thousands of years of Confucian social discipline, of Hindu mysticism, of Buddhist charity and compassion, have had no significance and were not intended to give their own special light to the general illumination of mankind. For the philosophers and scholars of Christianity today the task is, then, still the task of Paul interpreting Greek philosophy to the Hebrews and Hebrew tradition to the Greeks. For all religions and for all mankind, the intervention in time of the Incarnate God and the initiation of a new humanity is the central fact of history. But this supreme event may be interpreted in a future Asian Christianity in a form of ritual and tradition as apparently alien to Latin or Anglo-Saxon Christianity as was the concept of the Greek Logos to the Jewish expectation of a Messiah. The reconciliation in Christ of the great traditions of a Mediterranean world united under Roman rule may be repeated in the wider world of our own day, which the energy of the West has drawn into closer physical contact than the peoples of Rome ever knew. And it may be, too, that the task of interpretation and understanding will be undertaken with all the greater fervor and charity since now for the first time all the religions of the world confront in Communism a secular faith based upon the explicit denial of God and upon the worship of the material order.

It cannot be too often repeated that one of the chief reasons why Communism exercises such power in the modern world is because it has unashamedly made a religion of its political objectives. Some of the jargon may be scientific. The aims may seem, in many ways, highly prosaic—fifty new power stations, a hundred-per-cent rise in coal production, canals across the desert, irrigation to make the wastelands fertile. But behind these material aims there lurks a lyrical passion for physical expansion, an impassioned belief that men will be brothers and society a classless paradise once the problems of production are mastered and every man works, not for "monopolists and exploiters," but for the single master, the state. There is no fear of enthusiasm, no deprecation of faith and vision in Soviet propaganda, and the appeal it has often made in the West has been above all to those who feel intensely the need in life for an explanation of reality, for an ideal and for a path to follow. Adolescents asking their first questions of life, young men and women at college grappling for the first time with philosophy and sociology, educated workingmen who look for a status and a role in life denied them in industrial society— these are the natural converts to the faith of Communism. The more irrational and indifferent Western society appears—as it must appear in the throes of depression or war—the more entire their conversion to a visionary materialist religion which offers them the disciplines and the guidance that will make them co-workers in the coming of an earthly kingdom. And in the world of Asia, these attractions are doubled by the old deep-rooted suspicion of the West, the belief that its way of life is imperialist and exploitative, and the desire to assert a new-found independence even if it involves imminent risk from the Soviet side.

In this contest with the attractions of Communism the Western world cannot rely on the momentum of past achievements and relationships. It has to reassert its vision of a free and just society, of a humanity united as brothers under the Fatherhood of God. The reason for bringing the great vitalities of nationhood and of material possessions under rational control is not only that survival demands a reordering of Western institutions. It is, above all, because new experiments in international and social relations will show to the world at large— to the young, to the students, to the new voters in Asia and Africa, to the natural leaders of the world's masses—that the traditional faith of the West is strong enough to remold society, strong enough to fulfill the promise of brotherhood which, whatever the blindness of nationalism or the selfishness of property, remains imbedded in our society as a judgment and a challenge.

Nor can we doubt, as the Western world shows signs of recovering the faith which lies at its foundation, that Communism will begin to give ground even in the territories it has already conquered. Whatever the material achievements of the Communist system—and they are likely to be immense— a society which is imprisoned within the limits of time and which systematically debars its citizens from any sense of a more than human destiny will, when the first excitement of material creation has worn away, become a closed order of deadening monotony. At best, it will achieve the mummified survival of the great planned experiment of Egyptian society. But the Egyptian experiment took place before the cycle of Western history had opened to mankind the vistas of freedom and growth and creation inherent in the vision of man as son and co-worker of the eternal and omnipotent Godhead. This phase of history cannot be canceled. The "immortal longings" implanted in the human soul, of which Communism in this its first untried phase of activity takes advantage, will not be satisfied by bread and metallurgy and atomic power alone. Indeed, even now, the fact of freedom in the West is so explosive that the Soviet regime does not permit its citizens to travel at will abroad and encounter freedom at first hand. How much more certain would be the infiltration and reconversion of Soviet society if the Western world were not only free but patently generous and brotherly and unafraid. It is useless to suppose that a reversal of pressure can come about solely through material competition. Today, the vast material superiority of the United States is not felt, in the rest of the world, as a moral as well as a physical challenge. The West will reassert its powers of attraction only if its material achievements are seen to express a vision of spiritual order.

No one can forecast the possibility of such a renewal of the springs of faith in the West. Freedom is the essence of any spiritual movement and freedom implies that unpredictability which belongs to the really creative activities of mankind. We cannot stand and prophesy "that these dry bones shall live." Nor can we expect to hear, above the braying of secular propaganda, the still, small voice with which the greatest inspirations of humanity—of saint and philosopher, of poet and scientist—have been breathed. Yet at least we can say that in human history it is often the days of greatest tribulation and deepest despair that are the preludes to a time of enlightenment. The world religions grew up in the collapse of archaic civilization. Christianity renewed a Mediterranean world disintegrating beneath the material load of the Roman empire. In the most arid decades of eighteenth-century rationalism, Wesley carried the gospel of salvation to the people. After the catastrophe of the French Revolution, the French Church recovered its soul of sanctity and learning. Today, the scale of our distress is certainly sufficient to prompt the question whether we have not, in the presumption of nationalism and the pride of material achievement, brought our society to the verge of annihilation. The roads we have followed in blind confidence have proved false roads. To realize this is the first step in the search for another route. And of that search, it can be said in the light of man's spiritual history that those who seek shall find, to those who ask shall be given, and those who knock shall have reopened to them the doors of creation, freedom, and spiritual life.

Index

Image Books

... MAKING THE WORLD'S FINEST CATHOLIC LITERATURE AVAILABLE TO ALL

Image Books

. . . making the world's finest
Catholic literature available to all

THE WORLD'S FIRST LOVE
by Fulton J. Sheen

The whole story of Mary, Mother of God, lovingly and reverently portrayed in the inimitable style of the great Bishop. **D30—75¢**

THE SIGN OF JONAS
by Thomas Merton

The absorbing day-by-day account of life in a Trappist monastery by one of the great spiritual writers of our times. **D31—95¢**

PARENTS, CHILDREN AND THE FACTS OF LIFE
by Henry V. Sattler, C.Ss.R.

An invaluable guide for parents and teachers for sex instruction of children, based on tested and approved Catholic methods and principles.

D32—75¢

LIGHT ON THE MOUNTAIN
The Story of LaSalette
by John S. Kennedy

The miraculous appearance of the Blessed Virgin Mary at LaSalette in 1846 dramatically and inspiringly portrayed.

D33—65¢

EDMUND CAMPION
by Evelyn Waugh

The heroic life of the great English Jesuit and martyr told in the matchless prose of one of England's greatest authors.

D34—65¢

HUMBLE POWERS
by Paul Horgan

Three beautifully told novelettes which magnificently emphasize the eternal power of faith, love and sacrifice.

D35—75¢

SAINT THOMAS AQUINAS
by G. K. Chesterton

A superb introduction to the work and personality of the Angelic Doctor by the scintillating and irresistible G.K.C.
D36—75¢

ON THE TRUTH OF THE CATHOLIC FAITH (SUMMA CONTRA GENTILES) BOOK TWO: CREATION
by St. Thomas Aquinas, newly translated, with an Introduction and notes, by James F. Anderson.

The second volume of the new translation of St. Thomas Aquinas' great classic *Summa Contra Gentiles*. **D27—95¢**

If your bookseller is unable to supply certain titles, write to Image Books, Department MIB, Garden City, New York, stating the titles you desire and enclosing the price of each book (plus 5¢ per book to cover cost of postage and handling). Prices are subject to change without notice.

Image Books

*. . . making the world's finest
Catholic literature available to all*

APOLOGIA PRO VITA SUA
by John Henry Newman
Introduction by Philip Hughes
Definitive edition of the great
English cardinal's superb spiritual autobiography. D37—95¢

A HANDBOOK OF THE CATHOLIC FAITH
by Dr. N. G. M. Van Doornik,
Rev. S. Jelsma, Rev. A. Van De
Lisdonk. Edited by Rev. John
Greenwood.
A complete summary of every
aspect of Catholic doctrine and
practice. 520 pp. D38—$1.35

THE NEW TESTAMENT
Official Catholic edition
Newly translated into English
by members of the Catholic
Biblical Association of America
under the supervision of the
Episcopal Committee of the
Archconfraternity of Christian
Doctrine. D39—95¢

ON THE TRUTH OF THE CATHOLIC FAITH (SUMMA CONTRA GENTILES) Book Three: *Providence,* **Part I**
by St. Thomas Aquinas, newly
translated, with an Introduction
and notes, by Vernon J. Bourke
The third book of the new
translation of St. Thomas' magnificent classic *Summa Contra
Gentiles.* Part 1 contains chapters 1 to 83. D28A—85¢

MARIA CHAPDELAINE
by Louis Hémon
A novel of French-Canadian
life which has justly been called
an idyllic epic. D40—65¢

SAINT AMONG THE HURONS
by Francis X. Talbot, S.J.
The stirring and inspiring story
of Jean de Brébeuf, one of the
American martyrs, who was
tortured and put to death by
the Indians. D41—95¢

THE PATH TO ROME
by Hilaire Belloc
The delightful account of a
most unusual pilgrimage on foot
to Rome. Illustrated by the
author. D42—85¢

SORROW BUILT A BRIDGE
by Katherine Burton
The biography of Nathaniel
Hawthorne's daughter—her conversion to Catholicism and her
work as Mother Alphonsa,
founder of a religious order.
D43—75¢

ON THE TRUTH OF THE CATHOLIC FAITH (SUMMA CONTRA GENTILES) Book Three: *Providence,* **Part 2**
by St. Thomas Aquinas, newly
translated, with an Introduction
and notes, by Vernon J. Bourke
Part 2 contains chapters 84 to
163. D28B—85¢

If your bookseller is unable to supply certain titles, write to Image
Books, Department MIB, Garden City, New York, stating the titles
you desire and enclosing the price of each book (plus 5¢ per book
to cover cost of postage and handling). Prices are subject to change
without notice.

Image Books

*. . . making the world's finest
Catholic literature available to all*

THE WISE MAN FROM THE WEST
by Vincent Cronin

A vivid, fascinating account of a remarkable priest who brought Christianity to the strange world of sixteenth century China.
D44—85¢

EXISTENCE AND THE EXISTENT
by Jacques Maritain

Existentialism, the most discussed trend in modern philosophy, examined in the light of Thomist thought by a world-famed Catholic philosopher.
D45—75¢

THE STORY OF THE TRAPP FAMILY SINGERS
by Maria Augusta Trapp

The delightful story of a remarkable family. "Engrossing, humorous, poignant," says Boston Traveler.
D46—85¢

THE WORLD, THE FLESH AND FATHER SMITH
by Bruce Marshall

The heartwarming story of a lovable priest. "Delightfully written," said the New York Times of this wise and witty book.
D47—65¢

THE CHRIST OF CATHOLICISM
by Dom Aelred Graham

A full, well-rounded study of Christ, His personality and teaching, by the distinguished Benedictine writer. **D48—95¢**

ST. FRANCIS XAVIER
by James Brodrick, S.J.

A new condensed version for modern readers of the biography of St. Francis that the New York Times calls: "the best book on Francis Xavier in any language." **D49—95¢**

ST. FRANCIS OF ASSISI
by G. K. Chesterton

A fresh, fascinating study of one of the best-loved saints—by one of the outstanding writers of our time. **D50—65¢**

ON THE TRUTH OF THE CATHOLIC FAITH (SUMMA CONTRA GENTILES) BOOK FOUR: SALVATION
by St. Thomas Aquinas. Translated, with an Introduction and notes, by Charles J. O'Neil

The final volume of the superb new English translation of this great Christian classic.
D29—95¢

If your bookseller is unable to supply certain titles, write to Image Books, Department MIB, Garden City, New York, stating the titles you desire and enclosing the price of each book (plus 5¢ per book to cover cost of postage and handling). Prices are subject to change without notice.

Image Books

VIPERS' TANGLE
by François Mauriac

A penetrating novel of evil and redemption by one of the world's greatest writers, and winner of the Nobel Prize.   **D51—75¢**

THE MANNER IS ORDINARY
by John LaFarge, S.J.

Delightful autobiography of a famous Jesuit priest and his full, rich life of service for God and his fellow man.   **D52—95¢**

MY LIFE FOR MY SHEEP
by Alfred Duggan

A fictionalized biography of St. Thomas à Becket, twelfth century Archbishop of Canterbury who was martyred by Henry II for opposing the King's efforts to bring the Church in England under royal domination.

D53—90¢

THE CHURCH AND THE RECONSTRUCTION OF THE MODERN WORLD
The Social Encyclicals of Pius XI, Edited by T. P. McLaughlin, C.S.B.

The definitive English edition of the major encyclicals of Pope Pius XI. These works are among the most important body of authoritative teaching on the attitude of the Catholic Church toward modern problems.

D54—$1.25

A GILSON READER:
Selections from the Writings of Etienne Gilson
Edited by Anton C. Pegis

This book distills all the writings of Etienne Gilson, one of the greatest living philosophers, into a single volume that captures the essence of his thought and presents it as an integrated system.   **D55—95¢**

THE AUTOBIOGRAPHY OF ST. THÉRÈSE OF LISIEUX:
The Story of a Soul
A new translation by John Beevers

A new and distinguished translation of the outstanding spiritual book of our century—a book that is ranked among the foremost spiritual classics of all time.   **D56—65¢**

HELENA
by Evelyn Waugh

Brilliant historical novel about St. Helena, mother of Constantine the Great and founder of Christ's Cross, by one of the foremost novelists in the English-speaking world.   **D57—65¢**

THE GREATEST BIBLE STORIES:
A Catholic Anthology from World Literature
Edited by Anne Fremantle

Imaginative re-creations of fifteen Bible stories by many of the foremost authors in world literature.   **D58—75¢**

Image Books

*. . . making the world's finest
Catholic literature available to all . . .*

THE CITY OF GOD
by St. Augustine; edited with Introduction by Vernon J. Bourke; Foreword by Etienne Gilson

A great Christian classic, specially abridged for modern readers.
D59—$1.45

SUPERSTITION CORNER
by Sheila Kaye-Smith

Fast-moving historical novel of a girl's lonely struggle for her Faith in Elizabethan England.
D60—65¢

SAINTS AND OURSELVES
Edited by Philip Caraman, S.J.

24 outstanding Catholic writers portray their favorite saints in vivid profiles written especially for today's Catholic. **D61—95¢**

CANA IS FOREVER
by Rev. Charles Hugo Doyle

The complete Catholic guide to dating, courtship, and marriage —a unique blend of the ideal and the practical. **D62—75¢**

ASCENT OF MOUNT CARMEL
by St. John of the Cross; translated and edited by E. Allison Peers.

A classic guide to the spiritual life by the saint who is widely regarded as the greatest of all mystical theologians.
D63—$1.25

RELIGION AND THE RISE OF WESTERN CULTURE
by Christopher Dawson

Brilliant interpretation, in terms of culture, of Europe from the late Roman Empire to the end of the Middle Ages. **D64—85¢**

PRINCE OF DARKNESS AND OTHER STORIES
by J. F. Powers

Eleven superb stories by one of America's finest writers.
D65—85¢

ST. THOMAS MORE
by E. E. Reynolds

Vivid biography of England's best-loved saint, portraying his court, family, social, and intellectual activity as well as his spiritual life. **D66—95¢**

If your bookseller is unable to supply certain titles, write to Image Books, Department MIB, Garden City, New York, stating the titles you desire and enclosing the price of each book (plus 5¢ per book to cover cost of postage and handling). Prices are subject to change without notice.

Image Books

...making the world's finest Catholic literature available to all...

JESUS AND HIS TIMES
by Henri Daniel-Rops

A magnificent and readable re-creation of the life and times of Our Lord. 2 volumes.
D67A & D67B—95¢ each

SAINT BENEDICT
by Abbot Justin McCann, O.S.B.

The finest modern life of the founder of Western monasticism and "Father of the West." Revised edition. **D68—85¢**

THE LITTLE FLOWERS OF ST. FRANCIS
translated, with an Introduction and notes, by Raphael Brown.

A new, modern translation of the beloved spiritual classic with addtional material never before available in English. **D69—95¢**

THE QUIET LIGHT
by Louis de Wohl

An exciting and fascinating novel of the life and times of St. Thomas Aquinas. **D70—95¢**

CHARACTERS OF THE REFORMATION
by Hilaire Belloc

Scintillating profiles of 23 key men and women of the Reformation. **D71—85¢**

THE BELIEF OF CATHOLICS
by Ronald Knox

A brilliant statement of the basic truths of Catholicism. **D72—75¢**

FAITH AND FREEDOM
by Barbara Ward

A stimulating inquiry into the history and relationship of political freedom and religious faith
D73—95¢

GOD AND INTELLIGENCE IN MODERN PHILOSOPHY
by Fulton J. Sheen

"May safely be called one of the most important contributions to philosophy which has appeared in the present century."—*Commonweal* **D74—95¢**

If your bookseller is unable to supply certain titles, write to Image Books, Department MIB, Garden City, New York, stating the titles you desire and enclosing the price of each book (plus 5¢ per book to cover cost of postage and handling). Prices are subject to change without notice.